JUDGES
A Commentary in the Wesleyan Tradition

*New Beacon Bible Commentary

JUDGES
A Commentary in the Wesleyan Tradition

Robert D. Branson

Copyright 2009
by Robert D. Branson and Beacon Hill Press of Kansas City

ISBN 978-0-8341-2407-3

Printed in the United States of America

Cover Design: J.R. Caines
Interior Design: Sharon Page

Unless otherwise indicated all Scripture quotations are the author's own translation.

The *New Revised Standard Version* (NRSV) of the Bible, copyright 1989 by the Division of Christian Education of the National Council of the Churches of Christ in the USA. Used by permission. All rights reserved.

Library of Congress Cataloging-in-Publication Data

Branson, Robert, 1941-
  Judges / Robert D. Branson.
    p. cm. — (New Beacon Bible commentary)
  Includes bibliographical references.
  ISBN 978-0-8341-2407-3 (pbk.)
  1. Bible. O.T. Judges—Commentaries. I. Title.

  BS1305.53.B73 2009
  222'.3207—dc22

2009008179

DEDICATION

This book is dedicated to our grandchildren, the next generation, for whom we pray daily: Brandon, Joshua, Emily, Melissa, Zachery, and Rebecca.

COMMENTARY EDITORS

General Editors

Alex Varughese
　Ph.D., Drew University
　Professor of Biblical Literature
　Mount Vernon Nazarene University
　Mount Vernon, Ohio

George Lyons
　Ph.D., Emory University
　Professor of New Testament
　Northwest Nazarene University
　Nampa, Idaho

Roger Hahn
　Ph.D., Duke University
　Dean of the Faculty
　Professor of New Testament
　Nazarene Theological Seminary
　Kansas City, Missouri

Section Editors

Joseph Coleson
　Ph.D., Brandeis University
　Professor of Old Testament
　Nazarene Theological Seminary
　Kansas City, Missouri

Robert Branson
　Ph.D., Boston University
　Independent Scholar

Alex Varughese
　Ph.D., Drew University
　Professor of Biblical Literature
　Mount Vernon Nazarene University
　Mount Vernon, Ohio

Jim Edlin
　Ph.D., Southern Baptist Theological
　　Seminary
　Professor of Biblical Literature and
　　Languages
　Chair of the Division of Religion and
　　Philosophy
　MidAmerica Nazarene University
　Olathe, Kansas

Kent Brower
　Ph.D., The University of Manchester
　Vice Principal
　Senior Lecturer in Biblical Studies
　Nazarene Theological College
　Manchester, England

George Lyons
　Ph.D., Emory University
　Professor of New Testament
　Northwest Nazarene University
　Nampa, Idaho

Jeanne Serrão
　Ph.D., Claremont Graduate University
　Dean of the School of Theology and
　　Philosophy
　Professor of Biblical Literature
　Mount Vernon Nazarene University
　Mount Vernon, Ohio

CONTENTS

General Editors' Preface	11
Acknowledgments	13
Abbreviations	15
Bibliography	17

INTRODUCTION	21
A. The Title	22
B. The Historical Setting	23
C. Chronology of the Book of Judges	25
D. The Deuteronomic History	26
1. Modern Theories	27
2. Themes	30
3. Supporting Themes That Flow Out of the Concept of Covenant	32
E. Writing and Compilation of the Book of Judges	33
F. Judges and the Inspiration of Scripture	35
G. Methodology	36
H. Theological Themes	37
1. Human Freedom	37
2. Sovereignty of God	38
3. Call for Total Loyalty	38

COMMENTARY	41
I. Overview (1:1—3:6)	41
A. A Geography of Failure (1:1—2:5)	43
1. Judah Goes Up (1:1-7)	44
2. Taking Jerusalem and Hebron (1:8-10)	46
3. Taking Debir (1:11-15)	47
4. Judah's Successes and Inadequacies (1:16-21)	48
5. Taking Bethel (1:22-26)	49
6. Living Among the Canaanites (1:27-36)	50
7. End of the Conquest (2:1-5)	51
B. Testing of Israel (2:6—3:6)	54
1. Death of Joshua (2:6-10)	55
2. The Next Generation (2:11-19)	56
3. Yahweh's Decision (2:20-23)	59
4. Reasons for the Nations to Remain (3:1-6)	60

II. Military Triumph: Spiritual Degeneration (3:7—16:31)	63
A. Othniel, Ehud, and Shamgar (3:7-31)	64
1. Othniel (3:7-11)	64
2. Ehud (3:12-30)	67
3. Shamgar (3:31)	70
B. Deborah, Barak, and Jael (4:1—5:31)	71
1. The Prose Story (4:1-24)	72
a. Sisera the Oppressor (4:1-3)	74
b. Deborah and Barak (4:4-10)	75
c. Heber the Kenite (4:11)	76
d. The Battle with Sisera (4:12-16)	77
e. Sisera and Jael (4:17-22)	77
f. Destruction of Jabin (4:23-24)	79
2. The Poem (5:1-31)	83
a. Introduction (5:1-11)	84
b. The Mustering of the Tribes (5:12-18)	85
c. The Battle (5:19-22)	86
d. Jael's Victory (5:23-27)	86
e. Sisera's Mother (5:28-31)	87
C. Gideon, Abimelech, Tola, and Jair (6:1—10:18)	89
1. Gideon, the Reluctant Judge (6:1—8:35)	89
a. Oppression of the Midianites (6:1-10)	89
b. The Call of Gideon (6:11-40)	91
c. God's Victory (7:1-23)	96
d. Gideon's Victory and Vengeance (7:24—8:21)	100
e. Gideon and Israel's Idolatry (8:22-35)	103
2. Abimelech's Failed Monarchy (9:1-57)	105
a. Abimelech as King (9:1-6)	106
b. Jotham's Parable of the Trees (9:7-21)	107
c. Plots Against Abimelech (9:22-33)	108
d. Abimelech's Battles (9:34-57)	109
3. Tola and Jair (10:1-5)	112
4. God's Rejection of Israel's Cry (10:6-18)	113
D. Jephthah, Ibzan, Elon, and Abdon (11:1—12:15)	116
1. Jephthah and the Ammonites (11:1-40)	117
2. The War with Ephraim (12:1-7)	122
3. Ibzan, Elon, and Abdon (12:8-15)	124
E. Samson (13:1—16:31)	126
1. The Birth of Samson (13:1-25)	128
2. Samson's Conflict with the Philistines (14:1—15:20)	133
3. Samson's Final Exploits (16:1-31)	140
III. Failure Complete (17:1—21:25)	149
A. Relocation of Dan (17:1—18:31)	151
1. Micah and the Levite (17:1-13)	151
2. New Home for the Tribe of Dan (18:1-31)	154

B. War Within Israel (19:1—21:25) 161
   1. The Levite and His Concubine (19:1-30) 162
   2. War Between the Tribes (20:1-48) 171
   3. Wives for the Men of Benjamin (21:1-25) 182

GENERAL EDITORS' PREFACE

The purpose of the New Beacon Bible Commentary is to make available to pastors and students in the twenty-first century a biblical commentary that reflects the best scholarship in the Wesleyan theological tradition. The commentary project aims to make this scholarship accessible to a wider audience to assist them in their understanding and proclamation of Scripture as God's Word.

Writers of the volumes in this series not only are scholars within the Wesleyan theological tradition and experts in their field but also have special interest in the books assigned to them. Their task is to communicate clearly the critical consensus and the full range of other credible voices who have commented on the Scriptures. Though scholarship and scholarly contribution to the understanding of the Scriptures are key concerns of this series, it is not intended as an academic dialogue within the scholarly community. Commentators of this series constantly aim to demonstrate in their work the significance of the Bible as the church's book and the contemporary relevance and application of the biblical message. The project's overall goal is to make available to the church and for her service the fruits of the labors of scholars who are committed to their Christian faith.

The *New International Version* (NIV) is the reference version of the Bible used in this series; however, the focus of exegetical study and comments is the biblical text in its original language. When the commentary uses the NIV, it is printed in bold. The text printed in bold italics is the translation of the author. Commentators also refer to other translations where the text may be difficult or ambiguous.

The structure and organization of the commentaries in this series seeks to facilitate the study of the biblical text in a systematic and methodical way. Study of each biblical book begins with an **Introduction** section that gives an overview of authorship, date, provenance, audience, occasion, purpose, sociological/cultural issues, textual history, literary features, hermeneutical issues, and theological themes necessary to understand the book. This section also includes a brief outline of the book and a list of general works and standard commentaries.

The commentary section for each biblical book follows the outline of the book presented in the introduction. In some volumes, readers will find section ***overviews*** of large portions of scripture with general comments on their overall literary structure and other literary features. A consistent feature of the commentary is the paragraph-by-paragraph study of biblical texts. This section has three parts: **Behind the Text**, **In the Text**, and **From the Text**.

The goal of the **Behind the Text** section is to provide the reader with all the relevant information necessary to understand the text. This includes specific historical situations reflected in the text, the literary context of the text, sociological and cultural issues, and literary features of the text.

In the Text explores what the text says, following its verse-by-verse structure. This section includes a discussion of grammatical details, word studies, and the connectedness of the text to other biblical books/passages or other parts of the book being studied (the canonical relationship). This section provides transliterations of key words in Hebrew and Greek and their literal meanings. The goal here is to explain what the author would have meant and/or what the audience would have understood as the meaning of the text. This is the largest section of the commentary.

The **From the Text** section examines the text in relation to the following areas: theological significance, intertextuality, the history of interpretation, use of the Old Testament scriptures in the New Testament, interpretation in later church history, actualization, and application.

The commentary provides ***sidebars*** on topics of interest that are important but not necessarily part of an explanation of the biblical text. These topics are informational items and may cover archaeological, historical, literary, cultural, and theological matters that have relevance to the biblical text. Occasionally, longer detailed discussions of special topics are included as ***excurses.***

We offer this series with our hope and prayer that readers will find it a valuable resource for their understanding of God's Word and an indispensable tool for their critical engagement with the biblical texts.

Roger Hahn, Centennial Initiative General Editor
Alex Varughese, General Editor (Old Testament)
George Lyons, General Editor (New Testament)

ACKNOWLEDGMENTS

The writing of a commentary is an engaging task that requires the writer to investigate diligently the literary and theological dynamics of the text. It is the hope of this writer that the commentary will enable the reader to better understand those dynamics and grow not only intellectually through a better knowledge of Scripture but also in devotion and commitment to God. The study of the Bible should be a spiritual exercise. As we examine God's word intently, we find it examining our values, lifestyles, presuppositions, and understanding of God's will for our lives. If the commentary helps the reader to hear the message of the book of Judges, both intellectually and spiritually, then it will have accomplished its purpose.

The writing of a commentary is not accomplished in isolation. I have benefited from the insights of other scholars, whose work I have carefully tried to document. In the last thirty years the amount of work that has been done on Judges has grown steadily and presents to the researcher a veritable feast of insight into the book. One of the foundational works that has shaped the recent scholarly discussion of Judges is the Yale dissertation of Lawson Stone. Lawson and I have worked together on a couple of projects, and I have come to respect his careful scholarship and spiritual insight. His work has been cited in this commentary a number of times. Beyond those specific places, it has also formed the framework of my understanding of the development of the book. I am deeply indebted to him. Several others have had a direct hand in the development of the book. I want to thank my student assistants: Angela Henzman Grupe, Nathan Yearian, and Steven Yearian for their careful work in proofreading the materials. My wife, Esther, beyond being patient with me during the many hours I worked on this project, has proofread the last five chapters of the book. Their suggestions have greatly improved its readability. I want also to thank Olivet Nazarene University School of Theology and Christian Ministry for giving me a reduced teaching load as a research professor. Their generosity enabled me to meet the writing deadlines established by Beacon Hill Press. The editor, Alex Varughese, has been particularly helpful in suggesting places where the work could be strengthened.

—Robert D. Branson

ABBREVIATIONS

With a few exceptions, these abbreviations follow those in *The SBL Handbook of Style* (Alexander 1999).

General

A.D.	anno Domini (precedes date) (equivalent to C.E.)
ABD	Anchor Bible Dictionary
ANE	Ancient Near East
ANET	*Ancient Near Eastern Texts Relating to the Old Testament.* Edited by James B. Pritchard.
BASOR	Bulletin of the American Schools of Oriental Research
B.C.	before Christ (follows date) (equivalent to B.C.E.)
B.C.E.	before the Common Era
BDB	*Hebrew and English Lexicon of the Old Testament*
ca.	circa
C.E.	Common Era
cf.	compare
ch	chapter
chs	chapters
DH	Deuteronomic History
Dtr	Deuteronomic Historian/Historians
e.g.	*exempli gratia*, for example
esp.	especially
etc.	*et cetera*, and the rest
f(f).	and the following one(s)
IDB	Interpreter's Dictionary of the Bible
i.e.	*id est*, that is
KBL	Koehler, L., and W. Baumgartner. *Lexicon in Veteris Testamenti Libros.*
lit.	literally
LXX	Septuagint
MS	manuscript
MSS	manuscripts
MT	Masoretic Text (of the OT)
n.	note
n.d.	no date
n.p.	no place; no publisher; no page
nn.	notes
NT	New Testament
OT	Old Testament
s.v.	*sub verbo*, under the word
v	verse
vv	verses

Modern English Versions

NRSV	New Revised Standard Version

Print Conventions for Translations

Bold font	NIV (bold without quotation marks in the text under study; elsewhere in the regular font, with quotation marks and no further identification)
Bold italic font	Author's translation (without quotation marks)

Behind the Text:	Literary or historical background information average readers might not know from reading the biblical text alone
In the Text:	Comments on the biblical text, words, phrases, grammar, and so forth
From the Text:	The use of the text by later interpreters, contemporary relevance, theological and ethical implications of the text, with particular emphasis on Wesleyan concerns

Old Testament

Gen	Genesis	Dan	Daniel		
Exod	Exodus	Hos	Hosea		
Lev	Leviticus	Joel	Joel		
Num	Numbers	Amos	Amos		
Deut	Deuteronomy	Obad	Obadiah		
Josh	Joshua	Jonah	Jonah		
Judg	Judges	Mic	Micah		
Ruth	Ruth	Nah	Nahum		
1—2 Sam	1—2 Samuel	Hab	Habakkuk		
1—2 Kgs	1—2 Kings	Zeph	Zephaniah		
1—2 Chr	1—2 Chronicles	Hag	Haggai		
Ezra	Ezra	Zech	Zechariah		
Neh	Nehemiah	Mal	Malachi		
Esth	Esther				
Job	Job				
Ps/Pss	Psalms				
Prov	Proverbs				
Eccl	Ecclesiastes				
Song	Song of Songs / Song of Solomon				
Isa	Isaiah				
Jer	Jeremiah				
Lam	Lamentations				
Ezek	Ezekiel				

(Note: Chapter and verse numbering in the MT and LXX often differ compared to those in English Bibles. To avoid confusion, all biblical references follow the chapter and verse numbering in English translations, even when the text in the MT and LXX is under discussion.)

New Testament

Matt	Matthew
Mark	Mark
Luke	Luke
John	John
Acts	Acts
Rom	Romans
1—2 Cor	1—2 Corinthians
Gal	Galatians
Eph	Ephesians
Phil	Philippians
Col	Colossians
1—2 Thess	1—2 Thessalonians
1—2 Tim	1—2 Timothy
Titus	Titus
Phlm	Philemon
Heb	Hebrews
Jas	James
1—2 Pet	1—2 Peter
1—2—3 John	1—2—3 John
Jude	Jude
Rev	Revelation

Greek Transliteration

Greek	Letter	English
α	alpha	a
β	bēta	b
γ	gamma	g
γ	gamma nasal	n (before γ, κ, ξ, χ)
δ	delta	d
ε	epsilon	e
ζ	zēta	z
η	ēta	ē
θ	thēta	th
ι	iōta	i
κ	kappa	k
λ	lambda	l
μ	my	m
ν	ny	n
ξ	xi	x
ο	omicron	o
π	pi	p
ρ	rhō	r
ρ	initial rhō	rh
σ/ς	sigma	s
τ	tau	t
υ	upsilon	y
υ	upsilon	u (in diphthongs: au, eu, ēu, ou, ui)
φ	phi	ph
χ	chi	ch
ψ	psi	ps
ω	ōmega	ō
ʼ	rough breathing	h (before initial vowels or diphthongs)

Hebrew Consonant Transliteration

Hebrew/Aramaic	Letter	English
א	alef	ʼ
ב	bet	b
ג	gimel	g
ד	dalet	d
ה	he	h
ו	vav	v or w
ז	zayin	z
ח	khet	ḥ
ט	tet	ṭ
י	yod	y
כ/ך	kaf	k
ל	lamed	l
מ/ם	mem	m
נ/ן	nun	n
ס	samek	s
ע	ayin	ʻ
פ/ף	pe	p
צ/ץ	tsade	ṣ
ק	qof	q
ר	resh	r
שׂ	sin	s
שׁ	shin	š
ת	tav	t

BIBLIOGRAPHY

COMMENTARIES

Boling, Robert G. 1975. *Judges: Introduction, Translation, and Commentary.* The Anchor Bible. Garden City, N.J.: Doubleday.
Gunn, David M. 2005. *Judges.* Blackwell Bible Commentaries. Malden, Mass.: Blackwell Publishing.
Matthews, Victor H. 2004. *Judges and Ruth.* The New Cambridge Bible Commentary. Cambridge: Cambridge University Press.
McCann, J. Clinton. 2002. *Judges. Interpretation: A Bible Commentary for Teaching and Preaching.* Louisville, Ky.: John Knox Press.
_____. 1996. The Book of Psalms. Vol. 4 of *New Interpreter's Bible.* Nashville: Abingdon.
Niditch, Susan. 2008. *Judges.* The Old Testament Library. Louisville, Ky.: Westminster John Knox Press.
Olson, Dennis T. 1998. The Book of Judges. Vol. 1 of *New Interpreter's Bible.* Nashville: Abingdon.
Schneider, Tammi J. 2000. *Judges.* Berit Olam: Studies in Hebrew Narrative and Poetry. Collegeville, Minn.: Liturgical Press.
Soggin, J. Alberto. 1981. *Judges.* Old Testament Library. Translated by John Bowden. Philadelphia: Westminster Press.
Stone, Lawson G. 1992. Judges. *Asbury Bible Commentary.* Grand Rapids: Zondervan.

MONOGRAPHS AND REFERENCES

Anderson, Bernard W. 1999. *Contours of Old Testament Theology.* Minneapolis: Fortress Press.
Arminius, James. 1956. *The Writings of James Arminius.* 3 vols. Reprint of 1858 edition translated by James Nichols and W. R. Bagnall. Grand Rapids: Baker Book House.
Beach, Waldo. 1979. *The Wheel and the Cross.* Atlanta: John Knox Press.
Binger, Tilde. 1997. *Asherah: Goddesses in Ugarit, Israel, and the Old Testament.* Journal for the Study of the Old Testament: Supplement series 232. Sheffield: Sheffield Academic Press.
Brown, Francis, S. R. Driver, and Charles A. Briggs. 1906. *Hebrew and English Lexicon.* Reprinted in 1979. Lafayette, Ind.: Associated Publishers and Authors.
Clendenen, Avis, and Troy Martin. 2002. *Forgiveness: Finding Freedom Through Reconciliation.* New York: Crossroad.
Cross, Frank Moore. 1973. *Canaanite Myth and Hebrew Epic: Essays in the History of the Religion of Israel.* Cambridge, Mass.: Harvard University Press.
Dever, William G. 2001. *What Did the Biblical Writers Know and When Did They Know It?* Grand Rapids: Eerdmans.
Fretheim, Terence E. 1983. *Deuteronomic History.* Nashville: Abingdon Press.
Grider, J. Kenneth. 1994. *A Wesleyan-Holiness Theology.* Kansas City: Beacon Hill Press of Kansas City.
Hills, A. M. 1931. *Fundamental Christian Theology.* 2 vols. Pasadena, Calif.: C. J. Kinne.
Koehler, Ludwig, and Walter Baumgartner, eds. 1985. *Lexicon in Veteris Testamenti Libros.* Leiden: E. J. Brill.
Matthews, Victor H., and Don C. Benjamin. 1997. *Old Testament Parallels.* Mahwah, N.J.: Paulist Press.
Mounce, Robert H. 1997. *The Book of Revelation.* Rev. ed. Grand Rapids: Eerdmans.
Noth, Martin. 1981. *The Deuteronomistic History.* 1943 *Ueberlieferungsgeschichtliche Studien,* pp. 1-110. Translated by Jane Doull. Reproduced by permission of The Continuum International Publishing Group. Eugene, Oreg.: Wipf and Stock Publishers.
Pope, William Burt. *A Compendium of Christian Theology.* 2nd ed. 3 vols. London: Wesleyan-Methodist Book-Room, 1880.
Pritchard, James B. ed. 1950. *Ancient Near Eastern Texts Relating to the Old Testament.* Princeton, N.J.: Princeton University Press.
Rad, Gerhard von. 1966. *The Problem of the Hexateuch: And Other Essays.* Translated by E. W. Trueman Dicken. New York: McGraw-Hill Book Company.
Stone, Lawson G. 1987. "From Tribal Confederation to Monarchic State: The Editorial Perspective of the Book of Judges." Ph.D. diss., Yale University. Ann Arbor, Mich.: University Microfilms, 1987.

Wiley, H. Orton. 1940-43. *Christian Theology*. 3 vols. Kansas City: Beacon Hill Press.
Yee, Gale A., ed. 1995. *Judges and Method: New Approaches in Biblical Studies*. Minneapolis: Fortress.
Young, Edward J. 1960. *An Introduction to the Old Testament*. Grand Rapids: Eerdmans.

ARTICLES

Arnold, Patrick M. 1997. Gibeah. *The Anchor Bible Dictionary on CD-ROM*. Logos Library System Series X. Print ed.: David Noel Freedman, ed. *ABD*. 6 vols. New York: Doubleday.

_____. 1997. Ramah. *The Anchor Bible Dictionary on CD-ROM*. Logos Library System Series X. Print ed.: David Noel Freedman, ed. *ABD*. 6 vols. New York: Doubleday.

_____. 1997. Mizpah. *The Anchor Bible Dictionary on CD-ROM*. Logos Library System Series X. Print ed.: David Noel Freedman, ed. *ABD*. 6 vols. New York: Doubleday.

Atkinson, Kenneth. 2008. The Salome No One Knows. *BAR* 34:04, July/August: 61-65, 72.

Beit-Arieh, Itzhaq. 1997. Negev: Iron Age. *The Anchor Bible Dictionary on CD-ROM*. Logos Library System Series X. Print ed.: David Noel Freedman, ed. *ABD*. 6 vols. New York: Doubleday.

Ben-Tor, Amnon, and Maria Teresa Rubiato. 1999. "Excavating Hazor, Part Two: Did the Israelites Destroy the Canaanite City?" *BAR* 25:03, May/June: online.

Boling, Robert G. 1997. Shamgar. *The Anchor Bible Dictionary on CD-ROM*. Logos Library System Series X. Print ed.: David Noel Freedman, ed. *ABD*. 6 vols. New York: Doubleday.

Brodsky, Harold. 1997. Shephelah. *The Anchor Bible Dictionary on CD-ROM*. Logos Library System Series X. Print ed.: David Noel Freedman, ed. *ABD*. 6 vols. New York: Doubleday.

Day, John. 1997. Asherah. *The Anchor Bible Dictionary on CD-ROM*. Logos Library System Series X. Print ed.: David Noel Freedman, ed. *ABD*. 6 vols. New York: Doubleday.

_____. 1997. Ashtoreth. *The Anchor Bible Dictionary on CD-ROM*. Logos Library System Series X. Print ed.: David Noel Freedman, ed. *ABD*. 6 vols. New York: Doubleday.

Dearman, J. Andrew. 2006. Ammon, Ammonites. Pages 131-33 in vol. 1 of *The New Interpreter's Dictionary of the Bible*. Edited by Katherine Doob Sakenfield. 5 vols. Nashville: Abingdon.

Dyck, Elmer H. 1997. Thebez. *The Anchor Bible Dictionary on CD-ROM*. Logos Library System Series X. Print ed.: David Noel Freedman, ed. *ABD*. 6 vols. New York: Doubleday.

Edelman, Diana V. 1997. Jabesh-gilead. *The Anchor Bible Dictionary on CD-ROM*. Logos Library System Series X. Print ed.: David Noel Freedman, ed. *ABD*. 6 vols. New York: Doubleday.

Ferris, Paul Wayne, Jr. 1997. Sorek, Valley of. *The Anchor Bible Dictionary on CD-ROM*. Logos Library System Series X. Print ed.: David Noel Freedman, ed. *ABD*. 6 vols. New York: Doubleday.

Fewell, Danna Nolan. 1995. Deconstructive Criticism: Achsah and the (E)razed City of Writing. *Judges and Methods: New Approaches in Biblical Studies*. Edited by Gale A. Yee. Minneapolis: Fortress Press.

Geocities.com/HotSprings/Bath/6482/english/plants/lycium. htm.

Gonlag, Mari. No date. Women in Ministry—The Wesleyan Church. http://www.wesleyan.org/em/women_ministry_main.

Halpern, Baruch. 1988. The Assassination of Eglon: The First Locked-Room Murder Mystery. *Bible Review* 4, no. 6:33-41, 44.

_____. 1997. Kenites. *The Anchor Bible Dictionary on CD-ROM*. Logos Library System Series X. Print ed.: David Noel Freedman, ed. *ABD*. 6 vols. New York: Doubleday.

_____. 1997. Shiloh. *The Anchor Bible Dictionary on CD-ROM*. Logos Library System Series X. Print ed.: David Noel Freedman, ed. *ABD*. 6 vols. New York: Doubleday.

Hawk, Daniel. 2006. Aroer. Pages 273-74 in vol. 1 of *The New Interpreter's Dictionary of the Bible*. Edited by Katherine Doob Sakenfield. 5 vols. Nashville: Abingdon.

Holladay, Carl R. 1994. Contemporary Methods of Reading the Bible. Pages 125-49 in *New Interpreter's Bible*. Edited by Leander E. Keck. Vol. 1. Nashville: Abingdon Press.

Houseal, Richard. 2003. Nazarene Clergy Women: A Statistical Analysis 1908 to 2003. Paper presented at the annual conference of Association of Nazarene Sociologists and Researchers. Kansas City. March 13-15.

Hunt, Melvin. 1997a. Harod. *The Anchor Bible Dictionary on CD-ROM*. Logos Library System Series X. Print ed.: David Noel Freedman, ed. *ABD*. 6 vols. New York: Doubleday.

_____. 1997b. Moreh. *The Anchor Bible Dictionary on CD-ROM*. Logos Library System Series X. Print ed.: David Noel Freedman, ed. *ABD*. 6 vols. New York: Doubleday.

Klouda, Sherri L. 2007. Gilead, Gileadites. Page 572 in vol. 2 of *The New Interpreter's Dictionary of the Bible*. Edited by Katherine Doob Sakenfield. 5 vols. Nashville: Abingdon.

Knauf, Ernst Axel. 2006. Abel-keramim. Page 7 in vol. 1 of *The New Interpreter's Dictionary of the Bible*. Edited by Katherine Doob Sakenfield. 5 vols. Nashville: Abingdon.

Koester, Craig R. 2006. Belial. Page 421 in vol. 1 of *The New Interpreter's Dictionary of the Bible*. Edited by Katherine Doob Sakenfield. 5 vols. Nashville: Abingdon.
Kotter, Wade B. 1997. Timnah. *The Anchor Bible Dictionary on CD-ROM*. Logos Library System Series X. Print ed.: David Noel Freedman, ed. *ABD*. 6 vols. New York: Doubleday.
Launderville, Dale F. 1997. Hobab. *The Anchor Bible Dictionary on CD-ROM*. Logos Library System Series X. Print ed.: David Noel Freedman, ed. *ABD*. 6 vols. New York: Doubleday.
Lemaire, Andre. 1984. "Who or What Was Yahweh's Asherah?" *BAR* 10:06, Nov/Dec: online.
Luker, Lamontte M. 2006. Beth-rehob. Page 445 in vol. 1 of *The New Interpreter's Dictionary of the Bible*. Edited by Katherine Doob Sakenfield. 5 vols. Nashville: Abingdon.
Martin, Lee Roy. 2008. Judging the Judges: Searching for Value in These Problematic Characters. Paper presented at the annual meeting of the Society for Pentecostal Studies. Raleigh, N.C. March 14.
Mazar, Amihal. 1983. "Bronze Bull Found in Israelite 'High Place' from the Time of the Judges." *BAR* 9:05, Sep/Oct: online.
McKenzie, Steven L. 2007. Dagon. Pages 3-4 in vol. 2 of *The New Interpreter's Dictionary of the Bible*. Edited by Katherine Doob Sakenfield. 5 vols. Nashville: Abingdon.
McMurry, Heather M. 2007. Gibeah. Pages 565-66 in vol. 2 of *The New Interpreter's Dictionary of the Bible*. Edited by Katherine Doob Sakenfield. 5 vols. Nashville: Abingdon.
Mendenhall, George E. 1997. Midian. *The Anchor Bible Dictionary on CD-ROM*. Logos Library System Series X. Print ed.: David Noel Freedman, ed. *ABD*. 6 vols. New York: Doubleday.
Meyers, Carol. 1997. Ephod. *The Anchor Bible Dictionary on CD-ROM*. Logos Library System Series X. Print ed.: David Noel Freedman, ed. *ABD*. 6 vols. New York: Doubleday.
Rainey, Anson F. 1996. Who Is a Canaanite? A Review of the Textual Evidence. *BASOR* 304:1-15.
Reed, Stephen A. 1997. Perizzites. *The Anchor Bible Dictionary on CD-ROM*. Logos Library System Series X. Print ed.: David Noel Freedman, ed. *ABD*. 6 vols. New York: Doubleday.
Robinson, H. Wheeler. 1935. The Hebrew Conception of Corporate Personality. *Werden und Wesen des Alten Testaments: Vortraege gehalten auf der Internationalen Tagung Alttestamenlicher Forscher zu Goettengen vom 4.-10. September*. Repr. pages 1-20 in *Corporate Personality in Ancient Israel*. Philadelphia: Fortress Press, 1964.
Shanks, Hershel. 2008. Bible and Archaeology. *Biblical Archaeology Review* 1:6, 84.
Smend, Rudolf. 2000. The Law and the Nations: A Contribution to Detueronomistic Tradition History. Translated by Peter T. Daniels. Pages 95-110 in *Reconsidering Israel and Judah: Recent Studies on the Deuteronomistic History*. Edited by Gary N. Knoppers and J. Gordon McConville. Winona Lake, Ind.: Eisenbrauns. Repr. from "Das Gesetz und die Völker: Ein Beitrag zur deuteronomistischen Redaktionsgeschichte," in *Probleme biblischer Theologie: Festschrift Gerhard von Rad*. Edited by H. W. Wolff. Munich: Chr. Kaiser, 1971. Pages 494-509.
Stone, Lawson G. 1991. Ethical and Apologetic Tendencies in the Redaction of the Book of Joshua. *The Catholic Biblical Quarterly* 53, no. 1:25-36.
Sweeney, Marvin A. 1997. Davidic Polemics in the Book of Judges. *Vetus Testamentum* 4:517-29.
Thompson, Henry O. 1997. Arumah. *The Anchor Bible Dictionary on CD-ROM*. Logos Library System Series X. Print ed.: David Noel Freedman, ed. *ABD*. 6 vols. New York: Doubleday.
Ussiskin, David. 1987. Lachish—Key to the Israelite Conquest of Canaan? *Biblical Archaeology Review* 13:1. Basarchieve.org.
Weippert, Helga. 2000. "Histories" and "History": Promise and Fulfillment in the Deuteronomistic Historical Work. Translated by Peter T. Daniels. Pages 47-61 in *Reconsidering Israel and Judah: Recent Studies on the Deuteronomistic History*. Edited by Gary N. Knoppers and J. Gordon McConville. Winona Lake, Ind.: Eisenbraus. Repr. from "Geschichten und Geschichte: Verheissung und Erfüllung im deuteronomistischen Geschichtswerk," in *Congress Volume: Leuven, 1989*. Pages 116-31.
Wolff, Hans Walter. 1975. The Kerygma of the Deuteronomistic Historical Work. Translated by Frederick C. Prussner. Pages 83-100 in *The Vitality of Old Testament Traditions*. Edited by Walter Brueggemann and Hans Walter Wolff. Atlanta: John Knox Press. Repr. from *Zeitschrift für die Alttestamentliche Wissenschaft*, 73 (1961): 171-86. Repr. from Hans Walter Wolff, *Gesammelte Studien Zum Alten Testament*. Munich: Chr. Kaiser Verlag, 1964.
Zertal, Adam. 1997. Bezek. *The Anchor Bible Dictionary on CD-ROM*. Logos Library System Series X. Print ed.: David Noel Freedman, ed. *ABD*. 6 vols. New York: Doubleday.
Zuckerman, Sharon. 2007. Hazor. Pages 753-54 in vol. 2 of *The New Interpreter's Dictionary of the Bible*. Edited by Katherine Doob Sakenfield. 5 vols. Nashville: Abingdon.

INTRODUCTION

The book of Judges both fires the imagination and chills the soul. Great victories over the strong were won by the weak. Oppressed and enslaved, the tribes of Israel struggled against opposing forces equipped with the most advanced technology. The foot soldiers of Barak fought the battalions of chariots commanded by Sisera. The Philistines who knew the secret of smelting iron equipped their armies with modern weapons while the Israelites had few weapons to fight with. Yet the God of Israel fought for his people. Led by a charismatic leader chosen by God, the victorious armies wrested their freedom from the hands of their oppressors. The book records not only the triumphs of war but also the depths of human depravity. A man slaughtered his brothers in order to grasp after a crown. A woman was sexually abused and her body dismembered. The devastation of war was not inflicted only on their enemies, for tribes fought against each other and one was almost entirely consumed. Women were kidnapped and forced into unwanted marriages. The people of God betrayed their God by seeking after other gods. The reader is confronted by stories of horror and triumph, saints and sinners, human depravity and the graciousness of God. This is a conflicted story of Israel's spiritual and social disintegration as the people struggled for survival while turning away from the God who offered them physical security and spiritual wholeness.

A. The Title

The book of Judges receives its name from the actions of its main characters. What is odd about the title is that with the exception of Deborah, the deliverers are never actually called judges. The noun "judge" (*šepet*) appears six times in 2:16-19 to describe those whom Yahweh would raise up to deliver Israel out of the hands of their oppressors. Here may be the source of the title for the book. The passage forms part of the Deuteronomistic introduction to the book (2:6—3:6) where the reader is informed that after the death of Joshua the Israelites repeatedly sinned against God and suffered oppression until God raised up a deliverer to overthrow the oppressor. The only other occurrence of the noun appears in the speech of Jephthah where he states, **Yahweh the Judge will judge this day** (11:27). The verb appears fourteen times, once as noted with Yahweh as the subject. In the other appearances, a deliverer is said to have judged Israel, for example, **And the Spirit of Yahweh was upon him [Othniel] and he judged Israel** (3:10).

These deliverers functioned in society like warlords, calling upon the militias of various tribes to do battle against their oppressors. The story of Othniel, a Judean and the first judge (3:7-11), gives the reader the prime example of how a judge should function. Israel was oppressed and cried out to Yahweh, who raised up Othniel to deliver them. He was moved by the Spirit to judge/deliver Israel and brought forth a time of rest. Ehud of Benjamin called upon Ephraim to attack the Moabites (3:15-29). While Barak commanded the forces of Zebulun and Naphtali, he answered to the leadership of Deborah (4:4-10). Jephthah had already organized a band of outlaws into a fighting force when the elders of Gilead called upon him to be their military commander (11:3-6). The judges achieved their place in society by military means. Elders and prophets had their separate functions, thus depriving judges of absolute power. When the Israelites wanted to give Gideon that power by making him king, he refused, stating that Yahweh was Israel's ruler (8:22-23). The judges do not fit the modern concept of court officials who in solemn attire preside over the administration of justice. Only about Deborah who is called a prophet is it said that she held sessions when persons could bring to her their disputes (4:4-5). Only after their battlefield successes did people seek them out to serve as arbitrators of justice.

While the word "judge" may also mean "ruler," Israel's administration of justice may give us another meaning for "judge." Witnesses were called to help determine the guilt or innocence of those accused of crimes. If a witness proved to be false, then the malicious witness was condemned to the same punishment that the accused would have suffered (Deut 19:16-20). The function of the judge was to determine and punish the one who was guilty (the wicked) and to deliver the one who was innocent (the righteous). It may be in this sense that those who delivered Israel from oppressors could be seen as judges—ones who delivered the people of God from the hands of the wicked.

B. The Historical Setting

The events of the book of Judges take place after the death of Joshua (1:1; 2:6-10) and prior to the birth of Samuel (1 Sam 1:20). The first chapter gives an account of the continuing conquest, with Judah taking the lead. Historically this time period is probably the end of what archaeologists call the Late Bronze Age II (1400-1200 B.C.) and extends into Iron Age I (1200 to 1000 B.C.). In the thirteenth century the central hill country, the area of Canaan that the tribes occupied, had a sparse population of about twelve thousand inhabitants. The next two centuries saw a rapid expansion of new inhabitants who built small villages scattered throughout the region. In the twelfth century the population had grown to about fifty-five thousand and then in the eleventh century to about seventy-five thousand (Dever 2001, 110). This rapid expansion cannot be explained by normal birth rates among the original inhabitants.

Several theories have been proposed to account for this sudden increase in population. It has been suggested that there might have been a gradual infiltration of pastoral nomads who settled in the sparsely populated areas of the central highlands. Dever, however, finds this suggestion inadequate to account for such a rapid rise in numbers (2001, 110). Another popular suggestion based on certain social theories is the peasant revolt theory. At the end of the Late Bronze Age there was a marked increase in social unrest as the cities were controlled by oppressive foreign hierarchies (see below). Many peasants escaped their bondage by fleeing the cities; some may even have revolted against the rulers and in the process destroyed the cities. They hoped to join a group of tribes who were in the process of settling in the central highlands and who had developed a more egalitarian lifestyle. It is well known that the languages, material cultures, and even worship practices (a number of the terms for various sacrifice are the same in both languages) of the Israelites and the Canaanites are quite similar. It is difficult to identify at this time period what archaeologically was distinctively Israelite. However, there is little biblical or archaeological evidence to suggest that the Canaanite peasants were in large numbers joining the Israelite tribes. The biblical account of a migration of the Israelites, a people new to the region, still represents the most probable explanation of the dramatic increase of population in the highlands.

Not only did the land experience at this time an influx of new peoples, but it was also a time of social turmoil. The end of the thirteenth century witnessed a period of social decay and political instability. The Egyptian control over the area was waning, and new peoples were taking control of different areas of the country. The "Sea Peoples" who had at the beginning of the twelfth century unsuccessfully tried to invade Egypt had

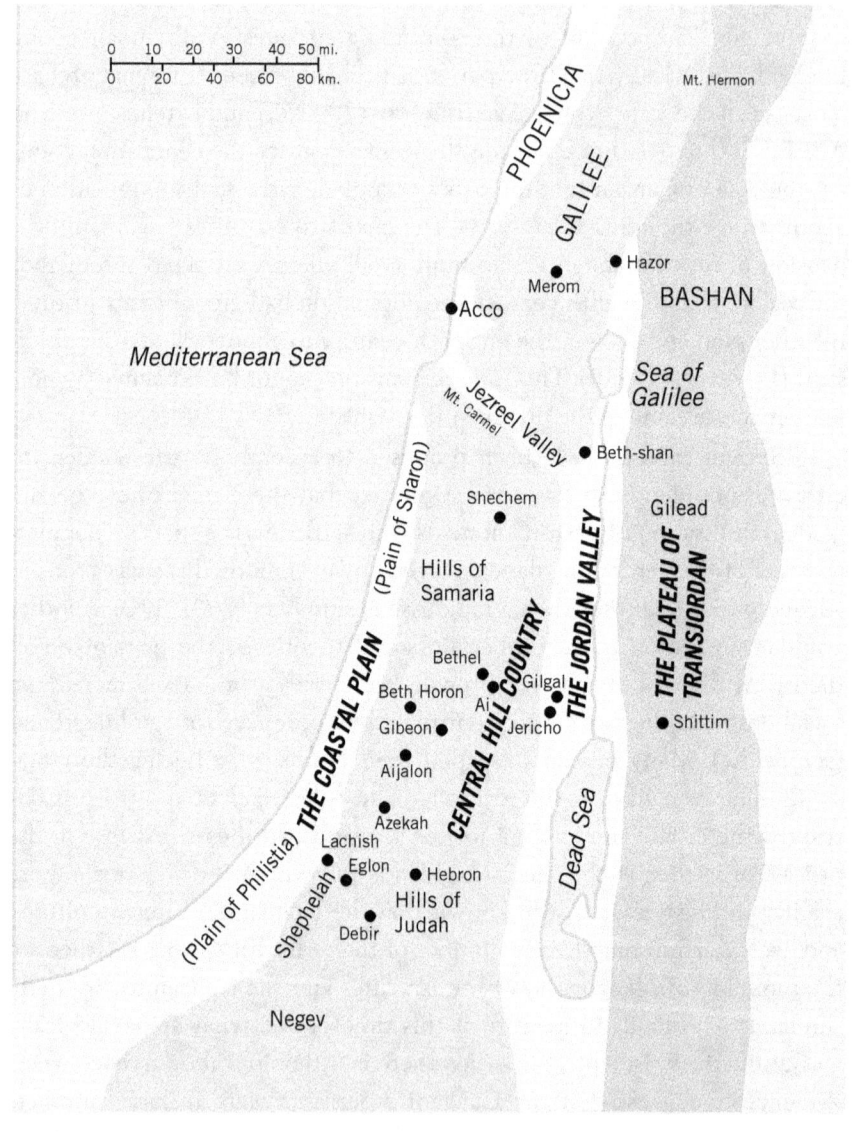

forcefully settled along the coast from Gaza to Dor. We know some of them as the Philistines who took control of Gaza, Ashkelon, Ekron, Ashdod, and Gath. A number of cities suffered destruction at this time, including such major cities as Lachish at the eastern edge of the Shephelah and Hazor in upper Galilee. It was a tumultuous time when rapid changes were taking place and various ethnic groups were seeking to exert control over weaker populations. This compares well with the description in Joshua of the Israelites settling in small villages in the central hill country, and of Judges when the Israelites repeatedly faced invasion by other groups who sought to plunder and enslave them.

C. Chronology of the Book of Judges

The chronology of Judges presents several challenges. It is a simple matter to add up the numbers for the periods of oppression and deliverance with the result that the book appears to cover a span of 410 years. The problem arises when this figure is compared to 1 Kgs 6:1, which notes that Solomon began to build the temple in his fourth year, 480 years after the escape from Egypt. By adding to the period of judges the 40 years in the wilderness, Saul's reign of 2 years (the text at 1 Sam 13:1 is difficult), David's reign of 40 years, and Solomon's 4 years, the total comes to 496. The lengths of Joshua's conquest and of Samuel's ministry are both missing. One approach to adjusting the figures is to suggest that when the Deuteronomic editor (see below) first compiled the material, the figures all agreed; it was the work of later editors that disturbed the chronology. The remedy is to determine by some means which figures were added and to adjust the chronology. Various arbitrary proposals have been made, but no clear rationale can be given for deleting certain figures and keeping others.

Another approach suggests correctly that the judges probably were not historically sequential in their periods of service, following one after another. Rather, some could have been contemporaries, as they came from different tribes and thus different parts of the land. However, the text as given places the careers of the judges in a back-to-back sequence. Who was contemporary with whom, and how do we know? Just asserting that some ruled at the same time does not solve the problem. Making arbitrary suggestions is an inadequate solution.

The fundamental weakness of such suggestions is that they start by assuming that the chronology presents a historical problem. The use of numbers in the Old Testament has several functions; giving accurate chronological order is only one of them. Numbers can serve ideological purposes as well. It is commonly accepted that the 480 years in 1 Kgs 6:1 represents twelve generations of 40 years each. In Judges rounded numbers appear often. In the accounts of Othniel, Deborah, and Gideon Israel enjoyed from each 40 years (biblically the length of a generation, Num 14:33) of rest, and in the Ehud story 80 years, the span of two generations. The unsuccessful judge Samson who only "began" to deliver Israel from the Philistines (13:5) judged Israel 20 years, half the length of the 40 years of the Philistine oppression. The five "minor" judges whose length of rule is given (Shamgar's is missing) have a combined total of 70 years. These rounded figures appear to have more to do with theology than with history. This concept will be filled out in more detail in the commentary.

After one has made all the calculations with the dates given in the book, there is one other notice that has to be considered. Judges 20:28 records that at the time of the war between the tribes and Benjamin, the priest who served before the ark of the covenant was Phinehas, the son of Eliazar, the son of Aaron. Aaron was a member of the generation that experienced the escape from Egypt but died in the wilderness. Eliazar's faithful generation began the conquest. Phinehas's generation, the third, proved unfaithful by not completing the conquest. The reader is brought back to the same time period as the beginning of the book. In final analysis the book in its canonical form cannot be squeezed into any historical matrix. It is not "history" as we understand that category today, but theology that uses historical events as carriers of meaning. Behind the accounts may lay actual historical events, but the writers and editors were more concerned with the theological meanings of the events and shaped the stories accordingly.

D. The Deuteronomic History

The book of Judges is part of what has come to be known as the Deuteronomic or Deuteronomistic History (DH). The first nine books of the Bible, from Genesis to Kings, present an unfolding story from creation to the destruction of Jerusalem and the exile of Judah to Babylon. The first five books (Genesis, Exodus, Leviticus, Numbers, and Deuteronomy) are referred to as the **book of the law** (Josh 1:8), the **law of Moses** (Luke 2:22), or commonly today as the Pentateuch, a Greek term that means "the five scrolls." The last four (Joshua, Judges, Samuel, and Kings) in Jewish tradition are called the "Former Prophets" and in Protestant tradition the "historical books." The books of Samuel and Kings were each divided into two books in the LXX. These books interpreted the history of the people of Israel in the manner of a prophetic discourse in that the actions of the people are praised or condemned according to the standards established in the Mosaic covenant. It recounts how they were continually called to repent and faithfully serve their God, Yahweh, who had rescued them from slavery in Egypt and given them the land of Canaan.

Deuteronomy functions as the pivotal work, looking both backward and forward. The first four books present the stories of creation, the patriarchal narratives, the deliverance of Israel from bondage, the giving of the covenant at Sinai, and their wanderings in the wilderness. The last four describe the fulfillment of the promise of God to give the people of Israel a land of their own and their subsequent history in the land. Deuteronomy looks backward through the sermons of Moses to Yahweh's actions of the giving of the Law and the journey to the land east of the Jordan (chs 1—4) and forward to the conquest through Moses exhorting Israel to obey faithfully the requirements of the covenant when they enter the land (chs 11—13) and designating Joshua as his successor (31:1-8).

The early church attributed the authorship of the historical books either to the major characters in the books (Joshua for the book of Joshua) or considered them anonymous (Kings). In modern times the books have come to be viewed as an extended theological work that was written to give a reason for the fall of Jerusalem and to look beyond its destruction for a basis for hope.

The books contain ancient materials, some passed down orally and others based on written documents. The stories of the judges probably originated as stories of tribal heroes that were told and retold for generations. The allotments of the tribes (Josh 13—22) reflect a written list of boundaries. There are a number of collections of stories that have been included, such as the ark narratives (1 Sam 4:2—6:21), the court history (2 Sam 9—20; 1 Kgs 1—2), the narrative on the reign of Solomon (1 Kgs 3—11), and the prophetic narratives (1 Kgs 17:1—2 Kgs 8:15). Court records from both Israel (***the Book of the Annals of the Kings of Israel***) and Judah (***the Book of the Annals of the Kings of Judah***) were used for 1 and 2 Kings.

I. Modern Theories

In 1981 Martin Noth first suggested what has now become generally accepted, that the four historical books were the product of an author/compiler who used the theology of Deuteronomy to give an explanation for the horrific destruction of Jerusalem and the subsequent exile. Noth designated this person "the Deuteronomic Historian" (abbreviated Dtr) and the work the "Deuteronomic History" (DH). He observed that speeches and summaries of varying lengths, looking both backward and forward, interpreted according to the theology of the book of Deuteronomy previous events and drew "the relevant practical conclusions about what people should do" (Josh 1; 23; 1 Sam 12; 1 Kgs 8:14 ff.; 2 Kgs 17:7 ff.). These editorial additions exhibit linguistic similarities such as vocabulary and writing style, as well as theological outlook (1981, 4-6).

Noth proposed that during the exile, around 560 B.C., Dtr gathered the materials together for the purpose of explaining why the nations of Israel and Judah were destroyed (1981, 79). The Deuteronomic Historian did not substantially change the materials but mostly incorporated them in their original form. However, as they were woven together to produce a coherent history, editorial additions were added to provide transitions between the various sources. These transitions also included Deuteronomistic theological comments that helped move the larger story forward. An editor later made some minor additions, but Dtr's basic work was not materially changed (1981, 7). The Deuteronomic Historian's central concern was to explain why the nations of Israel and Judah were destroyed. The people were commanded to keep with their whole heart the covenant with Yahweh their God. As Deut 6:4-5 states: **Listen, Israel! Yahweh is your God; Yahweh alone. And you shall love Yahweh your God with all your heart, and with all your soul, and with all your strength.**

The Israelites were to destroy the Canaanite places of worship and to centralize their worship; that is, their sacrificial offerings, at one location that Yahweh would choose (Deut 12:2-7). This became the fundamental test of loyalty to the covenant and Yahweh.

The Deuteronomic Historian described the long history of the failure of Israel to obey Yahweh and keep the covenant. While there were a few bright spots of obedience: Joshua, Samuel, David, Hezekiah, Josiah; for the most part the history is one of disobedience and seeking after other gods. Noth suggested that the purpose of Dtr was to explain to the exilic community that it was their history of disobedience that brought about the judgment of God and their present state of exile. The Deuteronomic Historian viewed their end as final, with no hope of restoration (1981, 97).

It is this last point of Noth that first drew criticism. Gerhard von Rad accepted the postexilic date of the writing of DH but suggested that the promises made to the line of David through the prophets provided a glimmer of hope. Von Rad compiled a list of prophecies of destruction and their fulfillments contained in the books of Kings (1966, 209-11). For Dtr the word of God given by the prophets was a sure word that worked out its fulfillment during the history of the nations. Von Rad further noted that Dtr viewed David as the model of kingship by which other kings were judged (1966, 216-17).

Second Kings ends with the account of Jehoiachin being released from prison and given preferential treatment by the king of Babylon (25:27-30). This von Rad suggests is a messianic note of hope that God had not forsaken the exiles but would in the future work in their behalf (1966, 220). Helga Weippert agreed with von Rad that the category of promise-fulfillment is a key to understanding DH. Her investigation found that a number of passages in Judges and Samuel as well as Kings contain promises, some that find fulfillment in immediate contexts and others that span greater lengths of history. This theological theme Weippert found in the early stories compiled by Dtr as well as in the editorial sections that were written to tie the stories into a coherent whole (2000, 47-61).

Hans Walter Wolff also thought that DH had a message of hope for the exiles. He disagreed, however, with von Rad that the note on the restoration of Jehoiachin was a sufficient basis for hope. He observed that at significant points in DH there appear calls for the people to repent. Of special note is Solomon's prayer at the dedication of the Temple (1 Kgs 8:46-50). Those who in the future might suffer exile for their sins were encouraged to repent so that God might again have compassion upon them. These calls to repent were a glimmer of grace that the exiles might grasp in hope. Later, an exilic editor in order to give the exiles an explicit hope added Deut 30:1-10, which promises to those who repent that God would gather them from the ends of the earth and restore them to the land (1975, 90-98).

Frank Moore Cross also agreed with von Rad that Dtr did have a message of hope, but he thought that it was more appropriately given to the people of Judah as a nation prior to the exile. Rather than being written to exilic Judah as a justification of the destruction of Jerusalem, Cross viewed DH as a preexilic work written to recall Judah back to covenant loyalty as modeled by King David (2 Sam 7). The Deuteronomic Historian developed two themes based on the concept of the blessings and curses of the covenant. Because Jeroboam I caused Israel to sin by establishing the alternate worship shrines in Bethel and Dan, the curses came upon that nation and its doom was inevitable. However, because the righteous David became a model of kingship for Judah, there was always hope that another righteous king would turn the nation back to the pure worship of Yahweh and gain his blessings. The Deuteronomic Historian wrote DH as a guide for King Josiah who did follow faithfully the Law of Moses as expressed in the book of Deuteronomy, even to the extent of destroying the illegitimate shrine erected by Jeroboam I in Bethel. An exilic editor whom Cross designated as Dtr² recorded the fall of Jerusalem and reshaped the history so as to make it more relevant for the exiles who had experienced the disappointment of the failed reforms of Josiah and the subsequent destruction of Judah. Cross thus made two significant contributions to the discussion, grounding the message of hope in the royal ideology of the House of David, and more importantly suggesting that DH was first written during the seventh century, prior to the exile, with a later editor around 550 B.C. reshaping the materials (1973, 278-87).

Rudolf Smend examined the problem of the authorship of DH from a different angle than did Cross who worked with major themes in the books of Kings. Smend examined individual texts and detected what he thought was another author (or several) in addition to the exilic Dtr, whom he designated DtrH. This author, or authors, whom he designated DtrN, reshaped the original work according to his (their) interest in the Law (2000, 98).

Subsequent to Smend's work it has become common to speak more of a Deuteronomistic school of writers or editors rather than one author. Their work spanned several centuries and their activities of collecting and editing extended to other books, particularly those of the prophets. Their work contributed significantly to what later came to be the Hebrew canon of Scripture. Scholars today are still divided over whether DH's earliest edition was written in the seventh century as a model for the Josianic reforms (primarily American scholars) or during the exile (primarily European scholars). It is generally accepted that the books of Joshua, Judges, Samuel, and Kings do form a coherent "historical-theological" work produced to explain the destruction of the nations of Israel and Judah and to give hope to the exiles.

2. Themes

The various compilers, writers, and editors of the books of Joshua through Kings were interested in adapting the historical materials for theological and political purposes. There was no thought of writing an objective history of "what happened." The basic materials were set forth to tell a story; a story that traced the interactions of a sovereign God with a humanity that was free to choose its own path and destiny. The overarching theme that binds the disparate materials of DH together is that of covenant.

Covenant

In the second millennium the Hittites, who ruled most of what is modern Turkey, developed an international treaty form that remained in use, particularly by the Assyrians, into the first millennium. Its purpose was designed to establish a covenantal as well as legal relationship between the overlord who granted the treaty and the vassal who received it. Those who were in covenant together enjoyed a peaceful relationship based on mutual commitment and loyalty to one another. A breach of the covenant would produce anger in the offended party, a legal response more than an emotional one, which led to the curses being invoked and eventually war or rebellion.

While over time there were variations in the form, it usually began with the identification of the overlord and was followed by a narrative describing the history of the relationship between the two parties. Next were recorded stipulations that the vassal had to adhere to, then regulations for the depositing and annual reading of the treaty, the calling upon the gods of both countries as witnesses, and a series of blessings for the vassal's obedience and curses for disobedience. This political form provided the model for the covenant established by Yahweh with Israel at Mount Sinai. The speeches of Moses in Deuteronomy are an explication of what this covenantal relationship between the two meant. The concept of covenant permeates the whole of the OT. Terms such as "love," "anger," "hatred," "fellowship," "peace," "prosperity," "friendship," "brother," as well as others are often grounded in the political/theological relationship established by the covenant. While this is not the place to discuss fully how pervasive the concept of covenant is in the OT, in the commentary it will be often referred to as the basis for understanding the relationship between the people of Israel and their God.

The speeches of Moses in Deuteronomy repeatedly call the Israelites to remain faithful to the covenant they entered into with Yahweh their God at Sinai. This Mosaic covenant was conditioned upon the people faithfully keeping the commandments and statutes of the covenant. Yahweh would keep the covenant and respond to the people in accordance with their actions. Disobedience would bring curses upon the nation. Obedience would bring blessings. Israel was urged to express their loyalty to Yahweh by diligently keeping the laws and commandments of the covenant. Their loyalty was to spring forth from love from their hearts (Deut 6:5), the center of their beings where will and thinking combined to motivate action. When Moses said, **You will love Yahweh your God with all your heart, and with all your soul, and with all your strength** (v 4), he was not saying that one should feel positive affections for God. To love someone was understood as an action. Those who kept the covenant loved God. Those who disobeyed and broke the covenant hated God (5:9). As an expression of their love the Israelites were to teach the commandments to their children (6:2, 7, 20-25) so that succeeding generations would be blessed. The keeping of the commandments and regulations (14:1-2) indicated that they were a holy people, chosen by Yahweh from among all the earth and separated from the other peoples.

3. Supporting Themes That Flow Out of the Concept of Covenant

The first commandment (Deut 5:7), restated in 6:4-5 (see above), was of primary importance and foundational for all the others. The breaking of the other commandments was symptomatic of forsaking or forgetting Yahweh. The people were to worship Yahweh alone and keep his commandments (Jer 7:8-10). To seek after and worship the other gods indicated a lack of trust that Yahweh could meet their needs and protect them. Israel was called to the exclusive worship of one God in one location chosen by Yahweh (Deut 12:2-19). Early in Israel's history many places of worship were tolerated (Exod 20:24-26; 1 Kgs 3:2); however, after the temple in Jerusalem had been built, Dtr viewed the worship at other shrines as idolatry. Jeroboam I was strongly condemned for establishing the shrines at Bethel and Dan as royal sanctuaries (1 Kgs 13:33-34), even though both had been worship centers for Israel for many years (Gen 28:18-22; Judg 18:30; 20:18). The kings of both Israel and Judah were judged by the first commandment as epitomized in the centralizing of worship in Jerusalem and remaining faithful in the worship of Yahweh alone. This inflexible rule led to all the kings of Israel being condemned and only a few of Judah receiving passing marks.

The blessings and curses of the covenant (Deut 27:15—28:68) were not like independent laws of nature that operated autonomously. They expressed the will of God who acted in response to the obedience or disobedience of his people. The people were viewed as a corporate unity so that blessings or curses came upon all, not on individuals. A wicked individual could enjoy the blessings of a community that was committed to keeping the covenant, and a righteous individual could suffer the curses inflicted upon a disobedient community. Thus it was important for the communities or the people as a whole to enforce compliance with the Law (Deut 13:1-18). The purpose of the curses was remedial, to recall the people back to obedience and thus blessings. It was not God's desire to punish, but to be gracious and forgiving, listening for the cry of repentance in order to restore (Deut 30:1-5). God would restore his blessings upon the community when sin was removed (Josh 7—8), or they cried out to him as they were oppressed (Judg 3:8, 15; 4:3; 6:7); or they humbled themselves and instituted reforms (2 Kgs 22:19-20). Yet there was the possibility of entering too deeply into sin so that Yahweh would refuse to listen to the people and judgment would inexorably come (1 Sam 15:23; 28:6; 2 Kgs 22:15-17).

The key to faithful obedience to the covenant was **leadership.** The right person, usually male but on occasion female (Deborah), who could maintain early the tribes' and later the nation's commitment to fidelity to Yahweh became God's instrument for blessing. Yet repeatedly this instrument failed as the nation forgot that Yahweh was their true king and continued to drift into apostasy by worshipping the Canaanite gods. When Moses the servant of Yahweh died, Joshua had already been commissioned to succeed him (Deut 31:23). Joshua became a model of faithful obedience during the conquest of Canaan, and God blessed the people by giving them victory over their enemies (Josh 11:16-23). Israel continued to serve God during the life of Joshua and the next generation of elders (Judg 2:6-10). However, the period of the judges became a downward spiral of moral and spiritual disintegration that led to the near extinction of the tribe of Benjamin (chs 19—21). The book of Judges looks forward for stable leadership with the establishment of kingship (17:6; 18:1; 19:1; 21:25). Saul's dismal reign preceded Israel's golden age of the reigns of David and Solomon. In response to David's faithfulness God granted him a new covenant, an eternal covenant assuring continued rule of the Davidic house (2 Sam 7:11*b*-16). But even this covenant became subject to the Mosaic covenant and the continual decline of the nation into apostasy could not be halted by those few good kings such as Asa, Jehoshaphat, Hezekiah, and Josiah. Only in a late addition to Jeremiah is the Davidic covenant lifted up as a message of hope for the exiles (33:14-22).

The Deuteronomic Historian demonstrates a strong interest in the **prophetic word.** A prophet like Moses was expected, one who could speak God's word directly (Deut 18:15-18). The Deuteronomic Historian records the appearance of many prophets, some unnamed (Judg 6:8-10; 1 Kgs 13:1-10) and others well known: Nathan, Elijah, and Elisha. A good deal of space is dedicated to the stories of the prophets, particularly Elijah and Elisha (1 Kgs 17—2 Kgs 9:10). The prophetic word served to interpret the course of the history of Israel as well as to call the people to repentance. They proclaimed not only judgment for sin but also that Yahweh was a gracious God who was slow to anger and ready to grant forgiveness and reconciliation if they repented. It was a message unheeded as both nations, Israel and Judah, willfully plunged headlong into destruction.

E. Writing and Compilation of the Book of Judges

The Talmud credits Samuel with the authorship of the book of Judges, along with that of Ruth and Samuel. Even Edward J. Young, a very conservative writer, found that position difficult to maintain and suggested that the book was compiled during the time of the united monarchy (1960, 180).

With the understanding that Judges forms part of a larger work compiled and edited according to the theology of Deuteronomy, the question of authorship is replaced with an inquiry into what are the sources of the materials and how did the editing process combine them to produce the book. The book came into its final form in four stages. First, the oral traditions about local heroes were told and passed on over several generations. The stories described the exploits of the individual warriors, known as "major" judges who lived at different times and came from different tribes: Ehud of Benjamin, Barak of Naphtali, Gideon of Manasseh, Jephthah of the Transjordan half tribe of Manasseh, and Samson of Dan. Second, at some point in the history of Israel, the stories of these judges were collected and then reduced to writing. When the stories were collected is unknown, but probably sometime after the rise of the monarchy, but not too late as the song of Deborah and Barak (5:2-31) represents some of the earliest poetry in the Bible.

In the third phase, the stories that had already taken a fixed form were incorporated into the larger work of DH by Dtr, either an individual or possibly a group who worked after the fall of Samaria (721 B.C.). Some minor editing of the stories placed them in a chronological sequence and structured them around the Deuteronomistic cyclical of sin, oppression, cry to Yahweh, and the raising up of a deliver (2:11-19). An introduction (2:6—3:6) provided a setting for the stories, after the death of Joshua, and explained why the conquest did not eliminate all the original inhabitants (2:22—3:2, 4).

The book as we have it today is the product of the fourth and final phase. Sometime after the writing of the book of Joshua but before the fall of Jerusalem (586 B.C.) a final editor(s) completed the book and gave to it its final shape and distinctive interpretation of the period of the judges. The additions include the present introduction (1:1—2:5) and concluding stories (chs 17—21), as well as the judgeship of Othniel (3:7-11) and of those of the "minor" judges, the judgment speeches (6:7-11; 10:6-16), the Abimelech story (ch 9 with transition comments in ch 8), and the death of Samson (ch 16). This final editing was theologically significant. While Joshua describes how God gave to a faithful Israel triumph after triumph, Judges chronicles how the next generations succumbed to the temptations to worship the Canaanite gods and suffered defeat as Yahweh gave them into the hands of their enemies. Failure to keep the covenant brought about a spiral of spiritual and social disintegration until the tribes turned against each other in internecine slaughter.

When all this literary activity took place is difficult to pinpoint. The final editing borrows from the book of Joshua and forms a transition to the book of Samuel, which records the beginning of the institution of kingship. Suffice it to say that the book came into its final form sometime during the seventh century, possibly during the reign of Josiah (640-609 B.C.). (See Stone 1987 for a full discussion of the redaction critical issues.)

F. Judges and the Inspiration of Scripture

The results of the examination of the introductory issues of the book of Judges have implications for the theological doctrine of the inspiration of Scripture. The internal chronology of the book is not consistent with statements found in other texts (see above). The numbers of warriors given for the various military excursions and battles are quite high. According to the Moabite Stone (mid ninth century), King Mesha attacked and destroyed the Israelite town of Jahaz with only 200 warriors (Matthews and Benjamin 1997, 158). Armies of 135,000 soldiers (8:10) and the slaughter of 42,000 Ephraimites (12:6), 22,000 Israelites (20:21), and 25,000 Benjamites (21:46) appear inflated for the twelfth and eleventh centuries. The stories of Judges circulated orally for generations before being collected and written down. The retelling of the accounts by professional storytellers and various family members would have provided occasions to inflate the numbers to heighten the effect of the stories. The compilers probably recorded the stories as they found them at the end of an extended period of oral transmission.

Wesleyan theologians have maintained a dynamic theory of inspiration that takes into account the cultural backgrounds of the people and the various sources that the writers had at their disposal. As early as 1880 W. B. Pope noted that the writers sometimes "have to register facts, or supposed facts, which they gather from public records; sometimes to record traditions, legends, current opinions, or uninspired predictions handed down by tradition: in these cases they are only witnesses of what they found" (1:172). Taking into account the various sources the writers used, he goes on to describe the authority of Holy Scripture as "the absolute and final authority, all-sufficient as the supreme Standard of Faith, Directory of Morals, and Charter of Privileges to the Church of God" (1:174). Similarly A. M. Hills recognized that "in spite of all discrepancies, and disagreements, and errors, and minor inaccuracies, the Bible still remains God's inspired and infallible book. . . . It infallibly guides all honest, and willing and seeking souls to Christ, to holiness, and to heaven" (1931, 1:134). This concept of inspiration was held by H. Orton Wiley, who limited the inerrancy of Scripture to "the authoritative rule of faith and practice in the Church" (1940, 1:171) and by J. Kenneth Grider who noted that "Wesleyan-holiness evangelicals hold the confidence that Scripture is inerrant on doctrine and practice but that it might contain error on matters relating to mathematics, science, geography or such like" (1994, 75). In summary then, we should not look for strict historical accuracy as to chronology and numbers, for the writers were accurately recording the materials that had been handed down to them at that time. This is consistent with the historic Wesleyan teachings on inspiration.

G. Methodology

The dominant method used by commentators of the twentieth century was based in the historical critical paradigm (Holladay 1994, 125-49). Commentators attempted to recover the original meaning of the text using such approaches as textual criticism, source criticism, comparative literature, form criticism, and redaction criticism. The application of such methodologies has been fruitful, but incomplete. The last third of the century found scholars exploring the literary paradigm with such methods as rhetorical criticism, narrative criticism, and reader response. While these methods have been helpful in understanding the literary structure of Scripture, especially its aesthetic value, they, too, are incomplete. Canonical criticism, also a more recent development, asserts that whatever editorial process a book might have gone through, it is its final form that has been recognized by the synagogue and church as inspired by God. It is the completed form of a book that is canonical and that must be taken into account when studying Scripture.

An incarnational approach will be taken in this study. Comments will be based on the Hebrew text with the author's translation placed in bold and italic font. Methods drawn from both the historical and literary paradigms will be used to analyze the process that has produced the text, as well as the text itself. The text records humanity's response to God's interaction with humanity. As such it is a human product. Yet the people of God have for generations also recognized and given witness to the divine dimension, the work of the Holy Spirit who was active in the shaping and the writing of the book. This work of the Holy Spirit makes it the word of God, an authentic and true record of God and humanity's interaction. As McCann has noted:

To be sure, such an incarnational view of Scripture is scandalously particularistic, but no more so than the fundamental Jewish and Christian convictions that God chose Israel or that God is fully known finally in one Jesus of Nazareth, who was "fully human"—"the word became flesh and lived among us" (John 1:14 NRSV). (1996, 643)

H. Theological Themes

The center section of Judges narrates cycles of sin, oppression, crying out to God, and the raising up of saviors to deliver Israel. The six cycles develop a pattern of an increasing downward spiral away from God and toward social disintegration. The first three cycles (Othniel, Ehud, and Deborah) depict Israel seeking other gods but being delivered and given periods of peace. The fourth cycle (Gideon) is pivotal for the overall story as it begins a downward trend toward destruction. In the fifth cycle the elders, not Yahweh, chose Jephthah as a leader, and in the sixth (Samson) there is neither crying out nor full deliverance. Framing the center section are first the opening chapters (1:1—3:6), which describe Israel's limited success in inheriting the land due to Yahweh's refusal to assist them because they had turned to other gods. Second, the final stories describe the depths of Israel's social and moral disintegration (chs 17—21).

I. Human Freedom

Israel was free to choose its path, either to follow Yahweh or to seek other gods. This freedom carried with it great potential for both blessings and curses. There was no attempt on God's part to limit Israel's freedom. Although he sent messengers to warn them (2:1-5; 6:7-10; 10:10-16) and allowed others to oppress them, he never revoked their power to choose their own paths of behavior. Their choosing to follow after other gods resulted in destructive behaviors that led to their being oppressed by other nations (2:14), their failure to inherit the land (2:3), and their turning on each other in war (12:1-6), even to the point of almost destroying one of their own tribes (20:36-48). Yet even in their sin, the character of the nation was not fixed. In the midst of their bondage they cried out to God who heard and responded graciously by raising up a deliverer.

The Israelites had the freedom to choose whom they would serve, but serve they would. The concept of absolute human autonomy is an illusion. The Israelites were free to serve the God of Israel and thus become his servants, obeying his commandments and enjoying his blessings. Or, they could serve the gods of the land, obeying their requirements but falling under the judgment of Yahweh. Paul rightly described humanity's choices: to become the slaves of sin, which leads to death, or to become the slaves of obedience to God, which leads to righteousness and life (Rom 6:15-16). The teachings of Judges and the NT are one at this point.

2. Sovereignty of God

While Israel was free to follow or transgress the covenant, Yahweh kept the covenant by blessing them in periods when they followed the leadership of a judge and bringing the curses of the covenant upon them when the people went after other gods. Yahweh was also free to act in behalf of Israel or to reject their cries (10:10-16). No covenant or agreement to which he was party could force God to respond either in deliverance or destruction. While he was still free in his sovereignty, yet he was torn by his compassion for them and repeatedly heard their cry for help and raised up a judge to save them.

The sovereignty of God is ultimately informed not by power, but by love. The Creator who holds absolute power over his creation can and will use his power to judge the sin of humanity (Gen 6—9; 19:1-26; Matt 25:31-46). However, he prefers to forgive the repentant sinner and restore him or her to covenantal relationship (Exod 34:6-7; John 1:10-13). The crucifixion of Jesus demonstrates the extreme to which God's love will reach out to a rebellious and sinful humanity to woo them back from the false gods who may promise life but can deliver only death. Though the Israelites during the time of the judges turned away from obeying God and sought after the gods of the land, he never rejected them. The curses of the covenant came as instruments of discipline in the attempt to draw them back to real repentance and redemption that he might bless them again (Deut 30:1-10). A sovereign God who tempered his power with love and covenantal faithfulness listened to the cry of the oppressed and moved in compassion to redeem them.

3. Call for Total Loyalty

The Deuteronomic covenant forms the theological foundation for the book of Judges. God graciously delivered Israel from the bondage of slavery in Egypt and brought them into the land. Israel was his people through redemption. The covenant with its commandments was given to provide the community and the individual a distinct way of life, a life given in devotion to this one God. This way of life meant that they were to worship no other gods, to maintain the sanctity of the name of Yahweh, not to lie or steal or commit adultery. These requirements revealed the very nature of Israel's God; One who is holy, and thus to be respected and worshipped; and who is just, and thus who dealt faithfully with the people of Israel. The individual was to respond by giving total loyalty to Yahweh; **you will love Yahweh your God with your whole heart and life and strength** (Deut 6:5). In a world given to the worship of many gods, this people was to be distinct; not by their actions alone, but by the presence in their midst of this one God (Exod 33:16). His presence would call them to holiness, to become in their existence and actions holy like Yahweh and thus to show to the world the possibility of a different way of being and living.

The failure of the people to respond to God in complete trust and loyalty led to the tragedy of their social and spiritual disintegration. The people cried out to the divine warrior Yahweh when they needed deliverance, but they failed to trust him to provide for their daily needs. Instead they turned to other gods who falsely promised prosperity and security. The people of Israel could not bring themselves to fully trust Yahweh to meet their spiritual and material needs.

This same God extends the same invitation to people today. He graciously offers redemption from the bondage of sin to all who truly repent. Beyond the act of forgiveness, he claims the lives of his redeemed people. His Spirit calls us to trust in the love and faithfulness of God. We are to turn from the idols of this world and make a total commitment to his will for our lives. He is faithful and takes our consecrated life and seals it with the gracious cleansing and empowering of the Spirit. We are called to live the life of the Spirit, being transformed daily into the person (individual) and people (community) who reflect the holiness of our God. In so doing we witness to the world a better way of life, a life free from the bondage of the false gods who can only enslave, but never free and save.

COMMENTARY

I. OVERVIEW (1:1—3:6)

The book of Judges begins with the introductory statement *and it was after the death of Joshua* (1:1). However, the death and burial of Joshua is also later recorded in 2:6-9, in wording very similar to Josh 24:28-30. It has long been recognized that Judges has two introductory passages, 1:1—2:5, added by the last editor/writer at the end of a long editorial process, and 2:6—3:6, part of the work of the Deuteronomic Historian (DH, see the Introduction). This is not unlike the beginning of the book of Isaiah with its two introductory superscriptions at 1:1 and 2:1. The passage recorded first, 2:6—3:6, is the work of the DH who edited the stories of the judges to reflect the theology of Deuteronomy. It begins with the account of Joshua's death and burial and the raising up of the next generation, which was ignorant of the works of Yahweh. It concludes with a list of the nations that were left in the land. God's purpose for leaving them was to test Israel to see if the people would be faithful to the covenant. The closing statement, however, describes how the Israelites violated the covenant by intermarrying with the other peoples.

The first chapter describes the tribes' failure to conquer the land. Moving geographically from south to north, the story moves from the success of Judah to the increasing failure of the northern tribes. In the final section (2:1-5) God indicted the tribes for failing to obey the commandments of the covenant and refused to drive out the other nations. This left the conquest unfulfilled.

The first introduction comes from the hand of the final redactor who also edited some of the accounts of the judges and added the concluding stories (chs 17—21) (see the Introduction). This final editing imparted a unity to the entire book through the use of catchphrases and words, parallel actions, and overarching literary themes. The obedient and successful tribe of Judah is contrasted with the northern tribes, which slowly incorporated Canaanite culture and beliefs in a downward spiral of disobedience to the covenant. The success of Judah is specifically contrasted with the failure of Benjamin. Judah conquered the city of Jerusalem and burned it (1:8), but Benjamin could not maintain control of the city by dislodging the Jebusites from it (1:21). Judah took the lead not only in the conquest (1:1-2) but also in the war against Benjamin (20:18). The ascendancy of Judah over Benjamin foreshadows the David/Saul conflict in 1 Samuel where the Benjamite house of Saul was displaced by the Judean David (Sweeney 1997, 517-29). Some of the other parallels include the notes that the Levite who joined the migration of the tribe of Dan (17:7), and the concubine who was abused by the men of Gibeah both came from the Judean town of Bethlehem (19:1). Dan was unable to take possession of its inheritance (1:34) and had to relocate to the north (ch 18). Two women in the book rode donkeys, Achsah the daughter of Caleb dismounted one (1:14) and the body of the presumably dead concubine was loaded on one (19:28). The significant theological word *ḥesed* (loyalty, steadfast love) appears only in 1:24 and v 35 of the late editorial addition of 8:33-35. These types of literary ties help integrate the total work so that in its final form, even though it contains various voices from different time periods, it speaks more as a harmonious whole.

Each introduction describes the downward movement of Israel, which brought to an end the conquest (2:1-5) and placed the covenant in jeopardy (3:1-6). With the death of Joshua the story of Israel turns from one of obedience and success to one of disobedience and failure.

A. A Geography of Failure (1:1—2:5)

BEHIND THE TEXT

This passage contains several instances of intertextual exegesis, borrowing material from Josh 14, 15, and 17 and adapting it to form subtle changes in the passage for theological purposes. The changes serve the interest of highlighting the successes of Judah in contrast with the failures of the "house of Joseph," a term that appears in vv 22 and 35 to frame the account of the conquest by the northern tribes. The passages borrowed include the following:

1. In Josh 14:6, 13-15; 15:13-15 Caleb conquered the city of Hebron and drove out the sons of Anak. In Judg 1:10 Judah conquered Hebron and killed Sheshai, Ahiman, and Talmai. In v 20 Caleb was given the city and drove out the sons of Anak.

2. In Josh 15:15-19 Caleb gave his daughter Achsah as a wife to Othniel, his younger brother. In Judg 1:11-15 Othniel is identified as the nephew of Caleb, the son of his younger brother Kenaz. This makes Othniel a member of the faithful generation who began the conquest under Joshua and who continued to serve God after Joshua's death (Judg 2:7).

3. According to Josh 15:63 Judah was not able to drive the Jebusites out of Jerusalem, but in Judg 1:21 the failure was attributed to Benjamin.

4. In Josh 17:16 the tribe of Joseph excused their failure to take the cities of the valley because the Canaanites had chariots of iron. In Judg 1:19 Judah is excused for not conquering the inhabitants of the valley because they had chariots of iron.

5. Manasseh's failure to take possession of a number of cities is recorded in Josh 17:11-13 and again in Judg 1:27 with only minor variations.

6. Ephraim's failure to drive out the Canaanites from Gezer is noted in Josh 16:10 and Judg 1:29.

The writer has recast the story of the conquest to emphasize Judah and Simeon's success in conquering their inheritances while the northern tribes floundered in their efforts. As the story moves geographically from south to north, it describes how the tribes became less and less successful in possessing the land. Manasseh, Ephraim, and Zebulun could not drive the inhabitants out but allowed the Canaanites to live among them, eventually reducing their status to forced labor. Asher and Naphtali lived among the Canaanites **because they [Asher] did not drive them out** (v 32). The failure to rid the land of its former inhabitants climaxes with Dan being driven out of its inheritance by the Amorites; a situation not resolved until ch 18 (Stone 1992, 332).

Joshua 13:2 notes that Joshua was not able to take the Philistine cities, yet in Judg 1:18 it is stated that Judah took the cities of Gaza, Ashkelon, and Ekron with their surrounding territories. The next verse (v 19) states that Judah was not able to dispossess the inhabitants of the plain. The LXX reads v 18 as a negative: **Judah was not able to take Gaza.** This reading relieves the apparent contradictions between Josh 13:2 and Judg 1:18 and between vv 18 and 19. However, 1:18 as it stands is in keeping with the context in which Judah's success is heightened in contrast with the failures of the northern tribes.

IN THE TEXT

1. Judah Goes Up (1:1-7)

■ **1-7** With the death of Joshua a new chapter in the story of Israel began. Moses at the command of God had designated Joshua to be his successor (Deut 31:7-8, 14-23), but no successor to Joshua had been chosen. Joshua belonged to the first generation, which had witnessed the mighty acts of God in bringing Israel out of the bondage of Egypt. Because this generation refused to obey God and invade the land from the south, it had been cursed by God to die in the wilderness; only Joshua and Caleb were allowed to enter the land with the next generation (Num 14:26-38). The next generation under the leadership of Joshua successfully began the conquest. This second generation remained faithful to God during both the life of Joshua and the lives of their elders (2:7). Then a third generation arose. The first chapters of Judges address the questions of who would lead it; and would it remain faithful to the covenant given by God?

The sons of Israel or Israelites *inquired of Yahweh* (v 1); that is, they sought by some means an oracle or direct word from God as to which tribe should **go up** against **the Canaanite** (singular).

Who Were the Canaanites?

The term "Canaanite," occurring in the OT almost always in the singular as a collective term, may refer to a specific ethnic or cultural group as distinct from other groups. It may also refer in general to the inhabitants of the area along the southeastern coast of the Mediterranean, up to the city of Tyre, and extending inland beyond the city of Damascus. Legal and administrative documents from the Late Bronze era (1550-1200 B.C.) from Egypt, Babylon, and other areas refer to inhabitants of this area as "sons of Canaan," "men of Canaan," "sons of the land of

Canaan," or Canaanites (Rainey 1996, 1-15). In Judges it refers to the inhabitants of the land as a whole, even when it is paired with another specific ethnic group (e.g., the Perizzites in v 4).

The term ʿālāh ("to go up") appears in vv 1, 2, 3, 4, 16, 22, and 2:1 and ties the unit together. With the exception of 2:1, it carries the meaning of going into battle or war. In 20:18 the tribes again inquired of Yahweh who should go up or lead in battle. The same terminology is used and the same answer was given, Judah. In both the opening chapter of the book and in the closing story Judah was given the place of prominence in going to war.

Yahweh's response to the inquiry was that Judah would lead the invasion. The second half of the verse is a promise, **I have given the land into his hand** (v 2). This was not spoken as an accomplished fact but rather an assurance that God would be with Judah to bless the tribe's efforts.

Judah invited his brother-tribe Simeon to form a coalition in order to assist each other in their war efforts. Simeon would in the time of the monarchy be absorbed by Judah and lose its separate identity. Their first attack was against the **Canaanites and Perizzites** whom **Yahweh gave into their hands** (v 4). The victory was assured by divine help. The Perizzites were a pre-Israelite group located in the wooded hills between Jerusalem and the inheritance of Ephraim (Josh 11:3; 17:15), an area originally given to Benjamin, not Judah (Josh 18:11). Nothing is known about the Perizzites other than what is contained in the OT, and that is very little. The name the Perizzite, always a collective term with an article and singular in number, probably is non-Semitic, possibly Hurrian, an ethnic group whose homeland was located in the mountains north of Mesopotamia (Reed 1997, ABD-CD). They were one of the peoples that the Israelites intermarried with (Judg 3:5-6), in violation of the commands given by Moses (Deut 7:1-3).

Bezek (Judg 1:4) is generally located north of Jerusalem, possibly in the area of Manasseh. Zertal suggests that Judah and Simeon may have taken a more northern route into the hill country and were opposed by the lord/ruler of Bezek, or rather translated as a name, **Adoni-bezek** (v 5) (Zertal 1997, ABD-CD). In Josh 10:1 the king of Jerusalem is identified as Adoni-zedek. It is not certain if the name "Bezek" has been corrupted from the original form "Zedek," however, they were two different kings. **Adoni-bezek** was taken to Jerusalem to die (Judg 1:7). The king of Jerusalem, Adoni-zedek, met a different fate, being struck down and his body hung on a tree (Josh 10:26).

When the Judeans captured Adoni-bezek **they cut off the thumbs of his hands and the big toes of his feet** (Judg 1:6). This would immobilize him as a warrior, for he would not be able to grasp a sword or run swiftly. There is no other account in Judges of the Israelites mutilating a living captive. Later David removed the head of Goliath (1 Sam 17:47-51) and after executing the men who killed Ish-baal had their hands and feet cut off and their bodies hung (2 Sam 4:12), but accounts of the Israelites mutilating their captives are rare. The Judeans inflicted upon Adoni-bezek that same cruelty he had used on others. This action produces a tension in the story. Were the Judeans becoming like the Canaanites they were displacing? Adoni-bezek acknowledged that what he had done to **seventy kings** (a round number used to mean "many") God had justly brought upon him (Judg 1:7). However, that confession does not relieve the tension in the story. Later the body of the concubine who had been sexually abused would be dismembered (19:29). When Saul called upon the Israelites to gather at Bezek to go and lift the siege of Jabesh-gilead (1 Sam 11:7-11), he dismembered his oxen as a symbol to the tribes of the seriousness of the situation. The mutilation of Adoni-bezek foreshadows both the dismemberment of the concubine (Judg 19:29) and of Saul's oxen (Schneider 2000, 6).

The verse ends with the sobering note that **they took him to Jerusalem, and he died there** (1:7). Who took him? The Judeans in order to strike fear into the inhabitants of Jerusalem? Or, his own people seeking refuge? The text does not tell us.

2. Taking Jerusalem and Hebron (1:8-10)

■ **8-10** The account of the attack on Jerusalem is concise but descriptive. The Judeans seized the city, put its inhabitants to death by the sword, and set the city ablaze. While the account is at variance with Josh 15:63, which states that the Judeans were unable to take the city, it serves the function of heightening the success of Judah to give it more prominence among the tribes. The Judeans then moved against the Canaanites **in the hill country, the Negev, and the Shephelah** (Judg 1:9). The hill country as it extends south of Jerusalem becomes less rugged. The Negev, which means "dry," lays at the end of the hill country as the terrain becomes flat and arid. It includes the Arad and Beer-sheba valleys, about a 40 by 40 km region. It was thinly populated during the time of the judges (Beit-Arieh 1997, ABD-CD). The Shephelah of Judah is an area of lower hills that runs southwest to northeast about 50 miles along the western edge of the Judean hills. It is good farmland and a number of major cities—such as

Lachish, Mareshah, Azekah, and Beth-shemesh—were located there (Brodsky 1997, ABD-CD).

In v 10 the tribe of Judah rather than Caleb took the active role in capturing Hebron (Josh 14:6, 13-14) and is credited with both the capture of Hebron and for striking down the three sons of Anak (Josh 15:13-15). Sheshai, Ahiman, and Talmai have non-Semitic names, indicating that their family was not indigenous to the area. They may have been Philistine. Caleb is not mentioned until he is introduced in Judg 1:12 in conjunction with the destruction of Kiriath-sepher. Ascribing the conquest of Hebron to Judah, not Caleb, continues the pattern of highlighting the successes of Judah.

Hebron was a significant political and sacred city located in the central hill country about 20 miles south of Jerusalem. It later became the first royal residence of David (2 Sam 2:1). Joshua had set it aside as a sacred city to which a person who had accidentally killed someone could flee for safety (Josh 20:7). It continued as a sacred center into the reign of David. His son Absalom, as a cover for launching his revolt, secured David's permission to go to Hebron to worship Yahweh (2 Sam 15:7-12).

3. Taking Debir (1:11-15)

■ **11-15** The town of Debir (v 11) was probably located southwest of Hebron in the Shephelah. Its former name was Kiriath-sepher, or "Town of the Book." In Josh 15:49 the city is called Kiriath-sannah, or "Town of Learning." The names indicate that the town was known as a center of learning or scribal activity. A city of learning and culture was taken and destroyed by the Israelites. As Fewell notes, "A city of learning was simply erased" (1995, 132).

Caleb offered his daughter Achsah as a wife to the warrior who would take the city. The identification of Othniel is ambiguous. Was he ***the son of Kenaz who is the younger brother of Caleb*** (v 13), and thus the cousin of Achsah? Or, was he ***the son of Kenizzite [a Kenite], the younger brother of Caleb,*** and thus the uncle of Achsah? The early Greek translations vary while the Vulgate has the latter. Since a marriage between an uncle and niece was considered improper, early commentators such as Poole (1685) and Scott (1702) suggested that "brother" be taken in the expanded sense of kinsman (Gunn 2005, 21-22). Stone argues that Kenaz should be read as the father of Othniel and the younger brother of Caleb. This would make Othniel a member of the second generation, the faithful generation of the conquest (1987, 204-7).

The beginning of v 14 should be read ***he went in to her,*** reading the ending *h* of the Hebrew verb as indicating direction. The terminology has sexual overtones and indicates the consummation of the marriage between Othniel and Achsah (Schneider 2000, 12). The second verb *sût* also has sexual overtones, to allure, incite (KBL 1985, 654) or seduce. Since Achsah subsequently approached her father with a request, the LXX and Vulgate read "he urged her to ask her father for a field" (Boling 1975, 56-57). It is better to follow the MT and read **she seduced him.** Achsah had been given without her consent to a warrior as a prize of war. She was under the authority first of her father and then her husband. It would be in keeping with her social position to use her sexuality to persuade her husband to seek further advantages from her father. Themes that are introduced in this first chapter are further developed later in the book. The motif of a woman using her sexuality for advantage over a man appears again in the Samson story where Delilah sought to discover the secret of his strength (16:4-22) (Schneider 2000, 13-14).

In the next scene Achsah traveled a good distance, riding on a donkey rather than walking, to see her father, Caleb. He realized that this was no casual visit as he asked, literally, **"What to you?"** or more smoothly, **"What do you want?"** (v 14). She demanded (the verb is in the imperative) that Caleb give her a blessing. She had been placed by him on water-poor land in the dry region of the Negev. Specifically she wanted springs of water. Her assertive manner in confronting her father over the poor quality of the land shamed Caleb, forcing him to respond. Caleb complied with her request. Achsah was not willing to accept a passive role in a male-dominated society (Matthews 2004, 40). She used her sexuality to prod her husband to ask for a field and then confronted her father over the poor quality of the land. She is the first of the women in Judges who stepped outside the traditional role established by society.

4. Judah's Successes and Inadequacies (1:16-21)

■ **16-21** This section completes the story of Judah's part in the conquest. It also includes several notes on those who were associated with Judah. The Kenites were related to Moses by marriage. Some part of the tribe went with Judah from Jericho, the City of Palms, into the Negev and **lived among the people** (v 16), an ambiguous term that could mean the indigenous people of the area or the people of the tribe of Judah or Simeon who were also moving into the area. The Jerahmeelites, another tribe that was related to Israel, also lived in the Negev (1 Sam 27:10).

Judah fulfilled its pledge to assist Simeon in occupying his inheritance (Judg 1:17). The Canaanites at Zephath were placed under the ban of total destruction, *ḥāram*. The city was then renamed Hormah, *ḥārmāh*, which is a play on the two words.

According to the MT Judah then seized the Philistine cities of Gaza, Ashkelon, and Ekron (v 18). However, the beginning of v 18 in LXX reads, **and Judah did not acquire Gaza**. The MT reading is probably better since it continues the theme of the success of Judah. In Josh 10:33 Joshua killed the king of Gezer who came to assist the city of Lachish, which the Israelites had placed under siege. However, the Philistine cities were not taken by Joshua (13:2). Both Gaza and Ashkelon were sea ports located on the coastal plain of the Mediterranean. Ekron was on the eastern edge of the plain. The next verse, however, notes that Judah did not conquer the cities in the valleys, as the inhabitants had chariots strengthened with iron (Judg 1:19).

Military Use of Chariots

The chariot served the same military purposes as the modern tank. Along with the one who handled the horses, there were one or two persons with bows or lances. It was highly maneuverable and with its greater fire power it produced shock and panic in the opposing infantry. The chariot was made of wood and then had iron bands and fittings to give it strength. One made wholly of iron would have been very expensive and too heavy to maneuver.

The beginning of v 19, **And Yahweh was with Judah**, forms a concluding remark, which with the last half of v 2, *I will give the land into his hand*, forms a frame or envelope around the narrative.

Caleb received the city of Hebron (v 20) as Moses had promised (Josh 14:9). However, he is associated with the tribe of Judah as his victory is an extension of the conquest of Judah.

This section closes (Judg 1:21) with the note that Benjamin did not take possession of Jerusalem because the Jebusites were there. What Judah had destroyed (v 8), Benjamin could not take. The Judah/Benjamin comparison forms the final note of the Judah narrative.

5. Taking Bethel (1:22-26)

■ **22-26** *The house of Joseph* (v 22) may refer specifically to the two tribes of Ephraim and Manasseh whose ancestor was the patriarch Joseph (Gen 48:8-20; Josh 17:17). It may also stand for the northern tribes in general, as it does in this passage. The town of Bethel belonged to the tribe of Benjamin (Josh 18:22). The concluding phrase of Judg 1:22, **and Yahweh was with them**, expresses the same commitment by God to the northern tribes as he made to the tribe of Judah (v 2). Since God was willing to assist each of the tribes to take possession of its territory, the tribe's success or failure was determined by its actions, not some failure on God's part.

Verse 23 begins with the verb *tûr* ("to spy, or reconnoiter"). The word links this story with the account in Num 13—14 where twelve were sent to spy out the land. The same word occurs there eleven times. The report that the men brought back was not positive. The Israelites refused to trust God and enter the land. Thus that generation proved unfaithful and died in the wilderness (Num 14:26-35). This new generation would succeed where the earlier one failed.

When the spies saw a man departing the city (Judg 1:24), they approached him with an offer to deal faithfully (*ḥesed*) with him and his family if he would show them an entrance into the city. The city probably had not only a main gate that would be heavily fortified but also smaller entrances or posterns more readily concealed and thus less heavily guarded. The offer of *ḥesed* echoes the story of Jericho where Rahab requested and received loyalty from the men she had hidden (Josh 2:12, 14). *Ḥesed* is a significant theological word that expresses faithful loyalty within a relationship. In modern versions it is often translated unfailing or steadfast love. Its only other occurrence in Judges is in 8:35 where the Israelites did not deal loyally with the family of Gideon after his death. The man agreed and showed the sons of Joseph an entrance. The inhabitants of the city were slaughtered, but the man with his family was permitted to leave in safety. The man then journeyed north of Lebanon, **to the land of the Hittites** (v 26), leaving the Canaanite area entirely to build a new city name Luz. While the story parallels the account of Rahab and the fall of Jericho, it also foreshadows the Danite conquest of Laish/Dan where a peaceful and unsuspecting people were slaughtered (18:27-29).

6. Living Among the Canaanites (1:27-36)

■ **27-36** As the narrative keeps moving topographically north, the success rate of the tribes diminishes. The tribes of Manasseh, Ephraim, and Zebulun were not able to fully possess the land but allowed the Canaanites to live among them. Next Asher and Naphtali lived among the Canaanites. Lastly, Dan was driven out of his inheritance by the Amorites.

The list of towns that Manasseh was unable to take (v 27) includes also the villages surrounding each town. Major towns like Beth-shean formed an economic district with the smaller villages. The surplus goods produced by the villages, both in the form of crops and material goods such as pottery, were taken as taxes by the hierarchical elite who lived in the larger towns. These towns were not major cities as we think of them today. The city of Jerusalem at the time of David may have had a population of less than a thousand.

When the Israelites became militarily stronger (v 28), they were able to subject the Canaanites to forced labor (*mas*). Israel had experienced the same subjugation in Egypt (Exod 1:11). Later Solomon conscripted native Israelites themselves into forced labor gangs (1 Kgs 5:13). Israel had learned from the Egyptians how to deal with a non-Israelite people, and without compassion they became like their teachers.

Neither Ephraim nor Zebulun were able to possess their inheritance but allowed the Canaanites to live among them (Judg 1:29-30).

The tribe of Asher (vv 31-32) suffered a different set of circumstances. In addition to not being able to dislodge the Canaanites, they **dwelt among the Canaanites** (v 32). Here is a shift of situation, from allowing the Canaanites to dwell among the tribe, to the tribe dwelling among the Canaanites. Naphtali endured the same situation (v 33), but at some point did become strong enough to subjugate the Canaanites and use them as forced labor.

Dan was driven out of his inheritance (v 34) by the Amorites. Thus the conquest ended. At first the tribes were unable to dislodge the inhabitants but allowed them to dwell among them. Then the tribes had to dwell among the Canaanites. Finally, Dan was driven out of the plains and into the hills, a reversal of what should have happened in the conquest.

The Amorites are listed among the earlier inhabitants that were to be driven out of the land (Deut 7:1). Israel first came into contact with them in the Transjordan area when Sihon attacked them (Num 21:21-31). His attack failed and Israel took possession of that area. The term "Amorite" was also used in the same manner as Canaanite, to designate all the inhabitants of the land, regardless of ethnic group (Gen 15:16). However, in Judg 1:34-36 they were a distinct group with identifiable boundaries. The use of the phrase **house of Joseph** in both vv 35 and 22 forms a frame or literary boundary for this passage.

7. End of the Conquest (2:1-5)

■ **1-5** This passage contains an oracle from Yahweh, delivered by a messenger designated as an angel/messenger of Yahweh. A *malʾak*, usually translated "angel" from the Greek *angelos*, "a messenger," was a member of the heavenly court who did the bidding of Yahweh. The oracle first rehearses the past actions of deliverance performed by God on behalf of the people and the commitment he made to their fathers (Judg 2:1). It next moves to an indictment of the people for not keeping the covenant (v 2). The oracle concludes with the passing of a sentence on the people in accordance with what God had previously said (v 3). This is in the style of a prophetic oracle seen commonly in the works of the classical prophets. The last two verses describe the reactions of the people, weeping and sacrificing.

The angel of Yahweh came up from Gilgal (v 1), the first encampment that the Israelites made after crossing the Jordan (Josh 4:19-20) and their base of operations for subsequent military actions (Josh 10:6-7). Boling suggests that this was an angelic being who took on human form (1975, 62). Later a prophet will bring a message of rebuke (Judg 6:7-10) and then the angel of Yahweh will foretell the birth of Samson to his parents (13:3). **Bochim,** which means "weepers," is identified by the LXX with Bethel. Also, the "Oak of Weeping" was located near Bethel (Gen 35:8). The name Bochim appears in both Judg 2:1 and 5 to form a literary frame for this passage. McCann notes, "The people are still weeping at the end of the book of Judges" (2002, 30), for they appear before Yahweh at Bethel again to weep before him after having been defeated by Benjamin (20:23).

The messenger stated inclusively, **I caused you to go up from Egypt, and I brought you into the land** (v 1). The word "you" in both clauses is emphatic. It is also in keeping with Deuteronomic expressions of being inclusive of later generations (Deut 5:3). Israel's obligation (Judg 2:2) was to keep the covenant, specifically by not forming covenants with the people in Canaan and by tearing down the altars erected to their gods. The Israelites were not chastised for leaving Canaanites alive, or not chasing them out of the land, but for entering into covenantal relationships with them and not destroying their places of worship. The violation shifts from not exterminating the people to becoming like them in both social intercourse and worship.

In v 3 the messenger recalls God's threat to Israel (Exod 23:21, 33; Josh 23:13), that if they did not obey, God would not drive out the peoples. Instead, the Canaanites would become thorns to them, discomforting barriers to Israel achieving God's will for them. Also, their gods would be traps, hidden fowlers' snares used to catch birds; a metaphor for enticing worshippers into the clutches of death. Israel's response was to lift up their voices in weeping and to offer a sacrifice to Yahweh. The sentence had been passed, and further action would not reverse it. The conquest had come to an end.

FROM THE TEXT

1. In Judges God is more of a reactor than an actor. God had chosen Moses and then Joshua to lead Israel and had given each direct orders on

how to proceed. While at times God dropped into the background and led through events, he was often seen as communicating directly; giving the commandments and laws, providing water and food, issuing battle plans. Judges opens with the tribes inquiring of God who should lead in battle. God responded by picking Judah to lead in battle and assured the tribe that he would be with them (1:2). The narrative notes twice more that God was with the tribes (vv 19, 22). The main actors in the story, however, were the tribes themselves. God did not intrude into the battles to give directions or to assure victory. At the end God sent a messenger to evaluate their actions and condemn their lack of obedience.

Humanity is given great freedom to respond to the challenges of life. God has given basic instructions and at times breaks in with specific directions, but most of life is lived with God in the shadows, working behind the scenes. This places great responsibility upon humanity. God allows us to shape the future, but we must also bear the consequences and live with the choices we make. If we fail to heed God's warnings about worshipping false gods, then we will experience the destructive consequences that come from disobedience.

This freedom of choice exists even in our spiritual life when God confronts us with the call to love him with all our body, mind, and strength. His Spirit does not call us to total commitment without enabling us to respond. However, we must be willing to tear down the altars to the false gods of power, wealth, sexuality, and self-centeredness, which try to seduce us. God is with his people (v 22), and it is only through his cleansing that the idols of the inner life can be destroyed. These last two statements speak of a great mystery. While it is the sovereign God who calls and his Spirit who empowers, he has through his grace enabled humans to choose. Therefore as in the days of Moses God still sets before us a choice, **life and goodness or death and evil** (Deut 30:15). While the choice is ours, God urges us to choose obedience and life.

2. Actions reveal who we are better than do our words. How different were the Judeans than Adoni-bezek? They did to him what he had done to others. The tribes lived among the Canaanites and did not destroy their places of worship. The Israelites had been slaves in Egypt and when in power reduced the Canaanites to the same forced labor they had experienced. While our ideals help shape our character, more telling is our actions. By acting like the Canaanites, do we become Canaanite? Recitations of creeds and public professions of faith help us sound religious, but it is our actions that truly define who we are and what we believe.

3. When the Israelites became powerful enough to overcome their

neighbors, they used the Canaanites as forced laborers. What they had been in Egypt, slaves, they in turn made the Canaanites. God's command to the Israelites was that they were to destroy the peoples of the land, not mix with them and become like them. The command, however, was capable of being modified, and it was possible for the Israelites to accept others into their community, if like Rahab (Josh 2:8-14) they were willing to acknowledge Yahweh as their God and make peace with the Israelites (Josh 11:19) (Stone 1991, 25-36). Instead, however, of incorporating them into the covenant community, Israel exploited them. The Israelites could not resist using such a valuable resource for their own profit. Economic gain triumphed over obedience to God. The exploitation of others for economic gain is a historically recurring injustice; one that is common to today's societies. We are driven by the desire not just for economic security but by a rapacious greed for more. This, as the apostle Paul stated, is idolatry (Col 3:5). Economic production must come under the judgment of God who demands that a community maintain economic justice especially for those in vulnerable circumstances (Isa 1:17; Amos 5:11-12; Mic 2:1-3).

B. Testing of Israel (2:6—3:6)

BEHIND THE TEXT

With 2:6 the reader is taken back to the time when Joshua dismissed Israel after the convocation at Shechem (Josh 24:28). The earlier edition of the book compiled by the Deuteronomic Historian (Dtr) began at this point. The first section (Judg 2:6-10) functions as a transition from the time of Joshua to the next generation. Joshua 24:28-31 is quoted almost exactly. One of the changes is that v 31, the last verse, is moved up to the second verse, Judg 2:7. This move emphasizes the obedience of the generation of elders and sets up the contrast with the unfaithfulness of the following generation.

With the later addition of 1:1—2:5, however, a shift is made in the setting of this passage. In Josh 24 the Israelites were at Shechem. In Judg 2:1-5 they were at Bochim, that is, Bethel, the location of the shrine established later by Jeroboam (1 Kgs 12:29—13:34). Reading the text (Judg 2:1-10) as it now stands (that is, in its canonical setting), the reader is alerted to the snare that Bethel became for the northern kingdom of Israel. While Judah continued to be ruled by the house of David, Israel experienced a tumultuous succession of nine different dynasties, none of which according to Dtr remained faithful to God and his covenant. Sweeney notes, "The narrative thereby serves Judean/Davidic polemics in that Bochim/Bethel becomes the site associated with YHWH's 'testing' or punishment of the people" (1997, 522).

Verses 10-20 introduce the cycle of sin, oppression, crying out to God, and deliverance in which each of the stories of the judges has been cast. The stories are not strictly cyclical, as each contains variations, and particularly with the later narratives become increasingly longer. There is also a progression downward. The Israelites continued to disobey God by worshipping the gods of the people who surround them and thus breached the covenant established at Sinai. What held the tribes together was not family ties or cultural solidarity, but the covenant of Yahweh. As the Israelites became more devoted to the false gods, their communal bonds became more frayed and the society became more fractured. At the end of the book the tribes will turn on each other in fratricidal wars.

The chapter ends (vv 21-23) with Yahweh's decision not to remove the peoples surrounding the Israelites. They would become a test to enable Yahweh to know whether or not Israel remained faithful to the path he had established for them. The last word of the chapter is the name Joshua, the second word in v 6. The references to Joshua form a frame or envelope for the narrative, beginning and ending it.

This section ends with a summary statement concerning the purposes of God (3:1-6). It contains a double listing of the nations/peoples God left in the land and also of the purposes of God for not removing them. The material may have originally come from two sources and been combined by the editor. God allowed the people to remain in order to teach the next generation the art of war (vv 1-2) and also to test the Israelites to see if they would remain faithful to the commandments given to them by Moses (v 4). The Israelites did not obey the covenant (Exod 34:15-16) but intermarried with the people and worshipped their gods. As Judg 1:1—2:5 concludes with the failure of the conquest, in like manner 2:6—3:6 ends with the failure of the covenant.

IN THE TEXT

1. Death of Joshua (2:6-10)

■ **6-10** When Joshua dismissed the Israelites, they departed **each to his inheritance to possess the land** (v 6). The people were engaged with the conquest, doing what God had commanded. Verse 7 begins, **and the people served Yahweh.** The verb "serve" (ʿābad) appears five times in this passage (2:7, 11, 13, 19, and 3:6) with a key function. It traces the religious affinities of the people. One serves a master/god by keeping his commandments. In v 11 they served the Baals, in v 13 Baal and Ashteroth, in v 19 the other gods, in 3:6 the gods of the people they intermarried with. While the people of the generation of the elders who outlived Joshua remained faithful, the next generation did not.

Another subtle shift in 2:7 notes that the generation of the elders that lived after Joshua died **saw all the great deeds of Yahweh.** Joshua 24:31 states that they **knew all the deeds of Yahweh.** To see an event means to experience it. To know something or someone can mean to have knowledge or to enter into a relationship, such as in Gen 4:1, Adam **knew his wife Eve and she conceived.** Both phrases emphasize that the generation of the conquest was committed to doing the will of God, for they had experienced both his grace and his power and were fully confident that he would help them succeed. The death and burial of Joshua is described in vv 8-10*a*.

Joshua died at the age of 110 years, slightly less than the 120 years Moses attained. He was also given the title **servant of Yahweh** (v 8) as had been Moses (Josh 1:1-2). The title and age symbolize that he was next to Moses not only as the next leader of Israel but also in faithfulness to Yahweh; next to, but not the same as. Others in Israel's history (David, Hezekiah, Josiah, Jeremiah, and Isaiah) were lauded for their righteousness and faithfulness, but none were held in higher regard than Moses. Joshua was buried (Judg 2:9) within the boundaries of his inheritance, indicating that he personally had successfully carried out God's command for the conquest.

Verse 10 describes the transition to the next generation. The faithful generation **was gathered to their fathers** (v 10). This is not just a euphemism for dying. It is that, but it also refers the burial custom of carving out of the soft limestone a burial chamber where the family members were buried. Several generations were often interred in the same chamber. The end of the verse states that the next generation **did not know Yahweh or the works he did for Israel** (v 10). The next generation was not ignorant of God's works of deliverance. Rather, unlike the previous generation, they refused to learn from them and to acknowledge Yahweh's sovereignty (Stone 1992, 333).

2. The Next Generation (2:11-19)

■ **11-19** This section sets forth a prelude of the cycle of sin, oppression, crying out to God, and raising up a deliverer that occupies the bulk of the book. No specific foe is mentioned nor is any judge named. This is more of a theological explanation rather than a historical narrative. It informs the reader what will be the pattern of events that play out in the following stories. This will not be a story of faithfulness and victory, but of seeking after other gods leading to political and spiritual failure. Yet Yahweh will not desert his people. He will graciously hear their cries and respond by raising up judges.

The opening line notes that the Israelites **did evil in the eyes of Yahweh** (v 11). At the end of the book the phrase **every person did what was right in his own eyes** appears twice (17:6; 21:25). The phrase indicates that the Israelites rejected the standards set by Yahweh but determined what was right or evil according to their desires (Deut 12:8). The theme of the individual determining for himself what is evil or right is established at the beginning of the book. The Israelites themselves established the standard of what is right or wrong, not God (Schneider 2000, 31). The specific evil mentioned is that of serving the baals, the various local manifestations of the Canaanite rain god Baal Hadad.

The Israelites abandoned or forsook Yahweh (Judg 2:12), in the sense that they also worshipped the god of the peoples who lived around them. Polytheism was not an exclusive religion. It made room for many gods. The covenant made between Israel and Yahweh, however, was exclusive. Polytheism allowed the worship of the various gods and Yahweh. Yahweh refused to be worshipped along with the other gods. Yahweh was **the God of their fathers, who had brought them out of the land of Egypt** (v 12). He asserted his sovereignty based on the act of redemption. He had entered into an exclusive relationship with the people because he had delivered them from slavery. Israel by worshipping the other gods **infuriated Yahweh** (v 12).

Yahweh became angry because they **served Baal and Ashtorot** (plural form) (v 13). Baal Hadad was an extremely important god for the Canaanites as he was the rain god, responsible for bringing rain at the right time of the year so that they might have bountiful harvests. Ashtoret, or more likely Ashtart, was a consort of Baal, probably to be identified with the Mesopotamian goddess Ishtar. The vocalization of the name in Hebrew has been conflated with the word for shame, *bōšet;* the vowels being inserted into the name so that the reader would understand that this was a shameful thing. Her name usually appears in the plural form, as in this verse (Day 1997, ABD-CD).

Why Did Israel Worship Other Gods?

Why did the Israelites continue to break the covenant by worshipping other gods? What made the other gods so attractive? To answer these questions we have to see the world through the eyes of ancient people. First, the common idea of cause-and-effect that drives our modern world did not exist. It was first stated by the Greek philosopher Aristotle in the fifth century B.C. Certainly events happened then as they do today, but the people did not explain them as we do. Instead, ancient peoples believed things happened because a god caused them. The sun came up because the sun god made it rise. Rain was caused by the rain god. Evil events came because someone angered a god, or an evil god/demon caused them. Since the world exhibited many forces, the people were polytheists, worshipping many gods. It was thought normal to worship many gods. The question was, what kind of gods did you worship? Israel identified Yahweh as a powerful God who delivered them from Egypt and supplied their needs in the wilderness. He could be called upon to deliver them from oppression. But, could he produce rain and make crops grow? Farmers depended on the crops they grew to feed their families. Drought, floods, locusts—all could spell starvation. So the question of what kind of a god one worshipped was a serious one. The neighbors of the Israelites believed that Baal Hadad caused the rain to come and that Ashtoret brought fertility. It was a serious matter not to worship the correct god or gods. If one insulted a god, then the angry god might ruin the crops and people, especially children would starve to death. Elijah's challenge to the prophets of Baal on Mount Carmel came after three years of drought (1 Kgs 18). The issue was, who made it rain, Yahweh or Baal? The one who answered by fire (lightning) was the true God. It is easy to sit comfortably in a modern setting and wonder why Israel could not trust Yahweh. It is harder when the lives of one's family are at stake and the neighbors are encouraging us to worship their god as the one who will meet our needs.

It was Yahweh who brought the Israelites victory in the battles against the Canaanites. When they angered Yahweh by worshipping other gods, he then **gave them into the hand of their oppressors . . . and sold them into the hand of their enemies** (v 14). The double statement adds emphasis. The expression "to give into the hand" means to deliver them into the power or control of another. "To sell them" refers to slavery. The tribes turned away from Yahweh to serve other gods. In response the God who freed them from the slavery from Egypt sold them to oppressive slavers. When they went out for war **the hand of Yahweh was against them for evil** (v 15). The curses in Deut 28:15-68 graphically portray the evils that would come upon Israel if they were disobedient to the covenant. Judges 2:15 states specifically that he would cause them to lose in war.

Yet Yahweh did not cast off his people. Graciously he raised up judges to save them (v 16). The motivation for God acting to save Israel was the pity he felt over their oppression (v 18). The word for **groaning** (ň'āqâ) appears also in Exod 2:24 and 6:5 where in both appearances God heard the groaning of his people who suffered oppression in Egypt. Judges 2:17 represents a later insertion that amplifies the sin of the people. Even when God had raised up judges, ***they did not listen for they went lusting after other gods and worshipped them*** (v 17). The word "lusting" (*zānâ*) has strong sexual connotations referring to illicit relationships. Again the generation is compared unfavorably to their fathers, the faithful generation that obeyed the commandments of God. This section closes with an emphatic description of the unfaithfulness of the Israelites. After the judge died, they greedily returned to the worship of other gods. They learned nothing from their previous experiences of oppression or from their periods of Yahweh's restful care. Rather in their own stubbornness they chose to serve other gods in violation of the covenant.

3. Yahweh's Decision (2:20-23)

■ **20-23** These verses summarize the message of the chapter. Joshua and the elders of that generation are exonerated for leaving the Canaanites in the land. The blame falls on the next generation, which failed in its obedience to the covenant. Yahweh himself speaks the judgment (vv 20*b*-21) and then the narrator explains Yahweh's motive (v 22). The last word of v 23 is the name Joshua, which ties the material not only back to 2:6 where Joshua dismissed the Israelite from the convocation at Bochim, but also to 1:1, which begins the book with the announcement of his death.

Yahweh was angry with Israel (2:20) because of their stubborn determination to serve other gods (v 19). The expression "became angry" literally reads ***Yahweh's anger grew hot.***

An Angry God

The act of becoming angry is a technical, covenant expression to describe the reaction of either an overlord or vassal when the other partner had violated a treaty/covenant. In the treaty between Mursilis and Duppi-Tessub, Mursilis states, "Aziras {father of Duppi-Tessub} remained loyal toward my father [as his overlord] and did not incite my father's anger; he did not take an unjust action against him or incite his or his country's anger in any way" (Goetze, ANET, 1969, 203). While the overlord or vassal might personally experience the emotion of anger, the term was used in a political context to indicate an objective reaction to the violation of the covenant. That reaction, unless the guilty party ceased violating the covenant, would lead to the curses of the covenant being invoked and war between the two parties. Modern-day interpreters should guard against making a psychological evaluation of how Yahweh felt about the Israelites worshipping other gods. The act of Yahweh becoming angry was a political/theological response to the disobedience of the Israelites. Unless they repented, Yahweh would act in accordance with the covenant and invoke the curses, which in this case meant allowing Israel's enemies to defeat and oppress them.

Since this nation had transgressed the covenant, he would not **continue to drive out the nations Joshua left when he died** (v 21). What had become a failure on Israel's part became an opportunity for God. The nations would become a means of testing Israel's faithfulness, to see whether or not they would follow God's commandments (v 22). His judgment was not a decision to destroy but a decision to establish a means for further testing, to see whether or not Israel would learn from their experiences. The last verse (v 23) indicates that this decision was made even before Joshua died, as God did not give the peoples into the hand of Joshua to drive them out hurriedly. Success was not ultimately determined by the size of armies or superiority of military technology but by the obedience to the will of Yahweh as expressed in the covenant.

4. Reasons for the Nations to Remain (3:1-6)

■ **1-6** This passage forms a conclusion to the two-part introduction to the book. The situation of the Israelites is openly acknowledged. The conquest did not rid the land of its former inhabitants (v 1), and Israel had to adjust its expectations to the reality that they were going to remain. Living close to other ethnic groups, all vying for control of the limited space and resources available, meant that there would be continued conflict. To survive, Israel had to prepare succeeding generations in the art of military conflict (v 2). The remaining nations became a means by which Yahweh might test (*nassôt*; also 2:22 and 3:4) Israel, that they might know war from experience.

The first list of peoples (v 3) begins with the five rulers of the Philistines. The word *seren* is only used of these rulers and can be translated "lords" or "tyrants" (BDB, 710). How it should be translated depends on one's perspective. The Philistines thought of their leaders as lords who would govern and protect them. The Israelites thought of them as tyrants who exploited them. The Philistines were part of a migration out of the Aegean area and took the cities of Gaza, Ashkelon, Ekron, Ashdod, and Gath in the early twelfth century. Their objective was the same as the Israelites, to rule the land of Canaan. Thus they were a constant military threat until the reign of David (2 Sam 5:17-25). The phrase **all the Canaanites** (Judg 3:3) is an inclusive term to refer to all the peoples in the area from Galilee in the north to the Negev in the south. The Sidonians and Hittites were located further north in what is today Lebanon and beyond.

The remaining peoples also provided Yahweh an opportunity to test whether or not Israel would **obey the commandments of Yahweh** (v 4). The list of six peoples (v 5) varies from that given in Deut 7:1 only with the omission of the Girgashites. Instead of obeying, the Israelites intermarried with the peoples and worshipped their gods (Judg 3:6).

FROM THE TEXT

1. It is difficult to reconcile the image of an angry God with that of a loving Heavenly Father. An angry God is not a popular one today. We like to hear messages about God's love, compassion, and grace; messages about a tame God who comforts us. If God makes no demands on us, lets us live as we choose, and then at the end of life says "I forgive," is he worth worshipping? If he is a cheery old fellow who stands for nothing, why bother with him?

Judges does not portray God as cruel but as one who is vulnerable. Of all the nations of the world, it was Israel that he had chosen to enter into a covenantal relationship. He had committed himself to deliver them from slavery, to provide for them in the wilderness, and to bring them into the land. Israel was to show God faithfulness by worshipping him alone and obeying his commandments. When Israel turned to other gods, they betrayed their relationship to God. In response God no longer protected Israel as he promised to do but gave them into the hands of their oppressors. His actions were just and righteous according to the covenant. However, God could not turn his back on his suffering people. He raised up judges to save them. This act of mercy is grace, the reaching out to the helpless who have nothing to offer in return.

We see both this same anger and this same vulnerability in Jesus who pronounced woes on both the cities that rejected his word (Matt 11:21) and the scribes and Pharisees (Matt 23:13-36). In Mark 3:5 he was both angry and grieved over the hardness of heart of the people. The Jesus of Revelation is the Lamb who will open the seals and unleash horrible devastations upon the earth (Rev 6:1-17). Yet he is the Lamb, the one who embraced suffering and death to provide salvation.

God calls us to be his people and graciously liberates us from our bondage to sin. In response he demands faithful obedience; a turning away from all the ancient and modern gods that allure us. Their calls are not to freedom but to slavery. Although he warns us against them, he does not prevent us from listening to their calls, or even from forsaking him for others. However, even when we find ourselves ensnared and trapped, if we cry out to God, he will hear and have compassion. No false god is so powerful that the God and Father of our Lord Jesus Christ cannot free and restore us.

2. And what of the next generation? How does one generation transmit its faith and practices to the next? The generation of the conquest had

witnessed God's mighty deeds, but the next generation had only heard about them. The older generation had learned the art of war, but the next needed training. The generation of the elders remained faithful to Yahweh, but their children did not. How does one generation communicate to their children the reality of their faith that has shaped their values, beliefs, and practices? The easy answer is to establish standards of behavior: "Don't do this, but do that." The rituals of worship can be normalized and creeds written. Such actions and responses can be monitored to ensure conformity. However, following the rules is not enough. The next generation has to be captivated by the reality behind the rules.

What must be communicated are not just the forms but the reality of faith; the hearing of the call of God and the responding in faithful obedience. We struggle with this task, but it is not of our own doing. We have to trust in the faithfulness of the One who calls. We may teach and witness about God, but only when the Spirit of God confronts, convicts, and transforms does a person find the essence of faith. Nor can we control the response of the next generation. The children themselves become responsible for their own decisions. Those who opt out of their childhood training to follow their own desires fall under the wrath of God, the severe mercy of God that seeks always to call them to repentance and restoration. Perhaps yet in their day God will raise up a "judge" to bring them salvation.

II. MILITARY TRIUMPH: SPIRITUAL DEGENERATION (3:7—16:31)

OVERVIEW

The majority of the book contains the stories of the individual judges beginning with Othniel and ending with Samson. As the accounts progress, more details about the individual is included. The story of Othniel is told in five verses and includes only minimal details about his family and personal life. The story of Samson is told in four chapters. It begins before his birth, traces his exploits on the battlefield and in the bedroom, and concludes with his death. As the stories progress, they also describe a downward spiral of spiritual and social disintegration. Othniel represents the model of judgeship as he was empowered by the spirit of Yahweh to lead Israel to victory and bring to Israel a period of rest. Ehud and then Deborah and Barak also with the support of God bring victory. Gideon becomes pivotal. He diplomatically avoided a confrontation with Ephraim and then rejected the offered kingship, but afterward made an ephod that led Israel into religious apostasy. Jephthah brought victory not only over the Ammonites but also over the tribe of Ephraim when forty-two thousand were slaughtered during an intertribal war. The last judge, Samson, who broke every Nazirite vow to which he had been committed, only "began" to deliver Israel (13:5) and did not bring to Israel a time of rest. Scattered among the accounts of these "major" judges are the short stories of the six minor judges. None of them are said to have brought a period of rest or peace to the people.

The commentary will examine the brief accounts (3:7-31) of the first three judges—Othniel, Ehud, and Shamgar—in one section, and then take up each major judge in succession. The stories of the other five minor judges will be taken up as they occur, at the beginning and end of the account of Jephthah.

A. Othniel, Ehud, and Shamgar (3:7-31)

BEHIND THE TEXT

The first of the judges was Othniel, a Judean, while Ehud of Benjamin comes second. As has already been noted, the book gives prominence to the tribe of Judah as it led the tribes in the conquest (1:2) and in the war against Benjamin (20:18). Judah was able to take and burn the city of Jerusalem (1:8), while in contrast Benjamin was unable to drive out the Jebusites who lived in Jerusalem (1:21). Othniel is described as the ideal judge who was empowered by the spirit to liberate Israel. The second judge, Ehud of Benjamin, was also successful in liberating Israel and bringing to it an extended period of rest. The account contains more details and is marked with elements of rather earthy humor. A long oral tradition has shaped the story. Ancient bards and storytellers delighted their audiences with the account of an unlikely hero who by stealth assassinated an evil king and rallied the warriors in a great victory. In one verse the exploits of Shamgar, the first of the "minor" judges, is told. His story seems out of place as the short accounts of the others bracket the story of Jephthah. It owes its location due to Shamgar being mentioned in the song of Deborah (5:6). Since he is mentioned there, it makes sense for his story to be told prior to the exploits of Deborah and Barak.

IN THE TEXT

1. Othniel (3:7-11)

■ **7-11** Othniel has already been introduced in the book as the nephew of Caleb, son of his younger brother Kenaz (1:12-15). The previous section (3:1-6) closed with the statement that the Israelites transgressed the covenant by intermarrying with the inhabitants of the land. However, the reader knows that Othniel's marriage was according to Mosaic regulations. His wife was Achsah, the daughter of Caleb. Othniel serves as the model for what a judge should be, including his heritage and family life (Schneider 2000, 37).

This section begins (v 7) with a three-part sentence that indicts the

Israelites for doing *the evil thing,* forgetting Yahweh, and serving/worshipping the Baals and Ashteroth (plural for Asherah).

The Goddess Asherah

Asherah was worshipped in most of the countries of the ancient Middle East, but her connection with Israel probably came through Canaanite sources. Documents found in the Canaanite city of Ugarit inform us that she was considered the mother of the gods and consort of the high god El (Day 1997, ABD-CD). In Israelite religion, which had become corrupted by Canaanite influences, Yahweh replaced El as the creator god and head of the pantheon (Josh 22:21) and Asherah became his consort. Asherah is only mentioned in Judges in this text and in 6:25, 26, 28, 30; all of the latter verses refer to her as a wooden object or pole that was next to the altar to Baal. Gideon cut it down to use as fuel to burn the sacrifice on the altar he made to Yahweh. Most of the other references to Asherah in the OT portray her as a wooden idol or pole or tree. The wooden object was a representative of the goddess, which in the mind of her devotees represented the goddess herself (Binger 1997, 141).

The evil thing probably refers to the actions of the Israelites described in the previous verse—intermarrying with the people of the land—which led to their worshipping other gods. Yahweh's reaction was to bring the covenant curses upon Israel. ***He sold them into the hand of Cushan-rishathaim of Mesopotamia*** (v 8). That is, he returned them to slavery, and the slave master was one Cushan-rishathaim or "Cushan of the double evil," probably a nickname given by the Israelites to express their hatred. He has not been identified with any known person in history.

After eight years of servitude the Israelites cried out (*zāʿaq*) to Yahweh. ***And Yahweh raised up a savior for the sons of Israel and Othniel saved them*** (v 9).

Crying Out to God

The verb *zāʿaq* means "to cry out" in the sense of summoning help. It occurs in the political-military context as the issuing of a call for the mustering of chariots and troops for combat (4:10, 13; 6:34, 35; 12:2). In the religious sphere it denotes a desperate cry to God for help. In ancient Mesopotamian literature the cry of the oppressed rose up to the solar god, Utu (Shamash) the guarantor of justice and defender of the oppressed. This was a strong appeal to the god when there was no possibility to obtain justice from human institutions. The desperate cry did not contain a note of repentance or remorse for sin or wrongdoing; rather, the cry itself brought forth a response from the god to punish the oppressor. Justice had been denied and the foundation of ordered existence was threatened. Utu was moved to respond by sending a deliverer in order to bring justice and thus to maintain the order of creation.

> When Israel was oppressed in Egypt, they cried out to God due to their heavy bondage in slavery (Exod 2:23). God was moved to remember his covenant with their fathers and raised up Moses to deliver them. In Judges the people cry out to Yahweh as the third part of the cycle of sin, oppression, crying out, and raising up a savior/deliver (3:9, 15; 6:6, 7; 10:10). Earlier exegetes combined an act of repentance with the cry that moved God to respond in pity to deliver them. This is incorrect. God was moved to respond by raising up a deliver due to the desperateness of the cry. While it could be argued that the Israelites deserved their punishment because they broke the covenant, still God responded to the cry. Yahweh as the guarantor of justice was still free to respond as he chose. He might or might not raise up a deliver. The cry did not obligate him to respond. At this point he differed from the Mesopotamian gods (Stone 1987, 311-26).

The Israelites had cried out to God when enslaved in Egypt (Exod 2:23), and he provided Moses as a deliverer. The word does not indicate that the Israelites repented of their sins, only that they in desperation turned for relief to Yahweh, the mighty God who had the power to deliver them from the hands of their oppressors. In the time of Gideon when the tribes were being oppressed by the Moabites, they also cried out to God for relief. In response Yahweh sent a prophet to warn them that they had not repented by turning away from the worship of other gods (6:6-10). The patience of God was being exhausted. When the Israelites were oppressed by the Ammonites and again cried out to Yahweh, he rejected their cry and told them to cry unto their other gods for deliverance (10:10-16). No deliverer was raised up by Yahweh, and the leaders had to seek out their own commander, Jephthah, to fight the Ammonites (10:17—11:11). Yahweh had not cast Israel off, but his patience had run out. The stable order founded upon the covenant was being undone.

Othniel was empowered by the **spirit of Yahweh** (v 10). Later understanding will see this as the Holy Spirit, who is more openly revealed in the NT. Here the spirit should be understood as the power of enablement that God gave on occasion to his servants. It would be a mistake to attribute some redemptive aspect to the spirit's work. The spirit also came upon Jephthah who made and kept a foolish vow and who also fought a bloody war against Ephraim (11:29—12:6). More references are made to the spirit empowering Samson than to any other judge. While Samson won victories through the power of the spirit, he was also the judge who broke all his vows. His power was squandered as he led a life not obedient to the God who gave him his power.

As the result of Othniel's victory, **the land had rest** (v 11) or was peaceful and undisturbed for forty years, the length of a generation. The account ends with the notice of Othniel's death.

2. Ehud (3:12-30)

■ **12-30** The story of Ehud and Eglon originated as a folk story told among the clans. It tells of the adventure of an unlikely hero who through trickery and deception killed a tyrant and overthrew an oppressive regime. Expressions with double meanings meant both to build tension and to delight the hearer appear throughout the story. While the written story has been shaped to fit the fixed Deuteronomic framework, it has still retained its earthy humor, which sets it apart from the other stories of the judges.

The main characters are Ehud, a Benjamite of the clan of Gera, and Eglon, the king of Moab. The name Eglon means "calf/ young bull," and he is described as being very fat or obese (v 17); like a fatted calf ready to be slaughtered. The name "Benjamin" means "son of the right hand," but Ehud is described as *restricted in his right hand* (v 15). Thus a man of the right-hand tribe was somehow affected in his right hand. Some take the phrase to mean that he was deformed. It is doubtful that the Israelites would give a person with a deformed hand the responsibility of delivering tribute to the king. Lawless factions might seize the opportunity to take the valuable tribute for themselves. The tribe of Benjamin had a military unit made up of left-handed warriors (*restricted in their right hands*) who were highly skilled at slinging stones (20:16). It is possible that some men of Benjamin, including Ehud, at an early age bound their right hand in order to develop better their left-handed fighting skills. Thus the LXX was probably correct when it translated the phrase as "ambidextrous." Ehud was a highly skilled warrior who could fight with either hand.

There is also an ominous note in the identification of Ehud. The model judge was Othniel of Judah. In keeping with the pattern of moving geographically from south to north, the second judge, Ehud, was from Benjamin, specifically of the clan of Gera. When David was forced into exile by his son Absalom, he was cursed by a member of the house of Saul, one Shimei of the clan of Gera (2 Sam 16:5). By identifying Ehud as a member of the same clan, the reader is again reminded of the David/Saul polemic that forms one of the lesser motifs of the book.

The story begins by noting that *the Israelites again did the evil in the eyes of Yahweh* (Judg 3:12). With the death of Othniel the Israelites again returned to the evil of intermarrying with the indigenous people who then enticed them to worship other gods (v 6). The indictment is stated twice in the verse for emphasis. The Israelites were supposed to follow the standards of conduct established by Yahweh, doing right in the eyes of Yahweh. However, they continued to reject those standards until in the end of the book they established their own standards of right and wrong, doing what was right in their own eyes (21:25). They themselves became the standard of right and wrong, rather than God. In response Yahweh strengthened Eglon's oppression of Israel. Then things got worse. Eglon having established a residence in **the City of Palms** (1:16) enlisted the Ammonites and the Amalekites to assist him (3:13). The City of Palms is generally understood to be Jericho, but this name is used so as not to confuse it with the city destroyed by Joshua (Josh 6) and not rebuilt until the ninth century (1 Kgs 16:34). However, some city did exist in that general area earlier, as even David was aware of its existence (2 Sam 10:5). The area has good water, a warm climate, and fertile soil—right conditions for building a town. It may be that another town was established on the fertile plain east of the Jordan, but not until later was one rebuilt on the site of the old Jericho, which was a high hill on the western edge of the Jordan valley and near the hills that began the central hill country.

Under the command of Ehud, the Israelites sent tribute to Eglon (v 15). But Ehud planned to deliver more than the tribute to Eglon. He made a two-edged short sword, about a cubit, or 18 inches in length, **and he strapped it on his right thigh under his cloak** (v 16). A right-handed person would wear a sword on his left thigh and reach across his body to pull it out of its scabbard. So Ehud placed the sword where he could reach it with his left hand. The placement would also help him hide it from Eglon's guards who would undoubtedly check to see that he was unarmed before admitting him into the presence of the king. If he wore a sword on this left thigh, they would have taken it from him and probably not searched under the clothes on his right side where he hid the weapon.

After delivering the tribute, Ehud dismissed the Israelites who had brought the tribute (v 18). Then Ehud **returned from the idols which were at Gilgal** (v 19). The word often translated "stones" actually means "idols." It occurs again in v 26 to form an envelope or frame called an inclusio, a beginning and ending, around this part of the story. What was Ehud doing at a place where there were idols? His excuse for seeking an audience with Eglon was that he had a word from God. Perhaps he visited the shrine to give his request credence. He had been to the holy place and had received a message for the king. As he had delivered the tribute, it was now his duty to deliver the divine message.

The story now takes an ominous turn (vv 19-25). When Ehud returned to the court, he told Eglon that he had a **secret word** for him (v 19). The word *deber* can mean "word" or "thing." Eglon expected secret information, either from a god or perhaps intelligence concerning subversive activities of the Israelites. Ehud had something far different in mind. Eglon silenced Ehud and sent his attendants out of the audience room to the portico antechamber. He then went up the steps to a private upper room where he sat upon a throne. The room would also contain a secluded section where the king could relieve himself. When Ehud told him that it was a ***word from God*** (v 20), Eglon rose up from the chair. Swiftly Ehud with his left hand took the sword and thrust it up into Eglon's abdomen, possibly piercing his heart. How fat was Eglon? The story humorously mocks the king. He was so obese that the handle of the sword sunk into the fat, which enveloped it entirely. The last word of v 22 (*happaršedonâ*) occurs only here in all of the OT. It generally is taken to mean feces. Matthews suggests that the death blow "caused his anal sphincter to explode" and the smell of the refuse would later cause the attendants to think that he was relieving himself (2004, 61).

Ehud then left. But how? He needed time to escape. The text uses another word found only here in the OT (*hammisděrônâ*). It refers to the area in the private upper room of the king where he could relieve himself. Since the room was elevated, it allowed servants to have access below to remove the waste. Ehud ***locked the doors behind himself*** (v 23) and then went out through this hole into the room below. He then walked as if nothing had happened through the portico area where the attendants were waiting (Halpern 1988, 39). After Ehud left, the attendants found the doors to the upper chamber locked. They waited because they thought that the king was relieving himself (v 24). The phrase is literally ***he covered his feet.*** Some older commentators such as Henry took the phrase to mean that he was resting and pulled covers over his feet. Others noting that the same expression is used of Saul (1 Sam 24:3) correctly understood it as a euphemism for relieving oneself (Gunn 2005, 41). The smell of the expelled feces probably suggested to the attendants this explanation for the locked doors. While they waited, Ehud made his escape. After an embarrassingly long time (Judg 3:25), the attendants retrieved another key, opened the door, and found their king dead.

The task was only partially finished. With Moab leaderless, the time was right for Israel to fight for their freedom (vv 27-30). Ehud summoned the troops of Ephraim (v 27) by blowing upon a ram's horn. This was the first of three occasions when Ephraim went to war. Gideon with diplomacy placated an angry Ephraim and won them to his cause (8:1-3). The Ephraimites confronted Jephthah and ended up being slaughtered (12:1-6). By seizing the fords across the Jordan, the Israelites cut off the Moabite warriors' escape (v 28). A final note of humor is given. The Israelites killed ***10,000 fat men, and each one was mighty, but none escaped*** (v 29). The troops were like their king, too fat. The account closes with nothing said about Ehud being a judge, only with the statement that ***the land was undisturbed for 80 years*** (v 30) or two generations.

3. Shamgar (3:31)

▪ **31** One verse tells us about the exploits of Shamgar. He single-handedly took on a military unit of 600 Philistines and with an ox goad, a long pole with a metal tip, slew them. His name is not Israelite, maybe Hurrian. The epithet ***son of Anat*** refers to the Canaanite goddess Anat, the consort of Baal Hadad, and thus may not be a family name but a designation of a station in life, that of a mercenary (Boling 1997, ABD-CD). He possibly was a convert to Israel's religion, like Uriah the Hittite (2 Sam 2:3 ff.). This verse mentions Shamgar as the first of the six minor judges and probably owes its location to his being mentioned in the Song of Deborah (Judg 5:6), where he is listed as a contemporary of Jael, and thus also of Barak and Deborah. It was a dangerous time when caravans ceased and travelers had to take circuitous routes. The verse closes with the note that ***he also saved Israel*** (v 31).

FROM THE TEXT

1. Waldo Beach comments that people today are no less religious than previous ages, "the shift is in the gods whom they worship and obey and count on to give meaning and direction to their lives." While our "official" religion is some version of Judaism or variation of Christianity, what "commands the loyalty and devotion of the heart may be one of a number of secular faiths." He continues with the indictment that "Americans are practicing polytheists, with a whole pantheon of gods" (1979, 10). Israel's gods took physical shape in images that represented forces of nature they wished to control. The offering of sacrifices and prayers were often attempts to persuade the gods to grant the desires of the worshippers. Our gods may not be represented by carved wooden or stone figures, but we still have our idols of power, wealth, and pleasure that we trust to give us meaning to life. We are caught up in the unending pursuit of more: more possessions, more money, more power, more self-indulgence. At the center of this pursuit is self, the ordering of all things in order that I might be in control. In final analysis, I want to be my own god.

Yahweh demanded the exclusive loyalty of Israel. He would not tolerate divided loyalty. Jesus was no less demanding. He required of his disciples obedience unto death. The Holy Spirit still calls his disciples to lay aside all other loyalties in full surrender to God. The path to complete commitment usually is not an easy one as the Spirit probes deeply within the personality to search out and bring to consciousness the secret idols we cling to. This is no hurried affair accomplished in a few minutes of prayer, but can take days or months of continued searching, probing, and yielding. The Spirit, however, can be trusted to faithfully work with an earnest seeker to purge the false gods and bring full cleansing. It is his will to bring us to the point where we love God with our whole heart, soul, and strength.

2. The actions of Ehud have occasioned a long debate over the rightness of killing a ruler. The poet John Milton (1608-74) used the example of Ehud as a justification for the execution of Charles I. Others such as Voltaire (1694-1778) and the Scot Sir George Mackenzie (1636-91) denounced those who appealed to the example of Ehud to justify their assassinations of sovereigns (Gunn 2005, 44). During World War II Dietrich Bonhoeffer agonized over the question of whether or not a Christian could participate in tyrannicide. In the end he joined the plot to assassinate Hitler.

What actions may a Christian take against evil rulers or systems of oppression? Many believe that Jesus teaches us to be submissive even to evil authorities and not to resort to violence. It is worthy of note, however, that when forty men plotted to take Paul's life he had no reservations about calling on soldiers to provide protection (Acts 23:12-22). While evil is real and must be resisted, Christians should be cautious about turning to violence as a solution. People who turn to violence usually are consumed by that violence. Ehud may have been used of God to liberate his people, but too often in history those who seek to overthrow oppressors become the new oppressors. Christians should choose a path that promotes justice, harmony, and compassion within a community. In so doing they make real the kingdom of God in the midst of present history. Yet evil is real and strikes at the root of a peaceful community. When people are oppressed by forces of evil, whether murderous political regimes or local drug gangs, what should be the response of Christians? If they refuse to use violent means, military or police, there may be no adequate response to oppression. Our hope is that in the future God will establish his reign of peace and justice, but until that day comes, we must live in a world where evil is real and unless resisted will destroy the lives of the innocent.

B. Deborah, Barak, and Jael (4:1—5:31)

OVERVIEW

The story of Deborah, Barak, and Jael is told in two versions, first a prose account (ch 4) and then a poem (ch 5). There has been an ongoing discussion about which of these is the earliest version of the story. However, most scholars now agree that the poem with its ancient poetic forms and rare words may be one of the earliest pieces of literature in the OT. Both versions complement each other by giving information omitted by the other. Without one or the other we would be less informed about the events of the story. Chapter 4 gives more details of the setting, such as Deborah's function as a judge, more specific geographic details, and more details surrounding the events that led up to the death of Sisera. Chapter 5 describes the divine intervention by means of a storm that led to the defeat of Sisera's forces, lists the tribes that joined in the battle and those that did not, and includes the scene of Sisera's mother who waited impatiently for what she thought would be her son's victorious return. Even with both accounts we are left with ambiguity. Who is the judge in the story? Is it Deborah the prophet, Barak the warrior, or Jael the assassin? Each has a function, but not one is designated as a deliverer of Israel. Why did Barak hesitate to obey Yahweh's commands and insist that Deborah accompany him? Why did Jael invite Sisera into her tent? Did she violate the rules of hospitality by murdering him or was she defending herself? The text gives no answers to such questions but invites the reader to ponder the ambiguities.

1. The Prose Story (4:1-24)

BEHIND THE TEXT

Jabin was a king of Hazor who led a coalition against the Israelites (Josh 11). Joshua defeated the coalition, killed Jabin (v 10), and burned the city of Hazor. The mention of Jabin as the Canaanite king from Hazor in Judg 4:2 and 24 frames the story of the defeat of Sisera, Jabin's general. The name "Jabin" may have been a throne name, passed down to successive kings. Whatever may have been the actual history that lies behind the two accounts, Jabin functions symbolically in this narrative as the ultimate power of oppression that was only gradually defeated by the Israelites.

Hazor was a major city during the Middle Bronze (1800-1550 B.C.) to Late Bronze Age (1550-1200 B.C.). Situated 8.5 miles north of the Sea of Galilee, it was located on one of the major trade routes between Egypt and Mesopotamia. The city was divided into two main districts. In the upper part (25 acres), which was well fortified, the palace, administrative buildings, and several temples were located. The lower part (75 acres), which stretched to the north, housed most of the residences and businesses. The entire city was enclosed with a wall (Zuckerman 2007, 753-54). The city was the largest and most powerful in the area. It was first excavated by Yigael Yadin in the 1950s. He determined that it was destroyed sometime in the thirteenth century. It is not always clear who was responsible for the destruction of a city, as the conquerors rarely left any stone monuments celebrating their victory. Babylonian, Assyrian, and Egyptian kings who ruled great empires erected in their own countries victory stones called steles to celebrate their deeds. Yadin claimed that the destruction of Hazor was consistent with the biblical account (Josh 11:10-11) and that the Israelites led by Joshua had destroyed the city. Other scholars disagreed. In the 1990s Amnon Ben-Tor led another team to continue Hazor's excavation. Ben-Tor's work confirmed that the city had been destroyed in the thirteenth century. The excavators found that when the city was taken a number of statuary in the palace had been deliberately destroyed. Six or seven Egyptian statues had been intentionally mutilated; three had their arms and heads chiseled off. A large Canaanite statue had been broken into nearly a hundred pieces. Ben-Tor and Rubiato argued that if the Egyptians conquered the city, it would be unlikely that they would destroy statues of their own kings. Nor was it likely that a Canaanite group, even if it was strong enough to conquer the city, would mutilate statues of Canaanite deities. The Philistines did not penetrate that far inland, nor was any distinctive Philistine pottery found at the site. Ben-Tor thus concluded that the Israelites seem "to be the most likely candidate for the violent destruction of Canaanite Hazor" (Ben-Tor and Rubiato 1999, online).

The narrative of the chapter consists of six parts. In vv 1-3 the writer describes the plight of the Israelites. They again did evil in the sight of God and were oppressed by King Jabin and his army commander, Sisera. In the second section (vv 4-10) the two main Israelite characters, Deborah and Barak, are introduced. Deborah commanded Barak to muster the troops, gave him a battle plan, and promised him that God would give him victory. An editorial interlude (v 11) disrupts the narrative to introduce Heber the Kenite. The battle is briefly described in vv 12-16. In the sixth section (vv 17-22) the fleeing Sisera took refuge in the tent of Jael, where he was slain by her. The chapter concludes with an editorial note describing the victory of the Israelites and how they continued to fight Jabin until they destroyed him. There are four main characters. Deborah the prophet represents God. Barak is the commander of Israel's forces. Sisera, the commander of the Canaanite forces, begins the narrative as the villain and ends up as the fool who gets himself killed. The final character is Jael, the wife of Heber who gains the glory by killing Sisera.

IN THE TEXT

a. Sisera the Oppressor (4:1-3)

■ **1-3** Verse 1 concludes the story of Ehud with the stylized notice of the Israelites returning to evil and of the death of Ehud. What is different is the order of the notice. The death of the judge normally precedes the description of the Israelites' return to sin (3:11; 8:33; 12:7). In this case the simple two-word statement of his death follows. The land enjoyed an extended, undisturbed period of two generations, eighty years (3:30), but even before Ehud died the Israelites did *evil in the eyes of Yahweh* (4:1). They rejected his guidance and returned to the worship of other gods before he died. God's response was to *sell* (*mākar*) *them into the hand of Jabin* (v 2), that is, to return them to slavery. If the Israelites would not serve Yahweh, then they would become the slaves of the Canaanite king.

The strength of the oppressors was counted in military might, nine hundred chariots (v 3) that were strengthened with iron fittings, the new technology of the day. The huge number and the reference to iron indicate numerical and technological superiority. Sisera was the military commander (*śar*) who answered to Jabin. His dwelling or headquarters was at Harosheth-haggoiim or **Forest of the Gentiles,** an unidentified place located in the Esdraelon plain. At the end of the battle Sisera did not flee to this city but ran north toward Kedesh in upper Galilee, which probably had an ancient history as a political sanctuary. Joshua designated it as a city of refuge (Josh 20:7). The Israelites cried out (*zāʿaq*) to Yahweh for deliverance, a word that means to cry for help (Judg 10:12) or to summons others for military assistance (7:23, 24; 10:17; 12:1). For twenty years or half a generation they had suffered under the military might of Sisera.

Who Was a Commander?

The Hebrew term *śar* (pl. *śārê*, feminine *śārâ*) appears ten times in the book of Judges. It designates one in authority but who is responsible to another in higher authority. In Judges it is primarily, but not always, used as a military term to designate a commander. It also describes the women who served Sisera's mother (5:29). She was their mistress and they her ladies-in-waiting. Sisera was the commander (4:2, 7) of the forces of Jabin, the king of the Canaanites in the area of Hazor. In the song of Deborah and Barak (5:15), the commanders (*śārê*) of Issachar supported Deborah while the tribes' solders followed Barak into battle. The soldiers from Ephraim captured the two commanders (*śārê*) Oreb and Zeeb (7:25; 8:3) who served in the armies of the kings of Midian Zebah and Zalmunna. The leaders of Succoth are also called *śārê* (8:6, 14). They were in authority in the city but were not the elders who ruled. Since they responded to Gideon's request for food for his soldiers, they may have been either civic leaders or possibly commanders of the defense forces of the city. Zebul was Abimelech's representative (*śar*) in Shechem (9:30), but again we do not know if he was a commander of a small force or a civic leader who answered to the king, not the elders of the city. When the Ammonites attacked Gilead, the commanders (*śarê*, 10:18) were perplexed as to who would be their leader. It was the elders of the tribe (11:5) who went to Jephthah to enlist him to lead the forces in battle. In each case the *śar* was subordinate to another authority, and in most cases, the male was a military commander.

b. Deborah and Barak (4:4-10)

■ **4-10** Deborah's identification is rather odd, **Deborah, a woman, a prophetess, the wife of Lappidoth, she was judging Israel** (v 4). The obvious is emphasized; she was a woman who functioned as a prophet and judge, offices normally reserved for men. The reader is immediately alerted to a situation that was unusual, but not unknown, in the patriarchal culture of Israel. Miriam the sister of Moses was a prophet (Exod 15:20), and Huldah while not given that title delivered an oracle from God like a prophet (2 Kgs 22:14-20). The husband's name means "torch" or "flashing." Deborah was the only judge to preside over judicial proceedings prior to delivering Israel from oppression. Palm trees (Judg 4:5) normally did not grow in the highlands of Ephraim. The Israelites brought their disputes to her for judgment. Her authority extended further than the tribe of Ephraim, for she summoned Barak who was of the tribe of Naphtali. Whether or not individuals or groups from every tribe consulted her is unknown. An unusual woman sat under an unusual tree dispensing justice.

Deborah (v 6) summoned Barak; a bold move for a woman. Because his name means "lightning," similar in meaning to that of "torch" for Lappidoth, some have suggested that Barak was actually her husband. It was not unusual for different persons to have similar or even the same name. Nothing more should be made of their names. Barak's headquarters were located at Kedesh of Naphtali, situated at the southern edge of the territory of Naphtali, just southwest of the Sea of Galilee. The commission she gave Barak begins with a rhetorical question expecting a positive answer, **"Has not Yahweh the God of Israel commanded you?"** (v 6). So also reads the LXX. Evidently Barak had received a previous command from God, possibly through Deborah, and he had been slow to obey. A commander would be reluctant to commit his infantry into battle against a large chariot force. Chariots moved quickly over the battlefield and with one or two persons using the bow or javelin they had increased firepower. The infantry would be overwhelmed and thrown into a panic. Deborah's instructions were specific. Barak was to recruit ten thousand men from the tribes of Naphtali, his own tribe, and Zebulun, its near neighbor. Then he was to **proceed** (*mašak*) to Mount Tabor on the northern side of the Esdraelon plain. There was considerable risk to the soldiers since a chariot force on a level plain could easily overwhelm an infantry. Coupled with the command, however, was the promise (v 7) that God would **draw out** (*mašak*) the chariot and infantry forces of Sisera to the area of the Kishon wadi and deliver them into the hand of Barak. A wadi is a normally dry riverbed that would flow with runoff water during the rainy season.

Barak hesitated, refusing to go unless Deborah went with him (v 8). No reason is given for his demand. The word of God normally was a sufficient warrant for a leader to act. His demand foreshadows Gideon's several requests for assurances from God (6:36-40). These incidents contribute to the overall theme of the progressive breakdown in leadership in Israel. Obedience to divine requirements was beginning to show cracks.

Deborah agreed to the requirement but pronounced a judgment (4:9). The army leader would not be able to boast about his victory because Yahweh would **sell** (*mākar*, see v 2) Sisera into the hand of a woman. Who the woman would be is not made clear. At this point in the story the reader might assume that the woman was Deborah herself. Hesitation on Barak's part when given a clear command by God became costly in an honor/shame culture where a warrior's honor was measured by the list of his deeds. Barak proceeded (v 10) to rally his troops to Kedesh and then with Deborah move them to Tabor.

c. Heber the Kenite (4:11)

■ 11 This brief interlude seems to disrupt the flow of the story. It serves the purpose of alerting the reader early to a later development. A clue is given as to the identity of the woman referred to in v 9. But it is a veiled clue. The Kenites were related to the Israelites through the marriage of Moses to Zipporah, the daughter of Hobab.

Name of Moses' Father-in-law

The name of Moses' father-in-law has long been a problem. In Exod 2:18 his name is Reuel, but in 3:1 and 18:2 he is referred to as the Midianite priest Jethro. In Num 10:29 the father-in-law is again called Reuel and Hobab is Moses' brother-in-law. In Judg 1:16 he is identified as Hobab the Kenite. There is no satisfactory solution proposed to this shifting of names (Launderville 1997, ABD-CD). The only consistent thread is that Moses was related by marriage to the tribe of Midian, and specifically the clan or subtribe of the Kenites.

Heber had migrated north to the upper Galilee area around Kedesh, pitching his tent at the oak of Zaanannim, a place presently unidentified.

d. The Battle with Sisera (4:12-16)

■ **12-16** Having been told that Barak had brought a fighting force to Mount Tabor, Sisera moved his forces, both chariots and infantry, to the wadi Kishon, southwest of Tabor (vv 12-13). The order to begin the battle was given by Deborah. ***Arise for this day Yahweh has given Sisera into your hand. Yahweh goes before you*** (v 14). This last phrase indicates that the troops were engaged in a holy war and that it was actually Yahweh who would bring victory. Success in battle is often determined not by the size of an army or its technologically advanced equipment, but by the attitudes of the combatants. Battles are disorderly affairs, and confidence can quickly be eroded. According to 5:20-21 Yahweh caused rain to turn the battleground into a field of mud, limiting the maneuverability of the chariots. This gave the advantage to Barak's infantry. Sisera's soldiers lost confidence and fled in panic. Sisera's own chariot was also mired in the mud, so he ***got down from the chariot and fled on foot*** (v 15). The ancient storyteller added this touch of humor to the story. The mighty commander of a huge chariot force was seen running on foot away in panic from the battle. Meanwhile Barak (v 16) and his army pursued the fleeing Canaanites and slaughtered them before they could reach the security of Harosheth-haggoiim.

e. Sisera and Jael (4:17-22)

■ **17-22** The next scene in the drama begins by repeating ***Sisera fled on foot*** (v 17), only this time the direction is given, ***to the tent of Jael the wife of Heber the Kenite*** (v 17). The purpose of introducing Heber the Kenite in v 11 is now made clear. Heber had settled somewhere along the road that led to the sacred city of Kedesh, the ultimate destination of Sisera who was looking for sanctuary. It is unlikely that Sisera would have headed for the Kedesh located in the territory of the tribe of Naphtali, as this was Barak's military headquarters (vv 6, 10). Heber had a conflicting loyalty, to the Israelites to whom his clan was related by marriage to Moses, and to Jabin the king of Hazor with whom Heber had established a relationship of peace, possibly, but not necessarily a formal covenant. Heber's family consisted of pastoralists who moved their flocks and herds to different grazing sites during the seasons of the year. The king may have allowed him to pitch his tents on his lands during certain seasons in exchange for trade, particularly in meats of beef and lamb (Halpern 1997, ABD-CD). If Sisera intended to seek sanctuary at the camp of Heber, he would have gone to Heber's tent. However, Jael initiated the contact by inviting Sisera into her tent with the promise of security (v 18). She had her own tent probably because Heber had more than one wife, each with her own tent. Sisera quickly accepted the invitation of Jael, for who would think to look for a military commander in the tent of a woman? She hid him under some type of rug or blanket. The word *śmk* occurs only here in the OT, so it is difficult to know precisely what is meant. Sisera then made two requests of her (vv 19-20); first to give him water to drink, and second to stand in the door of the tent and to lie if a pursuer asked if a man was in her tent. She responded to the first request by bringing him milk. Was it part of Jael's plan that the warm milk would help the exhausted Sisera fall asleep? Instead of complying with the second request, Jael picked up a tent peg and hammer (v 21) and approached him quietly. The mighty commander, weary from fighting a battle and running away, had drunk the milk and fallen asleep. Jael drove the tent peg through his head and into the ground.

Jael's actions have been the subject of much discussion throughout the centuries. Was she justified in her action, or was she a murderer? Deborah proclaimed her, "Most blessed among women" (5:24). She had destroyed Israel's oppressor. Early in the church this title gave rise to the thought that she was a forerunner of the Virgin Mary. After the Reformation her image became more ambiguous. Some saw her deed as necessary for victory, but not an action to be emulated; women, it was held, should not kill men. Deist philosopher Voltaire found her actions morally horrible (for an extensive survey of opinions, see Gunn 2005, 71-92). The text does not tell us what motivated her to kill Sisera. There was peace between her husband and Jabin, Sisera's lord. The Kenites, however, were related to the Israelites though the marriage of Hobab's daughter to Moses. Did Jael place the duties to blood kin above that of family obligation to a Canaanite ruler? Matthews defends Jael's actions by suggesting that Sisera violated the rules of hospitality. The seven rules of hospitality that he describes are based on biblical examples, plus parallels both to modern Arab and ancient Mediterranean customs (2004, 68-73).

Protocol of Hospitality, According to Matthews

The following are the "Protocol of Hospitality" given by Matthews:
1. Villages and individuals were obligated to provide hospitality for strangers when their travels brought them into areas.

2. By accepting the offer of hospitality, the stranger was transformed from a potential enemy to an ally.
3. The offer of hospitality was to be made only by the male who was either the head of the household or citizen of the town.
4. The hospitality was offered for a specifically stated time but could be extended by the host if both parties agreed.
5. The offer of hospitality might be refused, but this might be considered by the potential host as an insult to his honor. The stranger by refusing ran the risk of being attacked.
6. The rules of conduct for the host and guest were established by custom.
   a. The guest should not make requests.
   b. Whatever may have been the initial offer of hospitality, the host was to provide the best he could provide.
   c. It was expected that the guest would share news gathered in his or her travels, respond graciously to what the host offered, and express a blessing for the future.
   d. It was not considered proper for the host to ask the guest personal questions.
7. As long as the guest stayed, the host was obligated to provide protection. (2004, 68-69)

Matthews' analysis falters at two points. First, Jael initiated the contact with Sisera by inviting him into her tent and offering protection. This violated the rule that the husband should be the one to offer hospitality. Her invitation indicates that from the beginning Jael planned to kill Sisera. Her actions were premeditated. Second, it is not certain that rules drawn from the nonbiblical sources were followed during the time of the judges. Sisera had not violated such rigid rules of conduct that Jael was justified in murdering him. We are drawn back to Deborah's assessment. Jael had sided with Israel and killed an enemy. The glory was hers, not Barak's.

Barak belatedly pursued Sisera to the encampment of Heber. **Jael went out to call to him** (v 22), the same words used in v 18. While it would not be normal for a woman to invite a man into her tent, the circumstances overturned convention. Jael had sided with the Israelites in their war with Jabin and had slain Sisera. She needed to demonstrate her loyalty to the Israelite commander by showing him the body. Inside the tent Barak found Sisera dead, a tent peg in his head.

f. Destruction of Jabin (4:23-24)

■ **23-24** Barak and his troops fought, but the victory belonged to God. It was he who subdued Jabin before the Israelites. The balance of power now shifted to the Israelites, and they continued to strike against Jabin the king of the Canaanites until he was destroyed. The battle at the Kishon was a great victory, but continued military operations were needed to assure complete victory. It was necessary to continue making sacrifices until the enemy had been destroyed. To stop before winning a complete victory would have enabled the enemy to regroup and possibly reassert control over Israel. A partial release from oppression is no release at all.

FROM THE TEXT

1. Praise is given to God for delivering the Israelites from oppression. However, God was also responsible for placing them in bondage (4:2). The Israelites broke the covenant by worshipping other gods. God then brought the curses of the covenant upon them. We need to be cautious about assuming a direct cause-and-effect relationship between disobedience and divine punishment. Israel struggled with this problem (Ps 73) as they observed that the wicked were not always punished nor were the righteous always rewarded. Jesus rejected the argument of his disciples that the blindness of a man was caused by someone sinning before he was born (John 9:1-5). Sin does have its effects on people, but it is not always easy to see them. A person who rejects God may live a long, healthy life, serve in important positions in society, and enjoy economic prosperity. Paul noted, however, that when we yield ourselves to sin we become its slave (Rom 6:16). Whether or not that slavery produces observable effects, we are still slaves. From this type of oppression, only the grace of God is able to free us. The spiritual life of an individual or community does bear fruit in other areas of life. We cannot separate what we worship from what we become. What we worship also determines our spiritual destiny.

2. After the people had been delivered by Ehud (Judg 3:30), the land enjoyed a period of quietness (šāqaṭ), or being undisturbed. It was during this time (4:1) that the people began to worship other gods. Spirituality is generally not shaped during times of crisis. Crises points such as the death of a loved one or battling a disease may force one to reconsider his or her lifestyle and thus become a turning point spiritually. Many in such circumstances reexamine their lives and reach a decision to follow God. Unfortunately for a few, they become overwhelmed with their problems and reject his offered grace. Most of life, however, is lived in the in-between-times of normal activities. We cope with the small issues that periodically arise, but mostly we seem to handle them with relative ease. This leads to the temptation to live self-sufficient lives with little or no recognition of God's call upon us. It is easy to grow lax spiritually and find our main values being

shaped by the culture around us. The slow drift away from obedience to and fellowship with God takes us unaware. Like the Israelites we begin to follow other gods, our gods may not be those images formed by hands, but other values to which we give our loyalty: money, power, jobs, or family. But this need not be. The quiet times may also bring opportunities to steady our character and to learn to trust God for our everyday needs. When crises do come, they then become times that reveal the depths of our commitments to God.

3. Jael presents an example of conflicting loyalties. Her husband, Heber, had made peace with Jabin, yet the clan was also related by marriage to the Israelites. In a conflict between the two, she had to decide which relationship was more important. Life is made up of a multitude of relationships, each with its requirements of varying degrees of loyalty. A person may be a spouse, a parent, a child, a sibling, an employee, a citizen of a nation, or a member of a church, a community organization, and a social club. Add to that list a number of friends of varying degrees of closeness. We usually can navigate the requirements of the various relationships with little difficulty, but on occasion there may be conflicts. Jael had a difficult problem. To whom would she be loyal, the king with whom there was peace or the people of God? We may face similar issues. What if my country makes laws that conflict with my faith? Christians in many lands face the prospect of persecution for their faith. Jesus told us to give to the ruler the things that belong to the ruler and to God the things that belong to God (Luke 20:25). It is not always easy to decide what belongs to whom. There is a constant pull for loyalty, yet one command stands foremost: we are to love God with all our being (Deut 6:5). Working out how to balance the sometimes conflicting obligations is not easy. Our loyalty to God must take first place. That does not mean that we can neglect the other obligations. Our commitment to God demands that we take seriously our obligations to others as well. We live out our faith only within the bounds of relationships.

4. Deborah was an unusual woman. She functioned both as a prophet and as a judge. In the Israelite patriarchal society, women did not usually assume public roles. However, Miriam (Exod 15:20) and Isaiah's wife (Isa 8:3) were also prophets. Huldah (2 Kgs 22:14-22) confirmed that the scroll found in the temple during the reign of Josiah was indeed the word of God. God is not bound by gender roles in his choice of servants. While most of the Israelite society's leaders were men, on occasion a woman could rise to a position of leadership. During the time of the Maccabees (164-67 B.C.), Salome Alexandra ruled Judah as queen for nine

years (76-67 B.C.), "the most prosperous and peaceful time in her nation's history." Josephus recorded that Salome won the affection of the people while also securing peace with Judah's neighbors. In Jewish tradition recorded in the Talmud, the rabbis held her in high regard (Atkinson 2008, 61-65, 72).

Joel predicted that God would pour out his Spirit on all flesh and that both the sons and the daughters would prophesy (2:28). Peter identified the coming of the Spirit on the day of Pentecost as the fulfillment of Joel's prophecy (Acts 2:16-17). Philip, one of the seven chosen to assist the apostles (Acts 6:5), had four daughters who were prophets (Acts 21:8-9). In Gal 3:27-28 Paul laid down the principle that all those who are baptized in Christ are clothed with Christ and that God no longer makes distinctions based on race, social position, or gender. Cultures often identify various roles according to gender, yet there is no consistent pattern across all cultures. Many cultures are patriarchal, but some are matriarchal. The gospel must be presented in a way that is culture specific. For example, the political system of one culture may be democratic, another monarchial, a third tribal. The gospel does not sanction one political system over another. However, it does speak about Christ dying for all people and freeing them from their sins. The social implications of the gospel are significant. God clearly values the life of each person, regardless of social position (ruler, free, or slave) or gender.

As to leadership in the church, God is sovereign in his choice of leaders, whether men or women. The church should respond by recognizing and enabling those called by God to fulfill his purpose in their lives. This may not be an easy task in cultures where leadership roles are defined along gender lines; such as, when men are not normally in leadership positions in matriarchal cultures or women in patriarchal cultures. The church must work within the culture in ways that do not discredit the gospel while also being a counterculture witness to the full message of the gospel.

The Wesleyan tradition has a long history of women taking leadership roles. John Wesley, in a day when his society did not look favorably on women taking leadership positions, argued for the education of women and appointed a number to lead Methodist class meetings. The churches that maintain their Wesleyan heritage have long supported "authorizing" and ordaining women to the clergy.

Status of Women

When John Wesley wrote his comments on 1 Tim 2:13 in his *Explanatory Notes on the New Testament* (1754), he took a position that women were to be subordinate to men. The Anglican tradition in which he was raised, and which he early accepted, maintained that the early chapters of Genesis taught that Eve had been created subordinate to Adam. Wesley made a thorough examination of Genesis as he was preparing his *Explanatory Notes on the Old Testament* (1765) and changed his mind in regard to a hierarchal order established in creation. In spite of strong opposition to his new position, the mature Wesley supported the education of women and "allowed them to preach and teach with authority equal to that of the male Methodist preachers" (private communication from Randy Maddox). In 1819, Richard Allen, founder of the African Methodist Episcopal Church, authorized Jarena Lee to preach, the first woman to be so recognized (online: http://www.pbs.org/wgbh/aia/part3/3h1638.html). From the beginning, women in the Salvation Army (1865) assumed leadership roles. The example was set by Catherine Booth, who worked alongside her husband, William. The Free Methodist Church has been ordaining women for over 150 years. At present 14 percent of clergy of various orders are women (online: http://www.freemethodistchurch.org/sections/about_us/stats/home.shtml). As early as 1861, the Illinois District of the Wesleyan Church ordained Mrs. Mary A. Will as an elder (Gonlag n.d., http://www.wesleyan.org/em/women_ministry_main). Today about 5 percent of the active ordained elders of the Wesleyan Church are women (private communication from Jerry Brecheisen, director of Media, Wesleyan Church). The United Methodist Church, the largest and oldest denomination in the Wesleyan tradition, has 10,378 clergywomen; 23.1 percent of its clergy (private communication from Pearl Hann, United Methodist Information Service). From the earliest days of the formation of the Church of God (Anderson) (1881), the leaders worked diligently to include both women and African Americans in leadership positions. Presently 25.6 percent of its ministers are women, 1,980 out of a total of 7,728 (private communication from David Farlow, chief of Strategic Communication, Church of God [Anderson]). When the Church of the Nazarene was founded in 1908, 17.7 percent of the clergy were women. By 1930, 20.7 percent were women, but by 2003 only 10.7 percent were women (Houseal 2003, 10). Several of the churches in the Wesleyan tradition had a decline after 1950 in the percentage of clergy who were women, but an increase in the 1990s. The decrease and then increase reflect cultural shifts; however, even during the time when few women were entering the clergy, no church took the position that women should not be ordained. All maintained that those persons, male or female, who were called by God should be recognized and ordained.

2. The Poem (5:1-31)

BEHIND THE TEXT

The Song of Deborah and Barak is perhaps one of the oldest poems in the OT and, as such, it contains some of its most difficult Hebrew. Many scholars have worked with the archaic language, comparing it to cognate or closely related languages such as Ugaritic and Phoenician (for detailed analysis of the Hebrew and references to more critical studies, see Boling 1975, 105-16, and Soggin 1981, 79-92). The reader may feel frustrated when a precise meaning of a word is not given, or when comparing translations seeing that they differ significantly. However, this may reflect the poet's artistry, having chosen words that have multiple meanings and thus giving the poem a richness of insight.

The poem of ch 5 and the narrative of ch 4 work together to give a more complete picture of the events than if they are read separately. The poem gives little background about the main characters or Barak's reluctance to respond to Deborah's instruction. It does contain more detailed lists of the tribes that did or did not participate in the battle. The concluding scene of Sisera's mother waiting for her son's victorious return is full of irony. The reader knows that the delay is not due to the celebration of the victor, but because he is already dead. The poem celebrates the deeds of the tribes and individuals, yet the main actor in the drama is Yahweh. It is to him that the poem is directed (vv 2, 4), and it his actions that are acknowledged as the main resource for success in battle.

IN THE TEXT

a. Introduction (5:1-11)

■ 1-11 An editorial note (v 1) attributes the poem to both Deborah and Barak, although Deborah's voice seems to dominate. The poem proper begins (v 2) with a difficult phrase (*biprō'a pěrā'ōt*) having to do either with the leaders loosening the hair as in a vow to go to war or with casting off restraint (imposed by the oppressor) and offering themselves willingly (*hitādēb*) to go to war (BDB, 621, 828). In v 3, the formal introduction of the poem, the poet speaks to the rulers, asking them to give attention to what she has to say. These verses begin a victory hymn that is a type of poetry well known in the ANE.

Verses 4-5 are addressed to Yahweh, the God of Israel, and describe a theophany or disclosure of God. In standard Israelite style (see Hab 3:2-15) Yahweh is described as coming as a warrior from the south where Mount Sinai is located. The first two lines are in synonymous parallelism. As Yahweh comes from the south, he passes through Edom, which is located south of the Dead Sea. Seir is another name for Edom. All nature including heaven, earth, and even the mountains are disrupted. The reference to rain from the clouds is the first mention of the storm that caused the Kishon to flood (Judg 5:21), hampering the maneuvering of the chariots of Sisera.

A description of the situation prior to the battle is given in vv 6-9. Shamgar had achieved a great victory (3:31) but had not brought oppression to an end. It was an evil time and travelers/caravans had **ceased** (*ḥādal*) their journeys or had to keep to the less-traveled and thus less-watched roads. Those who dwelt in **unprotected open areas** (*pĕrāzâ*) usually in tents rather than in the more protected towns that had defensive walls, had also **ceased** (*ḥādal*) (KBL, 777). The Canaanite oppressors had disrupted normal life, and the unprotected had become victims. That is, **until Deborah arose, arose a mother in Israel** (v 7). Her title does not refer to her giving birth to children, but to her function as a deliverer who brings, like a mother, life to the community.

The first line of v 8 is difficult to understand, and several different readings have been proposed. The choosing of **new gods** may refer to the earlier idolatrous practices of the people. Boling suggests that in a time of disruption of travel, new treaties were being entered into. The standard procedure called for the gods of the parties to become witnesses to the treaties (1975, 109). Israel would call upon Yahweh and the surrounding inhabitants their gods. Another possibility is that Israelites living in the various towns were calling upon Yahweh and other gods to assist them in battling their oppressors. Given their continued practice of worshipping other gods, this would not be an unusual practice. At the time, however, Israel lacked military arms, which meant a desperate situation for a people preparing for battle. Deborah expressed sympathy for the commanders: **My heart (goes) to the commanders among the people** (v 9). They freely offered themselves to the task that had considerable risk. The closing phrase, **Bless Yahweh,** forms a literary frame with the end of v 2.

Local people did not travel much as their time was consumed with the task of scratching out a living by farming or shepherding. When travelers arrived at a town, they became a source of information about the broader world. The poet calls on the tribal poet-singers to compose songs and stories to tell the deeds of Yahweh (vv 10-11), those victories won especially by his vulnerable people (v 7). In an oral culture the stories of the people were handed down orally from generation to generation. In the Israelite culture those skilled in composing a story, especially in poetic form, were honored. Much of the OT is set in verse, particularly the Psalms, Proverbs, most of Job, as well as most of the Prophets. At some point in history, we are not sure when, scribes began to write down the stories and poetry.

b. The Mustering of the Tribes (5:12-18)

■ **12-18** The poem shifts with a dramatic call to Deborah to sing of victory and Barak to take captives (v 12). A third voice, neither that of Deborah nor Barak, summons both to action. To call to someone to awake is to rouse the person to act. It does not mean that the person is asleep, only not engaged. See Ps 44:23 and Isa 51:9 where God is called upon to awake. A *remnant* (*śārîd*, v 13), not the whole of the people, gathered for battle. The list of those who responded to the call to battle begins with tribes situated in the central hill country, Ephraim, Benjamin, and Machir, possibly a clan of Manasseh. These tribes are not mentioned in the narrative account of ch 4. Zebulun and Issachar were located north of the Jezreel valley. The tribes of Reuben and Gilead located east of the Jordan River did not respond. Neither did the two coastal tribes of Asher, located in the north, and Dan, located evidently at this time in the south close by the Philistines. Zebulun, mentioned a second time, and Naphtali, both praised for their heroism, conclude the list of tribes. Judah is conspicuously absent from the list.

c. The Battle (5:19-22)

■ **19-22** The reference to kings in v 19 is poetic hyperbole. The leader of the Canaanites was Sisera, the general of King Jabin who did not participate in the battle. Taanach and Megiddo were two major cities in the valley. The stars (v 20) were viewed in Canaanite religion as a source of rain (Boling 1975, 113). The poet uses irony to describe in Canaanite terms the source of their own defeat. The Kishon (v 21) flows with water only during the rainy seasons of the year. It has been known to be dry in the morning, but when a heavy rain came later in the day, the waters have overflowed their banks and turned the area into a quagmire. The poet uses repetition of the word "torrent" (*nahal*) to build in the mind of the audience the force of the water that God released against the chariots. The last line shouts encouragement, **March on, my soul, with strength!** (v 21). Irony is used again in v 22, which describes the thunderous beat of the hooves of the horses as they pulled the chariots into the softened ground. The audience would know that as they moved swiftly to battle, they also swept speedily into the mud, which clogged the wheels and made maneuvering impossible. They became an easy prey to the Israelite infantry.

d. Jael's Victory (5:23-27)

■ **23-27** This section begins with a curse (v 23) given by an angel or messenger of Yahweh, **Curse Meroz.** The inhabitants of the village Meroz did not come to the assistance of Yahweh in his fight against Sisera. The location of Meroz is unknown. The emphasis of the text is on the theological; it was Yahweh's battle and they failed to come to his assistance. As a poetic and literary device this verse stands in contrast with the praise given to Jael (v 24). Meroz refused to come to Israel's aid, but Jael helped them by killing Sisera.

Blessed are you among women Jael! (v 24). This saying has been incorporated into Elizabeth's greeting to Mary (Luke 1:42) and on this basis some Medieval writers saw Jael as a forerunner to Mary. Because Jael, the wife of Heber who had made peace with Jabin (Judg 4:17), chose to honor the relationship with Israel (v 11) and destroy its enemy she received such high praise.

Judges 5:25-26 describe the scene in the tent. Sisera asked for water (4:19-20). Jael brought him milk in a bowl. Sisera asked her to stand in the door of the tent and lie to protect him. Jael drove a tent peg through his skull.

Sisera's death is told in brief, repetitive, and graphic detail. **Between her feet he bowed down, he fell, he lay down. Between her feet he bowed down; he fell. Where he bowed down, there he fell violently destroyed!** (v 27). The expression **between her feet** has sexual overtones. Sisera's presence in Jael's tent was a compromising situation that could have placed Jael in jeopardy of being raped. But Sisera lay between her feet, not in sexual repose but dead. The description of Sisera falling down seems to conflict with the narrative in 4:21 where Sisera is described as already laying asleep when Jael killed him. A warrior, even a tired one, would be alert to someone approaching him with a mallet and peg in hand. Sisera would hardly be so distracted that while standing upright he would allow Jael to place a peg against his head and hit it with a mallet. Rather the poetic description is hyperbolic, emphasizing the disgrace of Sisera who was killed by a woman, and not an Israelite warrior.

e. *Sisera's Mother (5:28-31)*

■ **28-31** Dramatically the scene shifts to describe Sisera's anxious mother who waits for the return of her son. Touchingly (v 28) she looks out the lattice-covered window, wondering aloud why his chariot is delayed. The reader already knows what has delayed Sisera. He is dead. She, however, interprets his delay as a sign that the warriors are taking their time to divide the spoils. The word normally translated as "woman" or "maiden" (**girl**) is *raḥam* (v 30; *raḥam* means "womb"). The captured women were reduced to objects of sexual exploitation with the end result that they became not only the objects of pleasure for the men but also the producers of another generation of slaves for their new masters. The irony was that the actions she and her attendants described might with the defeat of Sisera become their fate, their fine clothes to become the spoil of the Israelites and the women reduced to slavery.

The poem closes with a benediction that Yahweh's enemies might so perish and his friends (ʾāhab) or **ones who love him be as the sun coming in its might** (v 31). The word ʾāhab is usually translated as love with the connotation of a commitment of deep loyalty. It is the word used in Deut 6:5, **You shall love Yahweh your God,** which in turn is quoted by Jesus as the greatest commandment (Matt 22:37). The last line closes with the standard statement that the land was undisturbed for a generation.

FROM THE TEXT

The image of God as the Divine Warrior troubles many. It stands in contrast with the nonviolent approach of Jesus in providing redemption. He took upon himself the violence of a cruel death but did not return violence for violence. Jesus instructed his disciples to overcome persecution by returning good for evil (Luke 6:27-31). Yet even he performed a violent act when he cleansed the temple (John 2:13-16). Also, when Paul was in prison he asked for the protection of the soldiers when his life was threatened (Acts 23:12-35). The larger question that has troubled God's people through the ages is, should violence be used to oppose evil? Jesus did not identify the kingdom of God with any kind of human government, be that monarchy or democracy. His disciples are citizens of the kingdom and also of the political states where they dwell. Both Jesus (Luke 20:25) and Paul (Rom 13:1-7) recognized the authority of government, even when that authority might use violence against evil. Evil is not an abstract concept. People are evil and devise evil actions against others, particularly the weak and poor (Mic 2:1). The list of horrors humans have inflicted upon each other is long and growing. The availability of technology multiplies a nation's or even a group's capability to destroy those it deems its enemies. It has become possible to exterminate the entire populations of cities in just a few minutes. We are left with the problem that if violence is not used against evil persons, millions of people will be killed and the remnant population subjected to continuing oppression. If God opposes injustice, exploitation of the weak, slaughter of the innocents, oppression of people, extermination of populations, how shall he stop this cruelty except through people who use violent means to end the violence? This is the situation with Sisera. God used the counsel of Deborah, the commander Barak with his troops, and the cunning of Jael to destroy the oppressing forces. While we may request that God destroy his enemies (Judg 5:31), it is by means of human instrumentality that he accomplishes his victory.

C. Gideon, Abimelech, Tola, and Jair (6:1—10:18)

OVERVIEW

The story of Gideon provides a pivot to the rest of the book. The previous judges successfully delivered Israel from oppression in spite of the people's continued drift into idolatry. The hesitation of Barak foreshadowed Gideon's request for signs before he felt assured of God's assistance. Gideon was successful in delivering Israel from their enemies, but in the end led Israel into idolatry. Jephthah, who was used by God to deliver Gilead, was not called by him. Samson would only begin to deliver Israel. The stories recount Israel's downward spiral toward spiritual and societal chaos. The book ends with the accounts of tribal displacement and warfare, which illustrate the moral and spiritual confusion that resulted from their rejection of God's laws in favor of the worship of other gods.

Gideon is an ambivalent character demonstrating both weaknesses and strengths. Called by God to deliver his people from the oppression of the Midianites, he was unsure of his call and his abilities. He needed signs from God to assure him of success. Once assured he bravely led his little band of warriors to victory. When Ephraimites (8:1) accused him of neglecting to call them to battle, he diplomatically defused the situation. He was brutal to his enemies and to those who refused to assist him. He refused to accept the offered crown of kingship, yet led his people into idolatry. The story of Gideon takes longer to tell than the previous judges and thus allows the reader to see the complexities of Gideon's personality. His life started obscurely, peaked with national recognition, and ended with the people betraying him and his family. Things then got worse. Abimelech grasped at the crown his father refused and slaughtered his brothers to get it. His rule ended in disgrace with the tribes at war. The seeds of intertribal warfare had been sown and were beginning to sprout.

This section concludes with the brief accounts of two of the minor judges, Tola and Jair. Their stories form a bridge to the next major figure, Jephthah.

1. Gideon, the Reluctant Judge (6:1—8:35)

a. Oppression of the Midianites (6:1-10)

BEHIND THE TEXT

The standard editorial introduction of Israel doing evil opens the story. Only this time the oppressor was the Midianites, the larger tribe with which the clan or subtribe of the Kenites was associated. In the previous chapter it was Jael who had married the Kenite Heber who gained praise for helping deliver Israel by slaying Sisera. Now the larger tribe ironically became the tool of God to bring punishment to Israel for their sin. The Midianites, like the Israelites, also traced their ancestry back to Abraham. Midian was the fourth son of Abraham by his wife/concubine Keturah (Gen 25:1-6). The introduction also contains a late editorial addition of an appearance of a prophet (Judg 6:8-10). This section repeats in Deuteronomistic form the history of God's gracious acts in behalf of Israel and their refusal to listen to him. The statement indicted Israel for failure to obey God and foreshadows the announcement of Yahweh in the days of Jephthah that he would refuse to listen to Israel's cry because they had abandoned him. Thus the editorial introduction ties the story of Gideon to the events of the past and anticipates God's action in the future.

IN THE TEXT

■ **1-10** Again *the Israelites did the evil in the eyes of Yahweh* (v 1), turning to other gods in worship. His response was to allow the Midianites to oppress them for seven years. The Midianites in the thirteenth century inhabited the region east of the Gulf of Aqabah and were known for their trading and pastoral activities (Mendenhall 1997, ABD-CD). Their ancestor was Midian, the fourth son of Abraham through Keturah (Gen 25:1-6). In v 1 she is designated as his woman/wife (*'iššâ*). In v 6 when Abraham divided his wealth among his sons, to the sons of his concubines (*hapîlagšîm*), Hagar and Keturah, he gave gifts. The rest belonged to Isaac. Another family tie between Israel and Midian was established when Moses married Zipporah, the daughter of Reuel, a priest of Midian (Exod 2:15-22).

The oppression of the Midianites was so strong (Judg 6:2) that the Israelites were forced to hide in caves and fortified areas. The reference in v 3 to Israelites sowing crops indicates that the Midianites along with the Amalekites and other peoples from the east came as raiding parties during the spring each year. They would let their animals forage in the fields, thus destroying the crops. The devastation described in v 4, the destruction of both crops and livestock, is couched in hyperbolic language, not to be understood in strictly literal terms. The description of Gideon preparing a kid for a meal (v 19) and of his father having two oxen (v 25) indicates that not all were totally destitute. The Midianites did, however, bring suffering and starvation to many. The path of their destruction extended all the way to Gaza, which belonged to the Philistines. The reference to camels (v 5) is significant as the animal gave the Midianites the ability to move quickly, thus providing them with the elements of surprise and shock in battle. Israel's response to the oppression (vv 6-7) was to cry out (*zāʿaq*) to Yahweh, the God of deliverance who had brought them out of Egypt.

Yahweh's immediate response was to send **a man, a prophet** (v 8); a phrase similar to the identification of **Deborah, a woman, a prophet** (4:4). The opening words of the prophet identify who had sent him, **Thus said Yahweh the God of Israel, I brought you up from Egypt and I brought you out of the house of servitude** (v 8). These words are adapted from the opening statement of the Ten Commandments (Exod 20:2) and form the identification statement of the beginning of the covenant. Judges 6:9-10 recount the history of Yahweh's gracious acts in behalf of his people, delivering them from Egypt and those who oppressed them, and then driving out the peoples of the land to give it to Israel. The prophet's message concludes with a stipulation, the people were not to fear, that is, reverence the gods of the Amorites who inhabited the land. However, they did not listen to God's voice; that is, did not obey him. The structure of the statement is that of a covenant lawsuit. The offended party is identified, Yahweh the God of Israel. Next followed an account of the deeds done in behalf of the people and a command the people were to keep. Normally the lawsuit would conclude with an indictment against the people and a threat of judgment. Here the indictment hangs suspended in the air. There is no threat. The reader is left to conclude that Midian's oppression of Israel was the threat of judgment, the judgment that they were already experiencing.

b. The Call of Gideon (6:11-40)

BEHIND THE TEXT

This section has several divisions: The appearance of the messenger or angel of Yahweh (vv 11-24), the destruction of the altar of Baal (vv 25-32), Gideon's call to the troops (vv 33-35), and Gideon's additional request for a sign (vv 36-40). The story seems disjunctive at points, particularly the last two sections. This is part of the storyteller's art, moving ahead with the story and then shifting back to previous events. What is more significant is the number of parallels the narrative has with other stories, particularly with the call of Moses. These parallels will be noted in the next section.

IN THE TEXT

■ **11-24** Verses 11-24 record the appearance of an angel/messenger of Yahweh. The messenger was a member of the heavenly court sent to represent the physical form of Yahweh. As the conversation progresses, it becomes apparent that the messenger could be interchangeable or identical to Yahweh (see also Gen 16:7-13; 21:17-19; 22:11-12; Exod 3:2, 4) (Soggin 1981, 114). Like Deborah (4:5) the messenger sat under a tree, in this case an oak located in Ophrah, a town of the half tribe of Manasseh that was located west of the Jordan. The father of Gideon was Joash, a descendant of Abiezer of the tribe of Manasseh (Josh 17:2). Joash apparently was a significant figure in the community, as the altar to Baal belonged to him (Judg 6:25) and he had the ability to deflect the anger of the people when they discovered that Gideon had destroyed the sacred shrine (vv 30-31).

Gideon **was beating,** that is, threshing the wheat (v 11), removing the kernels of grain from the stalks. The place of threshing was odd, a winepress. Some winepresses were a series of shallow, bowl-shaped areas carved in the limestone bedrock. In the first, higher area the grapes were crushed by people stomping on them. The juice ran out through a channel into a lower area where it was strained, and then through another channel into jugs placed to catch the juice. Because of the threat of the Midianites Gideon was using the winepress probably because he was working with smaller amounts that could be hidden more readily in the area of the winepress than that of a normal threshing floor.

The messenger greeted Gideon, **Yahweh is with you, mighty warrior,** or **Yahweh will be with you, mighty warrior** (v 12). The pronoun "you" is singular. Gideon responded with a term of respect, **My Lord,** or **Sir,** and then shifted the conversation away from himself to ask, **If Yahweh is with us, then why has all this come upon us?** He ended his statement with an indictment of God, **and now Yahweh has forsaken us and given us into the hand of Midian** (v 13). Yahweh himself responded in v 14, shifting back to the singular pronoun **you.** This is a call narrative, commissioning Gideon to **save Israel from the hand of Midian** (v 14). Gideon responded by pleading, like Moses, insignificance. **My family** (*'elep* is often translated by the number 1,000, but here it reflects the older usage referring to a family or clan) **is the weakest in Manasseh and I am the least significant in my father's house** (v 15). God's response (v 16) was **I am with you.** The word for **I am** is *'ehyeh*, the same term God used in identifying himself to Moses (Exod 3:14). Gideon's response, **if now I have found favor/grace in your eyes** (Judg 6:17), was the same as Moses' when he asked to see God's glory (Exod 33:18). Gideon, however, asked for a sign to prove that the messenger was indeed Yahweh. Gideon hospitably offered (Judg 6:18) a gift (*minĕhâ*) or offering (Exod 30:9; Lev 7:37) for the messenger and urged him to remain until he returned.

The meal that Gideon offered (Judg 6:19) would have taken several hours to prepare. The amount of flour, an ephah or about 10 liters or 9 quarts dry measure, is quite large. When Gideon brought the meat, unleavened bread (*maṣṣâ*), and broth, the messenger directed him to place them on a stone. He then touched the food with his staff, a flame consumed the food, and the messenger **departed from his sight** (v 21) (see the parallel experience of Manoah the father of Samson, 13:19-21). Gideon finally realized who his visitor was and cried out in fear to Yahweh because he had seen **the messenger of Yahweh face to face** (v 22; see Gen 32:31, Jacob at Penuel), an experience of the divine that could mean death for a mortal (Isa 6:5). Yet Yahweh was still present, although not in bodily form, and spoke peace to him, assuring him that he would not die (Judg 6:23). Gideon in response, like Abraham (Gen 12:8), built there an altar to God.

■ **25-32** The next section describes how Gideon destroyed the altar of Baal. The scene shifts to the night (Judg 6:25). Yahweh commanded Gideon to tear down the altar of Baal, cut down the sacred pole of Asherah for firewood (v 26), build a proper altar for Yahweh his God on top of the fortified sanctuary area, and sacrifice his father's second ox, the seven-year-old one. The Asherah was a pole or tree that stood beside the altar to Baal. As Baal represented the male function of the fertility cult, the tree represented the female part. Gideon's first act as a judge was to destroy the symbols of Canaanite worship that had snared the Israelites.

That Gideon's family had at least ten servants (v 27) indicates that they had wealth and power. Yet Gideon feared the anger of his family and the people of the town, so they carried out God's command at night. Gideon's fear in this passage contrasts with Yahweh's command to him in v 23 not to fear. When the men of the town (v 28) discovered that the worship area had been desecrated, they inquired as to who did it (v 29). Some unidentified person informed them that Gideon was responsible. They demanded (v 30) that Joash deliver his son to them that they might execute him. Joash's response (v 31) presents a play on the word *rîb*, to sue, to bring a lawsuit, to contend (KBL, 888-89). Why would a god need someone to contend for him? If Baal was a god, he should be able to prosecute the violator and execute sentence. Joash was mocking the ineffectiveness of Baal and thus demonstrating that Baal was not a god. Olson notes the contrast between the promise of Yahweh to defend Gideon (v 16) and Baal's inability to defend his own altar. If Baal was truly a god, he would defend his altar and punish Gideon. Yahweh protected Gideon so that he was not executed and thus demonstrated his power as a defender (1998, 797). The name Gideon comes from the word that means "to hew down" or "to hack." His new name (v 32), Jerubbaal, **Let Baal Contend,** plays on the idea of the ineffectiveness of Baal.

■ **33-35** The narrative (v 33) moves back to describe again the attack of the Midianites, Amalekites, and the people of the east. They camped in the Valley of Jezreel, which runs east from the forests of Mount Carmel toward the Jordan River. It is a fertile area, good for growing grains and vegetables. **The spirit of Yahweh clothed Gideon** (v 34a), took possession of him, but not in the sense of overriding his consciousness. The spirit empowered him to act, yet his actions were his own. Earlier the spirit of Yahweh had come upon Othniel (3:10). Later the spirit will endow Jephthah (11:29) and Samson (14:6 and 15:14) to perform mighty deeds, yet there will be a continued deterioration in leadership. Empowerment by the spirit will not lead to consistency in obedience or sanctity of the person. Gideon recruited (vv 34b-35) his father's clan, the Abiezrites. He also sent messengers to Manasseh, Asher, Zebulun, and Naphtali, northern tribes whose lands were close to the Jezreel valley where their enemies had encamped.

■ **36-40** Gideon is portrayed as a hesitant, weak leader, unsure if God will perform his word. He devised a test that God might assure him that the words God spoke to him would be fulfilled, **If you will save Israel by my hand like you said** (v 36). He placed a fleece (*gizzâ*, the word occurs only in these verses) of wool (v 37) on a threshing floor and asked that the next morning dew would be on it but not on the ground. The next morning (v 38) he found that enough water was in the fleece to fill a bowl. It would be a natural occurrence for dew to be on an item and not on a stone threshing floor. So, Gideon cautiously asked that the reverse might happen. His request was similar to that of Abraham in interceding for Sodom (Gen 18:32), **Do not let your anger burn against me and I will speak only once** (Judg 6:39). That night (v 40) God reversed the sign and the fleece was dry and the ground was wet.

FROM THE TEXT

1. Those whom God chooses as leaders do not necessarily reflect the qualities that the culture would require for leadership. Gideon was not bold and aggressive, but timid and fearful, continually in need of reassurance. His requests, like that of Moses, for demonstrations of God's power reflected insecurity. Moses had been afraid that the people would not believe that God had commissioned him. In response God gave him signs to authenticate his leadership: turning a staff into a snake, causing and healing leprosy, changing water into blood (Exod 4:1-9). God's signs could be refused. Isaiah offered to Ahaz the opportunity to see a sign from God, but Ahaz refused. He had made his plans and did not want to be obedient

to the word of God (Isa 7:10-12). The graciousness of God is demonstrated in his willingness to work gently with those whom he calls. For Gideon, God not only agreed to the tests of the fleece and dew, but even on the eve of battle sent him to spy out the camp where he could hear a message of victory (Judg 7:9-14).

The Gospel of John records a number of signs (*sēmeion*, often translated "miracle") that Jesus performed (2:11; 6:2, 14). These demonstrated to the people not only the power of Jesus but also his identity as the Christ. Many believed, but those who refused to believe that Jesus was the Christ rejected him. Signs must always be interpreted in faith. There is a natural tendency for people to seek after signs, to experience the miraculous. The miraculous, however, never fully satisfies the one whose faith has to be propped up by signs. Like an emotional high, the intensity of the experience soon wanes. Faith must take hold, faith in God and his promises. Our faith must rest in a good and faithful God who cares for his people. To place our faith in any other leads to idolatry.

2. When the messenger of Yahweh appeared to Gideon, the greeting prompted him to ask a question that many today could echo, **If Yahweh is with us, then why has all this come upon us?** (Judg 6:13). How do we know that God is with us? Do we identify times of prosperity, success, and triumph as signs of God's presence? Is he absent in times of loss, despair, and defeat? Is he to be identified with the good but not with the bad? How do we know? God assured Gideon, **I will be with you** (v 16), and later clothed him with the spirit (v 34), yet Gideon was still afraid and requested further assurances. The graciousness of God can be seen in the gentleness with which he supported Gideon. When God calls us to become his people, he does not expect us to be fully equipped to carry out his commission. It is only through his sustaining and equipping grace that we are able to serve him.

3. When God refused to lead the Israelites into the land, Moses interceded for them. For him the very identity of Israel depended upon the presence of God. That is what made Israel distinct (Exod 33:16). Yet his presence cannot be identified with any set of feelings or series of events. God is not necessarily in the times of joy or despair. Many Christians give testimony that they have gone through extended periods when they had no assurances that God was with them. Such times have been called "the dark night of the soul." Even Jesus felt abandoned during his crucifixion (Mark 16:34). Yet at the end he could confidently commit himself into the hands of his Father (Luke 23:46). It is in our faithful response of obedience that he is best known. Whether or not we feel his presence in private

devotions or inspiring worship services or recognize it in the Eucharist, we are called to continue to live faithfully regardless of the circumstances of life (Hab 3:17-19).

c. God's Victory (7:1-23)

BEHIND THE TEXT

The text of Judges is generally very secure, as it has been well preserved. There are, however, two places in this chapter where problems arise. The end of v 5 and beginning of v 6 appear to be disturbed. The fuller identification of how each group drank would be expected in v 5*b*. The text is reconstructed and then translated in various ways. Boling has used the LXX to reconstruct the text and has set the possibilities in a chart. He suggests that the words **with their hands to their mouths** were transposed by a scribe from v 5*b* to 6*a* and that in the process the words **with their tongues** were omitted. His translation thus reads, "(v 5b) 'and everyone who goes down on his knees to drink water, with hand to mouth set apart by himself.' (v 6a) The total of those who lapped with their tongues was three hundred men" (1975, 142, 145). In the discussion of the text, Boling's suggestion for translating the verses will be followed.

The other problem is in v 8. What is the subject of the verb **and they took** (*wāiyqḥû*)? It is a third person plural verb that would indicate that either the people or the three hundred men were the subject. It is unlikely that the people took their provisions and the horns as at least the horns would be needed by the remaining. It has been suggested that the verb should be singular, implying that Gideon took the provisions and horns from the people so that the three hundred might use them (Soggin 1981, 137-38). Still, why would the three hundred need the provisions of the others? A better understanding is that the three hundred took from the others that which they needed for the battle.

The numbers of soldiers recorded for both armies appear very high from what archaeological records tell us of the times. Midian had 135,000 and Israel 32,000. The high numbers in Judges are a source of continuing discussion. It is possible that during the period of oral transmission the numbers became inflated and that the editors simply recorded the traditions as they found them. The Wesleyan view of dynamic inspiration takes such procedures into account as W. B. Pope noted, "Sometimes they [the inspired writers] have to register facts, or supposed facts, which they gather from public records; sometimes to record traditions, legends, current opinions, or uninspired predictions handed down by tradition: in these cases they are only witnesses of what they found" (1880, 1:172) (see the discussion on inspiration in the Introduction).

IN THE TEXT

■ **1-8** These verses record how the army of Jerubbaal/Gideon was reduced in size. The 32,000 Israelite soldiers (v 1) moved to the southern edge of the Jezreel valley and camped by a spring called Harod, today known as Ain Jalud (Hunt 1997a, ABD-CD). The hill of Moreh, or "Hill of Seeing," is thought to be located at Nebi Dahi (Hunt 1997b, ABD-CD). The general locations of the events are known, but with the exception of the spring and the hill of Moreh, the named sites cannot be identified with any degree of certainty. The Midianites and their allies were camped in the Valley of Jezreel, just to the north of the Israelites. Yahweh was displeased with the large number of Israelite soldiers (v 2). A specific reason is given; he did not want the Israelites to be able to claim the honor for the victory and boast, **by our own hand we saved ourselves** (v 2). God would give the enemy into their hands, but the glory would be his. The first test (v 3) followed the requirement of Deut 20:8 that allowed anyone who was afraid to be exempt from battle. It is not stated exactly to where the 22,000 solders returned. Some translations add the words "to home," but the text is not specific as to where they went.

The 10,000 left were still too many (Judg 7:4), so Yahweh devised a test to reduce the number. Gideon took them to water to drink. A few lay down with their faces close to the water and lapped it like a dog. Others knelt down on their knees, took the water in their cupped hands, and raised it their mouths to drink. God had Gideon set aside the 300 who lapped the water. The end of v 5 is missing in Hebrew, the statement that Gideon separated the other 10,000. The Hebrew reads, **the number who lapped with their hand to their mouth was three hundred** (v 6). The reference to hands to the mouth confuses the identification and is better to read **lapped with their tongue** (see Boling above). God then promised Gideon that he would use the remaining solders to defeat the Midianites. The 300 (see discussion above) then took (v 8) what provisions or food supplies they needed. These 10,000, and possibly the other 22,000, were not sent home, but returned **to their tents,** possibly a staging area away from the battle area, but close enough to join the fight at the proper time (v 23). There has been much speculation as to what exactly the test was. Did those who lapped the water trust God to protect them while the others who rested on their knees, bringing the water in their hands, were watching fearfully? Or, were those who lapped careless and the others as trained warriors were watchfully ready to engage instantly in battle? The implication of this last suggestion is that God wanted the unprepared rather than the battle-ready. Such a choice would show clearly that the victory was of divine origin. Whatever the reason was, it was God who set the test to reduce the numbers. No reason is explicitly given as to why one group was chosen and the other dismissed. The troops were too numerous, and God wanted to reduce them (v 2). The victory was to belong to him, not humans. To take the few into battle and bring about victory would demonstrate that Israel should trust Yahweh to provide for their protection, not the Canaanite gods.

■ **9-18** Again Gideon is portrayed as fearful about the battle and personally insecure. God was ready and commanded Gideon, **Arise! Attack the camp, for I have given it into your hand!** (v 9). The verb *yārad* basically means "to come/go down" (BDB, 432). It is the context that gives it specific meaning of "attack." The word will occur several times in the following verses, switching back and forth from "go down" (vv 10, 11) to "attack" (vv 9, 10, 11). Yet Gideon was too afraid to attack (v 10), so God suggested that he go down to the camp with his **young man** (*na'ar*), or attendant, Purah. The purpose of their visit was to hear what the enemy was saying about Gideon. God told him that when he heard, **your hand will be strengthened and you will attack the camp** (v 11).

Who Was a Young Person?

The Hebrew term *na'ar* appears twenty-eight times in the book of Judges. Each time it refers to a person who is younger, not the full age of an adult. In 7:10, 11 Purah was an attendant of Gideon, possibly his armor bearer like Abimelech's young boy (8:54). It was a *na'ar* from Succoth who gave Gideon a list of the seventy-seven leaders of the city (8:14). Jether, Gideon's son (8:20), is described as a *na'ar*. Because of his youth he was afraid to kill the kings of Midian. Samson is repeatedly called a *na'ar* in the stories that foretell of his birth (13:5, 7, 8, 12, 24). And it was a *na'ar* who led Samson (16:26) to the pillars that supported the temple. The Levite who left Bethlehem and took up residence with Micah is referred to as a *na'ar* (17:7, 11, 12; 18:3, 5). In these instances the word is probably used as a derogatory term. He was the priest of Micah's shrine, and then of the illegitimate worship center in Dan. The Levite whose concubine left him had an unnamed servant who is referred to as a *na'ar* (19:3, 9, 11, 13, 19). His concubine is also called a *na'ărâ*, a feminine form (19:3, 4, 5, 6, 8, 9). Although she was married to the Levite, she was probably not considered a mature woman due to her age. Finally, the four hundred young women who were taken from Jabesh-gilead (21:12) were called *na'ărâ*. In each case the person so designated was not considered a mature adult. They often were servants. In most instances the term is used simply as a designation of youth. When the term is used in reference to Jether, the Levite from Bethlehem, and the Levite's concubine the term carries more ominous meanings.

Verse 12 heightens the impossibility of the situation. Gideon had three hundred. The enemy was like locusts and their camels without number. The hyperbole gives a reason for the fear of Gideon. It also functions to give glory to God when the enemy is defeated. Gideon heard (v 13) a man tell his neighbor a dream and his neighbor gave the interpretation. Not all dreams even in ancient cultures had significance, but an especially troubling dream was believed to be a message from a god. In this case the dream was from the God of Israel and foretold the destruction of the Midianites. The dream described a large, round loaf of barley bread smashing into the tent of Midian and collapsing it. The neighbor identified the loaf as **the sword of Gideon** (v 14) and that God had given to him the victory over Midian. When Gideon heard the dream and its interpretation (v 15), his first response was to worship God. His confidence was restored as he realized that God would give him victory. He returned to the Israelite camp. In speech like Deborah's command to Barak (4:14), Gideon commanded his troops, **Up, for Yahweh has given into your hand the camp of Midian!** (v 15).

Gideon strategically divided the three hundred soldiers in to three companies of one hundred each (v 16). Gideon commanded one company and told the others to follow his actions. Each soldier had a ram's horn and a clay pot, into which a torch (*lappîd*, the word used for Deborah's husband, Lappidoth, 4:4) was placed. The men were to follow Gideon's example (v 17). When he and his company blew their horns, the others were to blow theirs and shout, **For Yahweh and for Gideon** (v 18).

■ **19-23** The initial battle is briefly described in these verses. Gideon and his men (v 19) took their positions at the outskirts of the camp. The middle watch in Israelite reckoning was in the early hours before daybreak. A night attack was greatly feared. The inability to see clearly hindered troops forming ranks and marshalling the strength needed to repel an attacker. When the Israelites broke the pottery vessels revealing the lights, blew on the rams' horns, and shouted, **a sword of Yahweh and Gideon** (v 20), it produced panic in the Midian camp. Although the Israelites did not attack, but stood in place (v 21), it would appear to the Midianites as if they were attacking in full force. In the panic and the darkness the Midianites and their allies could not distinguish friend from foe. Consequently, **Yahweh set the sword of each against his neighbor** (v 22a) (see v 13 to note the ironic use of the term "neighbor" in the statement). This reference to Yahweh will be the last as an active participant. Gideon will refer to God in 8:3, 7, 23, but he no longer is described as taking an active part in the story. This is significant as the actions Gideon took became more vengeful and brutal. His personality changed from timid leader to revengeful conqueror as he acted independently of the guidance of God. The survivors of the initial attack fled eastward (vv 22b-23). The exact locations of Beth-shittah, Zererah, Abel-meholah, and Tabbath have not been identified. When the rout began Gideon called on the reserves of Naphtali, Asher, and Manasseh to pursue the fleeing troops.

FROM THE TEXT

God had Gideon reduce the number of his troops in order that the people would not be able to claim that they in their own strength gained victory. God gave the Israelites victory, not by allowing them to destroy their enemies, but by allowing their enemies to destroy themselves in panic. Yet we read that Gideon coveted the glory of victory when he commanded his troops to proclaim, **A sword for Yahweh and Gideon.** Subsequently Gideon treated with extreme cruelty not only the Midianites but also those who refused to assist him (8:10-21). Gideon secured for himself great honor in battle, but little for God. Even today some think that they honor God by killing those they disagree with. Evil must be opposed and violence must at times be used, but extreme brutality does not honor God. It does not honor the Christ who died to reconcile humanity not only to God but also to one another (Eph 3:13-22). Gideon's brutality is not an example of following God's command, but an example of humanity's lust for bloody violence. As much as is possible, we should live nonviolent lives. Those who guard society, police officers and military personnel, are called upon in extreme situations to use violence, but even then only sufficient force to restrain the persons committing the evil acts should be used. This is a difficult problem in society. Those who have given themselves to do evil seek to destroy and corrupt what is good. How much force must be used to restrain them is a continuing problem. To do nothing would be to allow evil to destroy the innocent. To give way to brutality would be to replace one evil with another.

d. Gideon's Victory and Vengeance (7:24—8:21)

This section describes Gideon's complete victory over the Midianites and their allies. It also injects some disturbing themes. Ephraim objected to their role in the battle, but Gideon diplomatically placated their anger. Jephthah was not as diplomatic and a civil war erupted (12:1-6). The disintegration of the tribal bonds eventually led to the near destruction of the tribe of Benjamin (ch 20). Gideon acted out of personal revenge in pursuing the kings of Midian. He also reacted vengefully to the leaders of Succoth and the people of Penuel who refused to extend hospitality to Gideon's weary troops. As the stories continue, the leaders of the tribes become more independent of God's guidance. They become more self-willed, seeking to fulfill their own pursuits more than the purposes of God.

IN THE TEXT

■ **24-25** Gideon sent messengers to Ephraim to enlist their aid in cutting off the escape of the Midianites (v 24). The troops of Ephraim were instructed to take control of fords of the Jordan River and thus block the escape route of the main body. The location of Beth-barah has not been identified. Ephraim was successful and captured two commanders (v 25) (*śar*, same term as for Sisera, see 4:2), Oreb (lit. "raven") and Zeeb (lit. "wolf"). Both commanders were executed and their names given to the places of execution, The **Rock of Oreb** and **The Wine Press of Zeeb** (v 25). The reference to a winepress recalls the opening scene of the story where Gideon was secretly threshing grain in a winepress for fear of the Midianites (6:11). Gideon was by this time across the Jordan in pursuit of the remnants of the Midianite army.

■ **8:1-3** The next problem Gideon faced was one concerning tribal honor. The men of Ephraim *disputed strongly* with Gideon (v 1) because he did not call them out to fight at the beginning of the battle. Ehud had called Ephraim first to seize the fords of the Jordan against the Moabites, and they had gained the great honor in the battle (3:27-29). When Gideon summoned them, the major battle had already been fought and Ephraim had caught only the escaping remnant of the army. They felt insulted. Gideon diplomatically responded (v 2) by depreciating his part in the battle and magnifying Ephraim's part. They had captured the commanders. What had he done in comparison? Gideon then created a proverb to strengthen his argument, **Are not the gleanings of the grapes of Ephraim better than the vintage** (a season's harvest) **of Abiezer?** (v 2). What he had done (v 3) was nothing, in the sense of bringing honor to the warriors, as their capturing the commanders (*śarê*) of the army of Midian. The words of Gideon satisfied the men and their anger subsided. The account, however, plays a larger role in the development of the book. Ephraim's involvement moves from being the primary combatants for Ehud, to secondary troops for Gideon, to not being summoned by Jephthah (12:1-6). While Gideon was able to placate their wounded honor, Jephthah later would speak harshly to them and war would break out. In the end Ephraim would be humiliated in battle. This is another example in the book of the continuing spiral downward toward societal disintegration.

7:24—8:3

■ **4-9** Another side of Gideon's personality appears, one that was vengeful and violent. Gideon and his smaller band of three hundred having crossed the Jordan **were weary yet were pursuing** the remnant of the Midian army (v 4). For the last word in the verse the LXX has "hungry" (*peináō*), which makes a better reading (see v 15 where Gideon says to the elders of Succoth that they refused to give his men bread). Gideon asked for food from the men of Succoth (v 5), stating that he and his troops were in pursuit of the kings of Midian. Soggin notes that the names of the two kings are symbolic of their fate and parallel to the names of the commanders. Zebah means "sacrifice" and Zalmunna is a composite name meaning "protection withheld" or "shelter refused" (1981, 149). The leaders (*śāre*) of Succoth (v 6) taunted Gideon with a play on words, asking if he had their hands in his hands. Gideon responded angrily (v 7) with a threat, that when he had captured the kings he would return and thresh (*dûš*) their flesh with thorns and briers. He went next (v 8) to Penuel where Jacob struggled with a man one night (Gen 32:22-32). His request was met with a similar response as at Succoth. Gideon threatened them (Judg 8:9) that when he returned in peace he would tear down their tower, a well-fortified building. The leaders of both towns were skeptical of Gideon's ability to defeat the Midianites and chose to wait for the final outcome. If they helped Gideon and the Midianites defeated his force, the towns could have suffered retribution.

■ **10-12** Gideon located the remnant of the army, 15,000 survivors of a total force of 135,000 (v 10). Gideon's force (v 11) marched along a caravan route that passed through the territories of Gad and Manasseh. Nobah of the tribe of Manasseh took the city of Kenath and renamed it after himself (Num 32:42). Jogbehah was given by Moses to the Gadites who rebuilt and fortified it (Num 32:33-36). The Midianite force evidently felt secure, for the camp was trusting/unsuspecting (*beṭaḥ*), from the same word used to describe the peaceful town of Laish, which the Danites conquered (Judg 18:10, 27). The attack (v 12) threw the camp into panic and all fled, enabling Gideon to capture the kings.

■ **13-17** Having captured the kings, Gideon and his soldiers (v 13) returned by way of the Ascent of the Heres (location unknown) to Succoth. He captured a **servant** (*na'ar*) **of the men of Succoth** (v 14). Gideon's attendant Purah was also called a *na'ar* (7:11). Upon being interrogated he wrote down for Gideon the seventy-seven names of the leaders (*śāre*) and elders (*zĕqēnîm*) of Succoth. The servant knew the names and how to write, which indicate that he probably served in some official capacity to record the actions of the town leaders. Gideon returned to the city (v 15) and flung back upon the leaders of the city the taunt with which they had taunted him. Then he carried out his threat to beat the elders (*zĕqēnîm*) with thorns and briers. Verse 16 ends with an odd expression, **and he taught** (*yādaʿ*, to know) **the men of the city**. While Soggin finds the MT an acceptable reading, both he and Boling follow the LXX in reading *kataxaiō*, **threshed the men of the city** (see v 7) (Soggin 1981, 155; Boling 1975, 157). Next (v 17) Gideon not only pulled down the tower of Penuel but also executed the men of the city. Gideon was not directed by God to seek his revenge on these two cities. The only reference to God in the passage is Gideon's response in v 7 to the men of Succoth. We see not a timid, insecure Gideon, but a strong, self-centered leader who wreaked a terrible vengeance upon those who refused him help.

■ **18-21** The next section describes Gideon's execution of the kings of Midian. At some time in the past they had executed his brothers at Mount Tabor, which is located in the Jezreel valley. The kings described them as like Gideon himself, **each one like the image of a son of a king** (v 18). Was this a straightforward answer or were the kings mocking Gideon? They knew that they were going to be executed, so they might have been defiant, seeing that they had nothing to lose. Gideon described his brothers as **sons of my mother** (v 19), an odd expression in a patriarchal culture. Gideon is always designated as the son of Joash, his father. The culture also allowed men to take more than one wife. While the bond between those born of both the same father and mother could be especially close, a strong bond still existed between those of the same father but different mother. Gideon ordered his firstborn son, Jether, to kill them (v 20). Jether was a *naʿar*, not fully grown. By having his son slay Zebah and Zalmunna Gideon was responding to their mocking of him. They would have been shamed by being killed by a young person, not a great warrior. Yet Jether, like his father in his earlier days, was afraid and did not draw his sword. Gideon (v 21) had to kill them. Afterward he took as spoils of war the crescent-shaped ornaments off of their camels.

e. *Gideon and Israel's Idolatry (8:22-35)*

BEHIND THE TEXT

This section is composed of three parts: Gideon's refusal of kingship (vv 22-28), Gideon's death (vv 29-32), and the Israelites' return to sin (vv 33-35). The first mention of kingship in the book is made in v 22. This will become a continuing theme. As the tribal confederation continued to deteriorate, the need for a king became more obvious, thus laying the foundation for the rise of the monarchy in 1 Samuel. Not only did Gideon refuse the crown, but he is never designated as one "who judged" Israel. This may be due to the editor's negative reaction of Gideon making the ephod, which unfortunately became an object of worship.

IN THE TEXT

■ **22-28** After the battle, possibly at a convocation called to celebrate Yahweh's victory (v 22), the Israelites offered to let Gideon and his family rule over them because he had **delivered/saved** (*yāšaʿ*) them from Midian. The word for **rule** in the text is *māšal*, "to rule, have dominion, reign" (BDB, 605), not the normal word for "to become king," *mālak*. Gideon refused, stating that **Yahweh will rule over you** (v 23). Gideon then requested (v 24) that each man might give to him one golden earring that was taken as spoil from the slain Ishmaelites. Ishmael was the son of Abraham by Hagar (Gen 16:15) and Midian his son by Keturah (Gen 25:2). In the story of Joseph the two tribes are interchangeable (Gen 37:25, 28, 37). It is possible that Midian was a confederation of tribes including the Ishmaelites and the Kenites.

They agreed (Judg 8:25) and the weight of the gold (v 26) was about twenty kg (forty-three pounds) (Soggin 1981, 159). With it Gideon made an ephod (v 27), a type of garment worn by a priest (Exod 28:6-8) (Meyers 1997, ABD-CD). Like the bronze serpent that Moses made in the wilderness (Num 21:4-9; 2 Kgs 18:4), it became an object of worship. The language is graphic. **All Israel prostituted themselves after it,** and for Gideon's house, **it became a fowler's snare** (v 27). The section closes with the note (v 28) that Midian had become subdued before the Israelites and the land was quiet for forty years, or a generation. There is sadness in the note. What should have been a peaceful relationship between the Israelites and Midianites, based on the bond of family ties through Moses' marriage (Exod 2:15-22; Judg 4:11) had degenerated to one of power, leading to war and destruction.

■ **29-32** Jerubbaal/Gideon returned home. He had a large harem (v 30) and fathered seventy sons or descendants, a round number meaning "many." The number may include grandsons as well. One of his sons, Abimelech (v 31), is specifically identified as his story will continue in the next chapter. His mother was a concubine from Shechem and his name means **my father is king.** It is not clear if the term "father" referred to Yahweh, as is common in names, or Gideon. If the former, then it was consistent with Gideon's refusal to rule since he declared that Yahweh was Israel's ruler (v 23). If the latter, then by Gideon giving him this name, it showed that he actually coveted becoming king. The ambiguity of the name may be intentional, leading the reader to ask, whom did Israel really want as their king, Yahweh or someone else? The mention of Abimelech forms one of several transitions to the next chapter, which recounts his abortive attempt to become a king.

■ **33-35** The account of Gideon closes with the editorial note that after his death the people returned to worshipping idols (vv 33-34). As in v 27 their actions are characterized as prostituting themselves with the Baals, and in particular Baal-berith, or "Lord of the Covenant," whose temple was located at Shechem (9:4). Two indictments are made. First, they ***did not remember Yahweh*** (v 34), a phrase that means that they did not obey his covenant. Second (v 35), they did not show loyalty (*hesed*, see 1:24 for the only other occurrence of this word in Judges) to the house of Gideon. The mention of Baal-berith and the lack of loyalty to Gideon's house also provide transitions to the next chapter. It foreshadows how Abimelech in trying to establish himself as king at Shechem had to kill his brothers, the sons of Gideon.

FROM THE TEXT

Gideon began his judgeship by destroying a false idol but ended it by erecting another object of false worship. Our desire to worship that which we can see, touch, and control leads us away from the true God and into the slavery of idolatry. We do not control our gods, but that which we worship will control us and lead us down a slippery path toward spiritual and social destruction. Israel did not even remember to remain loyal to Gideon and his family. The God of Israel required loyalty to him and to one another. Unfaithfulness disrupted both spiritual and community life. Jesus also emphasized the need for faithfulness when he stated that the highest commandments were to love God and to love our neighbor (Matt 22:36-40). Gideon represents the ambiguity of the judges. Empowered by God to bring deliverance, in the end he brought spiritual slavery. Israel's downward spiral of spiritual and social decay had gained momentum.

2. Abimelech's Failed Monarchy (9:1-57)

BEHIND THE TEXT

The story of Abimelech's failed attempt to establish a monarchy is closely connected to the story of Gideon. He was introduced at the close of the last chapter along with Gideon's other descendants. He was the son of Gideon's concubine from Shechem. The social status of a concubine is not specifically described. She evidently had an acceptable legal and social standing but lesser than that of a wife. Jephthah's brothers would not allow him to inherit since his mother was a prostitute (11:2), but the sons of Jacob who were born to the maids (not necessarily concubines) of his wives did inherit. The reader also has been told (8:33) that the Israelites worshipped Baal-berith whose temple was located at Shechem, the hometown of Abimelech's mother. In addition, the reader knows that the Israelites did not remain loyal to Gideon and his family (8:35). How that disloyalty was manifested is described in this chapter. This information establishes the background for the next events in the story.

The city of Shechem played a significant role in the history of the Israelites. In the days of Jacob (Gen 34) the ruler of Shechem was Hamor. His son Shechem (same name as the city) violated Jacob's daughter Dinah, but afterward asked Jacob and his sons for permission to marry her. They agreed with the stipulation that the men of the city be circumcised. The men agreed. On the third day after being circumcised, when the men were weak with pain, Jacob's sons Simeon and Levi attacked the city and killed the men. At the end of the conquest, Joshua assembled the tribes at Shechem to renew their covenant vows (Josh 24:1-28). What is odd is that in the book of Joshua there is no account of the tribes conquering the city. After the death of Solomon, his son Rehoboam met at Shechem with the northern tribes to hear their grievances. Unfortunately he rejected their requests and they revolted. They made Jeroboam king and he made Shechem his first residence (1 Kgs 12:1-25).

IN THE TEXT

a. Abimelech as King (9:1-6)

■ **1-3** The opening verses of the chapter describe Abimelech's political maneuvers to gain a crown. The passage is silent about God. This was a human, self-seeking power grab. Abimelech first went (v 1) to the kinsmen of his mother. The Hebrew is **brothers** (*'ăḥê*) **of his mother,** but "brothers" should be understood as a broader term; not just his uncles, but all the powerful men of the larger family. This is clarified by the last phrase of v 1, **to the whole clan of the house of the father of his mother.** He evidently did not have sufficient social standing, possibly due to being the son of a concubine, to address the lords (*ba'ălê*) or leaders of Shechem (v 2), so he asked his kinsmen to speak for him. Even though Gideon refused to rule over Israel, evidently his descendants did exercise some type of rule. This was common in the ANE and even is seen today; a son taking the place of leadership of the father, whether or not he has the qualifications to do so. Abimelech contrasted the rule (*māšal*) of the seventy to the rule of one,

one who was kin to them; **Remember that I am of your bone and your flesh** (see Gen 2:23; 29:14). The speech was accepted, and the leaders of Shechem declared, **he is our brother** (Judg 9:3). The irony of the statement should be noted. Abimelech was about to slaughter his own brothers, and later he would kill these, his brothers, the leaders of Shechem (v 49).

■ **4-6** Money was taken from the temple of Baal-berith and given to Abimelech to hire **worthless and reckless men** (v 4) to carry out the slaughter of the descendants of Gideon. The term "baal" means "lord" and could refer to an owner of land or slaves, a city leader, or even a husband. It was often used to refer to a god, particularly Baal Hadad, the rain god. It could even refer to the God of Israel. Saul named his son Ishbaal, "a man of the Lord," meaning Yahweh (1 Chr 9:39). The name **Baal-berith** means "Lord of the Covenant." This temple at Shechem may have been the site where Joshua held the covenant renewal ceremony (Josh 24:1-28).

The descendants of Gideon were executed by Abimelech **on one stone** (Judg 9:5). The phrase may be pointing forward to the death of Abimelech himself who was killed when his skull was crushed by a stone (v 53). However, one of Gideon's sons, Jotham, his youngest, escaped. Abimelech was crowned (v 6) king by all the rulers of Shechem and all the (male?) residents of Beth-millo, possibly a well-fortified section of the city of Shechem where the leaders lived.

b. Jotham's Parable of the Trees (9:7-21)

■ **7-15** Verse 7 forms a prose introduction to the poetic parable of Jotham (vv 8-15). He stood on Mount Gerizim, which was the mountain of blessing as established by Moses. The mountain of cursing was Ebal (Deut 27:12-13). However, his purpose was to utter a curse. He dramatically portrayed that the actions of the leaders of Shechem had reversed the mountains. That which should have been a blessing would become a curse.

In the parable the trees offered kingship to the olive tree, the fig tree, and the grape vine. Each refused. Each had a noble purpose that was more significant than being king. Finally (Judg 9:14), the trees turned to the bramble; scientific name *Lycium europaeum* (KBL, 34). It is a bush that grows to a height of 1 to 3 meters (3 to 10 feet) and is found in the northern Negev (Geocities.com). The end of the parable (v 15) contains a curse. The bramble would accept kingship if the offer was made in truth or **in good faith** (*'emet*). If so, then the trees would take refuge in its shade. The requirement was obviously absurd. If they did not, then a fire would come forth out of the bramble and consume the cedars of Lebanon, trees noted for their long age, height, and usefulness in building.

■ **16-21** In v 16 Jotham began his application of the parable. His address to the leaders of Shechem began with a conditional clause drawn from the parable, *if in truth* (*'emet*) *and in integrity* (*tāmîm*) *you have acted* (v 16). Joshua required that the Israelites show these same qualities (*'emet* and *tāmîm*) in their worship of Yahweh (24:14). These qualities were obviously lacking when they anointed Abimelech king and gave him the money to hire thugs to kill Gideon's descendants. This point is made in 9:17-18. Jotham declared to the rulers of Shechem that Gideon risked his life to deliver them from Midian. In contrast they had murdered the seventy sons of Gideon and made Abimelech king. As an insult he referred to Abimelech as the son of a slave (*'āmâ*), not even having the social status of a concubine. In the ANE as today in the Middle East, it is a great insult to question the legitimacy of one's birth. Jotham again questioned whether or not they had acted *in truth* (*'emet*) *and in integrity* (*tāmîm*) (v 19) in regard to Jerubbaal/Gideon. In v 20 Jotham's curse is stated. Fire, a metaphor for destruction, would come forth from both Abimelech and the lords of Shechem and they would devour each other. After uttering his curse, Jotham fled (v 21).

c. Plots Against Abimelech (9:22-33)

■ **22-24** Abimelech's reign of only three years (v 22) was short in contrast to the length of a judge's term, which was generally forty years or a generation. The actions of Abimelech and the leaders of Shechem had not gone unnoticed by God. The divine name used in this chapter is Elohim, not the covenant name Yahweh. A turning point in the story is signaled in v 23 with the statement, **God sent an evil spirit.** The spirit as a member of the heavenly court was sent to sow discord between the parties of this alliance. He is referred to as **an evil spirit,** not because he was himself evil, but because his actions were intended for evil and not good. The spirit was sent (v 24) to bring judgment upon both Abimelech and the leaders of Shechem for the evil they did to the family of Gideon.

■ **25** The rulers of Shechem made the first move. One of the duties of a king was to ensure safe passage to travelers. When the leaders of Shechem sent men in ambush to rob travelers, they were challenging Abimelech's authority.

■ **26-33** Gaal, the son of Ebed, and his brothers or kinsmen came to Shechem, and the leaders trusted him (v 26). The name Gaal comes from the verb meaning "to loathe, abhor." "Ebed" means "servant or slave." Thus the name "Loathed son of a slave" is probably symbolic. The events are dated (v 27) to the time of the grape harvest, early fall. Holding a feast in the presence of one's god to celebrate the grape harvest, from which new wine was made, was part of the liturgical calendar for this agricultural society. Israel observed it as the feast of booths or Succoth (Deut 16:13-15). The text makes a distinction. The feast was held *in the house of their god* (Judg 9:27), not the God of Israel. The people of Shechem along with Gaal and his family may have been Canaanites who were living among the Israelites. Gaal used the occasion to ridicule Abimelech and to suggest that he should be the leader of Shechem. Gaal asked rhetorically, **Who is Abimelech, and who is Shechem that we should serve him** [Abimelech]? (v 28). Gaal was tracing the lineage of the people of Shechem back to the days of Jacob. Shechem the son of Hamor, the ruler of the city of Shechem, had raped Dinah the daughter of Jacob (Gen 34:1-31). The ancestors of Gaal and his kinsmen, along with the rulers of Shechem, were Canaanites, not Israelites (Boling 1975, 178). Gaal ended his speech (Judg 9:29) by expressing his desire to be the ruler of Shechem and then calling on Abimelech to come fight. The boasts angered Zebul (name means "honorable") who (v 30) was a principal official of the city (*śar*, see comments about Sisera at 4:2) evidently appointed by the king. He alerted Abimelech (9:31-33) to the situation and advised him to bring his troops by night and lay in ambush (*'ārab*), the strategy that the Israelites would later employ to defeat the Benjamites (20:29). He was to attack the city in the early morning. Abimelech dwelt at Arumah, which was located about 5 miles southeast of Shechem, an easy march for his forces (Thompson 1997, ABD-CD).

d. Abimelech's Battles (9:34-57)

Three battles of Abimelech are recounted in quick succession (vv 34-41, 42-45, 50-55). In the first two Abimelech was victorious and many of his former supporters were killed. Like his father, Gideon, he was capable of cruel repression of his opposition, wreaking total destruction on his enemies. Verses 46-49 appear to describe another battle. However, the account is a more detailed description of the taking of the stronghold of Shechem. Part of the art of the writer is to retell an event from a different perspective, often with more detail. The last two verses (vv 56-57) contain the narrator's summary comments. God repaid Abimelech and the people of Shechem for the evil they had committed.

■ **34-41** Abimelech in the first battle attacked Shechem and defeated Gaal. He divided his forces into four companies (v 34), moved in force to Shechem, and **laid in ambush** (*'ārab*) until dawn. When Gaal saw the advancing troops, Zebul suggested that he was seeing the advancing shadows as the sun rose (vv 35-36). This ruse delayed Gaal's response to the threat and allowed the troops to move closer to the city. Gaal named two landmarks in v 37, Tabbur-erez or Naval of the Earth, a small mound southeast of Shechem, and Elon-meonenim or Diviner's Oak, a sacred site in the area. When Gaal recognized the troops (v 38), Zebul mocked him with the words of his earlier boast and challenged him to go out and fight. Gaal led the leaders of Shechem into the battle (v 39) but then fled. The victory (vv 40-41) strengthened Zebul's authority, and he drove the kinsmen of Gaal out of the city. Although he defeated Gaal's forces, Abimelech evidently did not capture the city itself. Zebul's position was strengthened, but he was limited to how much he could assist Abimelech, who withdrew his forces and returned to Arumah.

■ **42-45** After the first battle, the people of the city evidently felt secure enough to return to working in the fields (v 42). Abimelech again attacked Shechem, this time with three companies who laid in ambush (*'ārab*, v 43). The company with Abimelech (v 44) dashed forward to seize the open gate while the other two companies slaughtered the undefended field workers. This time he took the city (v 45), slaughtered the inhabitants, pulled down buildings, and sowed the ground with salt to make it unproductive (v 45). This chapter makes several references to working in the fields. The people were engaged in either harvesting (v 27) or possibly preparing the fields for sowing the next crop. As an agricultural-based society the production of food was of primary importance. A poor harvest would mean starvation. Sowing the soil with salt would be an especially cruel action as it would deprive the survivors of future harvests, dooming them either to starve or relocate.

■ **46-49** The destruction of Shechem is recounted from a different perspective, the assault on the more heavily fortified area where the leaders of the city lived. When the lords (*baʿălê*) of the tower (see v 2) heard that Abimelech had entered the city (v 46), they took refuge in the temple. Sacred places were often strongly built so that they could become sanctuaries in time of war. This fortified tower was part of the temple complex of El-berith, God of the Covenant, an alternate name for Baal-berith, Lord of the Covenant (v 4). Abimelech's strategy (vv 47-48) for taking the stone-built tower was to gather a large amount of wood and set it afire. The fire would not destroy the tower itself, although it could weaken the limestone materials. The stones would conduct the intense heat into the interior where flammable materials would then ignite. This was not an unknown practice. Jericho had at one time been so destroyed, leaving a 3 foot layer of ash (private communication from H. Neil Richardson, one of the excavators). The end result (v 49) was that about a thousand men and women, probably with their children also, perished.

■ **50-55** Abimelech's last battle (v 50) was at Thebez, probably located at modern Tubas, 13 miles northeast of Shechem (Dyck 1997, ABD-CD). No reason is given for the attack. Like the previous battle, the city was taken but the leaders of the city took refuge (v 51) in a fortified tower. This time Abimelech led his troops to the entrance (v 52) in an attempt to burn the wooden door. One of the defenders (v 53), a woman, threw a millstone and it crushed his skull. Immediately (v 54) he ordered his armor bearer, a young man (*na'ar*), to kill him lest he die at the hands of a woman. It was shameful for a warrior to be killed by a woman, as Jael killed Sisera. Yet Abimelech's death was so remembered. The messenger who took word to David of Uriah's death was told to anticipate his response: **Why did you go close to the city to fight? Did you not know that they would shoot arrows from the wall? Who killed Abimelech the son of Jerubbaal? Did not a woman throw upon him an upper millstone from the wall and he died at Thebez?** (2 Sam 11:20-21). When the soldiers (v 55) saw that Abimelech was dead, there was no longer any reason to continue the attack, and so they left.

■ **56-57** A theological epilogue (vv 56-57) closes the story of Abimelech. The evil that he did in slaughtering his brothers, as well as the evil of the men of Shechem, God caused to come back upon them. Jotham's curse became their destiny.

In the narrative, the only action ascribed to God was his sending an evil spirit (v 23) to cause strife between the rulers of Shechem and Abimelech. Yet the results of the conflicts are attributed to God. This explanation is typical of ANE thinking. All events are caused by God (or the gods), yet humans are free to make choices and are responsible for them. The rulers of Shechem were free to appoint Abimelech their ruler and to pay for the slaughter of Gideon's sons. But the justice of God held them accountable and brought the curse of Jotham upon them. Western thinking wants to see a single cause, either God or humans. Either God is sovereign or humans are free. The Bible asserts both; God is sovereign and humans are also free. What we may see as a contradiction was seen in that ancient culture as just the way things happened. It was not an either/or, but a both/and. Failure to recognize this way of thinking has led to theological confusion, setting the sovereignty of God over against human freedom.

FROM THE TEXT

The text does not explain why the rulers of Shechem became hostile toward Abimelech. Only a theological explanation is given. God sent an evil spirit to stir up trouble between them. While humans have the freedom to act as they choose, God still sits in judgment on their actions. Abimelech and the rulers had committed murder in slaying the sons of Gideon. We would like a description of the political, economical, and personal issues that gave rise to the hostility; however, they are irrelevant to the story. God sat in judgment and in accordance with Jotham's parable decided to cause the evil that they had done to return back upon their heads. There is not a rigid rule of retribution that everyone receives in this life rewards for good and punishment for evil. Yet there is a general pattern of retribution that Paul refers to when he wrote, **God is not mocked; whatever a person sows, this he will also reap** (Gal 6:7). This is not a popular concept. We like to think that God is always kind, loving, and gentle. Yet in dispensing justice, he brings evil upon people. As Paul wrote, **The wrath of God is revealed from heaven upon all the godlessness and wickedness of humanity** (Rom 1:18). God is good; not demonic. He does not delight in evil. He extends mercy to the sinner, calling him or her to repent. However, he is just, he condemns the unrepentant. As Lord of the whole earth, he uses the violence of humans to do his will. The exilic prophet expressed this truth when he bluntly stated, **I am Yahweh and there is no other; forming light and creating darkness; making prosperity and creating evil. I am Yahweh who does all these things** (Isa 45:6c-7). Jesus taught us that whether in this world or in eternity, justice will be done and evil will be judged by a righteous God (Matt 25:31-46). In the narrative we are told that the spirit of God redirected the wickedness of Abimelech and the rulers against themselves as punishment for their own evil. While God's justice is informed by his love, his love is also informed by his justice.

3. Tola and Jair (10:1-5)

IN THE TEXT

The brief accounts of two minor judges forms a bridge to the story of Jephthah's judgeship. It also provides an interlude of peace between the accounts of Abimelech's kingship and Jephthah's judgeship. The violence of both stories is horrific. Abimelech slaughtered not only his brothers but also the inhabitants of Shechem. Jephthah delivered the Transjordan tribes from the oppression of the Ammonites, but then fought an intertribal war with Ephraim. The times of Tola and Jair were peaceful with neither invasions from external forces nor hostilities between tribes.

■ **1-2** The note about Tola is brief. He was (v 1) of the tribe of Issachar, from the city of Shamir, which was located in the hills of Ephraim. There is some suggestion that Shamir was an earlier name for Samaria, which later became the capital of Israel, but the suggestion is doubtful as Omri named it after the owner Shemer (1 Kgs 16:24). How Tola saved/delivered (*yāšaʿ*) Israel and from whom is not recorded. He judged Israel (Judg 10:2) for twenty-three years and was buried in his hometown of Shamir.

■ **3-5** Jair (v 3) was a descendant of Manasseh and a kinsman of Machir to whom Gilead was given (Num 32:39-41; Deut 3:13-15). Both Deut 3:13-14 and Josh 13:30 locate Jair's cities in Bashan, but 1 Kgs 4:13 place them in Gilead. The two areas were located next to each other and over time there may have been some shifting of boundaries. He judged Israel for twenty-two years, giving a combined total of forty-five years for the two. The total number of years for the six so-called minor judges is seventy, a round number that may indicate that the latest editors chose specific persons to include so that the numbers fit their chronology (see the discussion of chronology in the Introduction). Jair (Judg 10:4) established a ruling dynasty of thirty sons who rode on donkeys and ruled thirty cities. He was from Gilead in the Transjordan area. Kamon, where he was buried (v 5), must also be somewhere in Gilead. His identification as a Gileadite leads into the story of Jephthah, who was also a Gileadite.

4. God's Rejection of Israel's Cry (10:6-18)

IN THE TEXT

■ **6-9** The Jephthah cycle begins (v 6) with the standard formula that the Israelites did evil in the sight of Yahweh. Only on this occasion the sin is enlarged. They served the **Baalim and Ashtarot,** the plural forms for the various manifestations of the fertility deities Baal and Ashtart (see comments on 2:13), and in addition the gods of the various peoples of the land. In their pursuit of the other gods **they abandoned Yahweh and did not serve him** (v 6). Polytheism allows the worship of many gods, and Israel often worshipped other gods in addition to Yahweh. In this instance as they turned to other gods they forsook the worship of the God who had brought them from slavery and had given them the land. In response (10:7) Yahweh sold them back into slavery, this time at the hands of the Philistines and the Ammonites, literally **the sons of Ammon.** The Philistines were part of a people movement that began in the Aegean Sea area at the end of the thirteenth century and spread to the area of modern-day Turkey and the eastern coast of the Mediterranean. They were a continual problem for the Israelites until David conquered them (2 Sam 5:17-25). Verse 8 begins with a play on words (the sounds r and $ṣ$ are repeated) to indicate the harshness of Israel's oppression. ***They were shattered*** (*rāʿaṣ*). This word appears in the OT only here and Exod 15:6 (BDB, 950) where it states that Yahweh shattered the Egyptians. What God had done to the Egyptians, the Ammonites were doing to the Israelites. ***And were crushed*** (*rāṣaṣ*, see 9:53 where Abimelech's skull was crushed). The land of Ammon lay just east of Gilead. The Transjordan area felt their cruelty for eighteen years. Ammon also crossed the Jordan (v 9) and attacked Judah to the south, the central hill country of Benjamin, and Ephraim.

■ **10-14** The normal cycle continues (v 10) with the Israelites crying out (*zāʿaq*) to Yahweh. Only this time they included a confession of sin, acknowledging that they had abandoned him to serve other gods. Yahweh's response was cast in the form of a covenantal lawsuit. It begins with a recounting of his gracious deeds of deliverance. Beginning with the exodus from Egypt (v 11), the history lists the nations Israel faced during the conquest and during the days of the earlier judges. The last people named are the Maonites (v 12). A better reading following LXX is the Midianites, Gideon's enemy. Verse 13 contains both the indictment, they had broken the covenant by worshipping other gods; and the threat, ***Therefore, I will no longer save*** (*yāšaʿ*, see v 1) ***you!*** God told the Israelites to cry after the gods that they had chosen. Israel was Yahweh's because he had chosen them. Yet they had chosen other gods and thus abandoned him.

■ **15-16** Israel pled with God a second time, confessing their sin and abandoning their false gods as a sign of repentance. The end of v 16 is difficult. It can be translated, ***His soul was impatient over the trouble of Israel.*** Two opposite interpretations are possible. God was "worn out" or "discouraged" (*qāṣēr*) by the "trouble" or "mischief" (*ʿāmāl*) of Israel and determined to allow them to suffer the consequences of their sin. Or, the "trouble" (*ʿāmāl*) afflicted upon Israel was more than God could **bear** (*qāṣēr*), and he would help them. The text may be purposefully ambiguous. It points toward the mystery of the judgments of God where both justice and mercy are mingled in ways that defy human categories of classification. While God rejects the repentance of Israel, he is still moved by their suffering. Olson notes, "It is Israel's *suffering*, not Israel's deep repentance, that motivates any potential change in the Lord's plans" (1998, 852). The following events also give evidence that the options are not necessarily an either/or, but both/and. God did not raise up a deliverer for Israel. The leaders of Gilead made their own choice. Yet God gave Jephthah victory in battle. He would not come to their rescue in like manner as the past, yet he did not abandon them.

■ **17-18** The last two verses of the chapter describe how the Ammonites moved against Gilead and how the commanders (*śārê*) of the people of Gilead were confused as to who would lead them. They did not inquire of God but like Caleb (1:12) offered a prize to the one who could lead them to victory. In this case it was not a daughter who was offered in marriage, but the right to rule over, **to be head over** (v 18) the Gileadites.

FROM THE TEXT

1. The popular belief that God will forgive because that is his business is difficult to reconcile with this passage. Israel repented, yet God would not forgive. The shallowness of Israel's repentance has been demonstrated a number of times in the book. When they were oppressed, Israel turned to Yahweh, their God of deliverance. When, however, the threat passed, they returned to the worship of the fertility gods. This shallowness of repentance was a continuing pattern in Israel's history. Olson notes that "God seems genuinely at a loss on how to turn Israel around" (1998, 826). Hosea knew that Israel's liturgy of repentance recorded in 6:1-3 was empty of meaning. Saying the right words and following the required liturgy was not enough.

> *What shall I do with you, Ephraim?*
> *What shall I do with you, Judah?*
> *Your steadfast love is like a morning cloud;*
> *even like the dew that goes away early.* (Hos 6:4)

Jeremiah similarly condemned the deceptive treatment of slaves when Babylon was besieging Jerusalem. In order to gain God's favor, the king and the people made a covenant to free their slaves. When, however, the Babylonians lifted the siege to meet the threat of the Egyptians, the people then reclaimed them (Jer 34:8-22).

The problem of insincere repentance is not limited to ancient times. In the movie *Gone with the Wind* Scarlet was distraught that God was going to send her to hell. Rhett taunted her, for he knew that she was not sorry for what she had done but afraid that she would be punished. It is common for those who abuse their spouses or children later to feel regret. They will plead with great emotion and tears for forgiveness, promising never again to commit such acts. Yet when they become angry, they again commit brutal acts against their families. Others are given to habitually lying, stealing, or cheating. Addiction to pornography is a growing concern. True repentance must be coupled with determination to reform, even if that means public confession and seeking the help of counselors to change habit patterns. The truth of one's behavior must be faced and acknowledged to God, oneself, and those who have been hurt. Repentance is an essential requirement for forgiveness and reconciliation. Clendenen and Martin state that, "The New Testament insists that genuine repentance is a necessary prerequisite for forgiveness. Jesus prescribes forgiveness for a repentant sinner (Matt. 18:15c), but expulsion and not forgiveness for a recalcitrant transgressor (Matt. 18:16-17)" (2002, 66).

2. There is an ambiguity in the judgment of God. Both justice and mercy must be done. These are not competing qualities, but complementary. Justice without mercy becomes legalism. Mercy without justice becomes sentimentalism. God proclaimed to Moses on Mount Sinai that he was merciful and gracious, one who kept covenant loyalty to the thousandth generation and who forgave sin. Yet he was also one who would not forgive the guilty; punishment would be visited on the whole family (Exod 34:6-7). For all the sins that Israel had committed Hosea announced that God had determined to send them into exile (11:5-7). This meant that the cities would be captured. Many would be slaughtered. The survivors would be horribly treated and then resettled in a foreign land. Yet in the midst of this proclamation God recoils at the horror. His compassion made room for mercy. This would not be the end of Israel. Why? *For I am God and not human, the Holy One in your midst* (Hos 11:9b). God does not stand off from his people, unmoved by their suffering, even if it is justified due to their sin. He suffers with them. This suffering is seen most clearly in the cross of Jesus. He did not desire death, yet it meant redemption and life for others. The scandal of the cross is that God in Jesus experienced suffering that he might thereby bring redemption to those who truly repent.

D. Jephthah, Ibzan, Elon, and Abdon (11:1—12:15)

OVERVIEW

The account of Israel's spiritual and social decline continues with hastening steps with the story of Jephthah. The standard opening describes the sin of Israel and their subsequent oppression. What is surprising is that their cry to God for deliverance was rejected. God's patience had run out. Having been rebuffed by God, the commanders acted on their own when they offered leadership to Jephthah. However, God did not annul the covenant. He enabled Jephthah to defeat the Ammonites, the description of the battle being told in one verse (11:33). More important to the story is Jephthah's foolish vow, which he kept by sacrificing his daughter. Jephthah had tried diplomatically to avoid the war with the Ammonites when he recounted the history of the two peoples (11:12-28). When the angry Ephraimites confronted him, he was not so diplomatic, but more confrontational. The end result was an intertribal war that left the tribe of Ephraim decimated. The bonds that held the tribes together were strained to the breaking point. Later they would almost disintegrate as Benjamin would be nearly annihilated (chs 20—21).

I. Jephthah and the Ammonites (11:1-40)

OVERVIEW

The crises facing Israel has already been identified as an impending invasion of the Ammonites. The commanders were at a loss as to who would lead them into battle. The present section introduces the next judge, Jephthah. The elders of Gilead offered him the leadership if he would defeat the Ammonites. There is no indication that they asked God to choose a leader. The actual battle is described in one verse. The story revolves around Jephthah's negotiations with the elders, the king of the Ammonites, and God. His foolish vow will become his undoing (vv 34-40), and his negotiating skills will fail him and lead to intertribal warfare (12:1-7).

BEHIND THE TEXT

Ammon was preparing to invade the area given to the tribes of Reuben and Gad by Moses (Num 32:33-42). The area in dispute stretched from the wadi Arnon, which flowed into the Dead Sea halfway up its east coast, to the wadi Jabbok, which flowed into the Jordan River about 25 miles north of the Dead Sea.

Jephthah's recounting of Israel's conquest of the Transjordan area agrees generally with Num 21:10-35. The mention of Moab (vv 17-18) rather than Ammon, Israel's immediate threat, and reference to Chemosh, the god of the Moabites, as the god of Ammon raise questions about the historical setting. The tribes of Ammon and Moab were closely associated, as they traced their ancestry back to Lot (Gen 19:30-38). Also, the claim that Israel had occupied the territory for three hundred years indicates that the passage is probably a late construction by the Deuteronomic editor (see discussion of the chronology of Judges in the Introduction). Ammon was flourishing about the time of the reign of Josiah (Dearman 2006, 130-33). It is possible that Ammon had claimed sovereignty over Moab and was taking the lead in asserting Moab's claims to the territory. The Moabite king Mesha had claimed the area in the ninth century (Boling 1975, 202). Jephthah's speech forms a theological and historical basis, not only for his defense of the territory but also for Josiah who later used military force to incorporate the Transjordan area back into "a greater Israelite" kingdom, as he did when he invaded the territory of the old kingdom of Israel (2 Kgs 23:15-20). There is no indication in the account of 2 Kings that Josiah campaigned in the Transjordan area, but it would not be unusual for the writer to omit material irrelevant to his purpose. However, Zephaniah who prophesied early in Josiah's reign condemned both Moab and Ammon (2:8-10). Thus while the story recounts how Jephthah's messages were sent to the king of Ammon, the initial readers of the book were probably the educated elite of the Josianic court. This transposes the account from a defense of Israel's occupation to a political claim for Josiah to reassert Israelite/Judean control of the Transjordan area.

IN THE TEXT

■ **1-3** The story jumps back in time to introduce Jephthah who is identified as ***a Gileadite, a powerful warrior*** (v 1). His qualities as a soldier are emphasized, as they will be the basis for his rise to power. The area of Gilead extended north from the Arnon to the Jabbok, and from the Jordan River valley in the west to the desert in the east. It took its name from Gilead, the son of Machir and grandson of Manasseh (Num 26:29). The father of Jephthah was also named Gilead (Klouda 2007, 2:572). His mother was not the wife of Gilead. She is described as a woman of $zôn\hat{a}$, often translated "prostitute," but it can also mean a woman involved in a sexual affair, but not necessarily for money. She is also described as ***another woman*** (Judg 11:2). She may have been what we would call a mistress, which gave her less social status than that of a concubine, but whose children the father would have accepted as his own. At the time of distributing the inheritance, however, Gilead's sons by his wife refused Jephthah a share. That he had to flee ($bārah$) indicates that he was in some danger (v 3). Tob, meaning "good," was a town northeast in Syria. Like Abimelech (9:4) he gathered men described as $rêq$, "empty, idle, or worthless men" (BDB, 938). In essence Jephthah became a warlord, surviving by raiding others.

■ **4-11** The story moves back again to the time of the Ammonite threat. The commanders ($śārê$, the plural of the same term used for Sisera, 4:7) of Gilead were unable to choose a leader (10:18), so the elders ($ziqnê$) of Gilead decided to offer to Jephthah command of the forces. His rank was to be that of a military leader, a $qāṣîn$ (Josh 10:24). Jephthah responded bluntly (Judg 11:7). He accused the elders of hating him and driving ($gāraš$) him out of his father's house. The word "hate" ($śānē^{\circ}$) is a covenant term meaning to act in such a way as to violate a relationship (Exod 20:5).

By disinheriting Jephthah and driving him away, the elders had expelled him from the tribe. As a result he had no obligation to assist them in their time of trouble. The elders countered that if he returned with them and fought the Ammonites, he would be the head (*rōʾš*) or ruler over those who lived in Gilead. His rise to power was based on the condition that he would be successful in battle (Judg 11:9). The elders invoked Yahweh as a witness to their words. Jephthah returned with them as both the commander and head, but before going to war he went to the sacred shrine at Mizpah to repeat the words in the presence of Yahweh. The words of the elders and the action of Jephthah going to the shrine of Mizpah formalized their relationship by entering again into a covenant. Several cities were named Mizpah, but this one was probably the sacred city located in the territory of the tribe of Benjamin. It will later play a prominent part in the war between the tribes of Israel and Benjamin (20:1; 21:1). The breach of the family relationship demanded that a formal covenant had to be established by calling on Yahweh as its guardian in order for both parties to be able to trust each other again.

■ **12-28** Jephthah attempted to negotiate with the king of Ammon (never named specifically) to avoid a war. Messengers were sent to the king asking why he wanted to go to war, ***in my land*** (v 12). Note the use of the first person pronoun. The king accused the Israelites after coming out of Egypt of ***taking my land*** (v 13). The second group of messengers began by denying that Israel took any of the land of Moab or Ammon (v 15). What follows is an abbreviated account of Israel's escape from Egypt, its journey around both Edom and Moab, as both had refused Israel passage through their lands, and the war with the Amorites who inhabited the land at that time (vv 16-22; see Num 20:14-21; 21:10-35). Three times Jephthah repeated that Israel took the land of the Amorites (vv 21, 22, 23). He then asked, **Since Yahweh, the God of Israel disposed the Amorites from before his people Israel, are you now to possess [it]?** (v 23). The implication of the statement was that since Yahweh had given the land to Israel, the king would be fighting not only Israel but also Yahweh.

The few references to God in the account are significant. The victory over the Amorites is attributed to **Yahweh, the God of Israel** (v 21). In vv 23 and 24 Jephthah asked a series of rhetorical questions. The point of them was that Yahweh, the God of Israel, helped the Israelites take the land by defeating the Amorites, not the Ammonites. The conclusion that Jephthah drew was that the Ammonites should stay in the land that Chemosh their god gave them and not try to take the land that Yahweh had given Israel. Little is known about the god Chemosh other than he was the national god of Moab, not of Ammon. Perhaps Ammon had usurped control over Moab and was pressing a claim to the land for Moab. In the ninth century the Moabite king Mesha had laid claim to the area and took several Israelite towns.

The argument shifts in vv 25 and 26 to a historical defense. King Balak of Moab did not try to fight Israel, nor did any of the Ammonites for over three hundred years. Jephthah denied (v 27) that he had sinned; that is, had done any wrong against the king, but that his going to war with Jephthah would be evil. The final request to avoid war was to submit the case before Yahweh the Judge who would judge between them. The proposal would be to go through a ritual to let God determine whose position was right. In the ANE such rituals were held to judge difficult cases involving individuals. A number of psalms also refer to such ritual trials (see Pss 7; 26; 43). The king rejected Jephthah's appeals. Matthews suggests that Jephthah's speech laid a basis for a "just war" with Yahweh deciding by battle who owned the land (2004, 122). This is contrary to the purpose of the negotiations, to avoid war if possible.

■ **29-33** With no other alternative left, Jephthah prepared for war. The text states that **the spirit of Yahweh was upon Jephthah** (v 29) (see comment on 3:10, p. 66, for "spirit" as the power of Yahweh). Yahweh did not abandon his people. Even though God had not chosen Jephthah, God empowered him with the gift of his spirit. He journeyed through Gilead and Manasseh collecting an army. Did Jephthah realize that God had given him the spirit? It is possible that he did not, for on the way to the battle (vv 30-31) he made a vow to God to assure victory. This was a common practice and took the form of, "if you do something for me, I will do something for you." In this case Jephthah pledged that if God gave him victory against Ammon, whatever came out of his house upon his return he would offer to Yahweh as a burnt offering. It is not at all clear that Jephthah meant that he would sacrifice a person. The typical Israelite house had two stories, and animals were given shelter at night in a section of the first floor area. What might come out of the house would include such animals as sheep, goats, donkeys, or oxen. Olson maintains that the vow is intentionally left ambivalent so that the reader is drawn into the story to wonder what will come out of the house (1998, 832). Yahweh did give the Ammonites into his hand and a great victory was gained (vv 32-33). Aroer was located on the wadi Arnon, the northern boundary of Moab (Hawk 2006, 273). Abel-keramim was possibly located just southeast of Ammon (Knauf 2006, 7). Jephthah's victory drove the Ammonites out of the southern part of Gilead and back to their own territory in the east. The section ends with the notice that **the Ammonites were**

subdued before the Israelites (v 33). Normally after such a statement a period of quiet or continued victory is described (3:30; 4:23; 8:28). This time the story continues to include two disturbing events.

■ **34-40** Jephthah's vow had horrific consequences. When he returned to his home in Mizpah of Gilead (Gen 31:43-55), first out of the door was his daughter, his only child. This was a tremendous shock to him. His first response (Judg 11:35) was an act of mourning, tearing his clothes (2 Kgs 22:11). Second, he blamed her for humbling (humiliating?) him. While he evidently believed that once the vow was given to Yahweh he could not take it back, he did not take the blame himself for making such a foolish vow. His daughter (Judg 11:36), who is never named, also believed that because God had given him victory over the Ammonites, he could not take back the vow. Their attitude reflected a belief that once a vow was spoken, if a god accepted it, it must be kept. Otherwise the deity would become angry and punish the vow-breaker. The function of this narrative is to describe the continuing spiritual disintegration of Israel. The characters thought that Yahweh was like the Canaanite gods and would require the fulfillment of the vow, even if it involved human sacrifice.

Jephthah's rash vow is similar to the foolish or rash (reading *yāʾal*, "to be foolish," BDB, 383) oath that Saul laid upon his troops (1 Sam 14:24). When it was discovered that Jonathan had transgressed the oath, Saul intended to carry out the oath and execute him. The troops objected and forced Saul to let him live (14:43-45). In both incidents the child of the father was at risk. While the daughter of Jephthah had no one to intercede for her, Jephthah should have known that the God of Israel was not like the Canaanite gods and would not have been pleased with her death.

The story is set at the time of the Judges, yet it was written for an audience in the seventh century when Manasseh burned his son as a sacrifice (2 Kgs 21:6) and when, at Topheth in the Valley of Ben-hinnom, the residents of Jerusalem were offering their children as burnt offerings to Molech, the god of the Ammonites (2 Kgs 23:10; Jer 7:31). Heard in that context, the story linked the action of Jephthah with the later practices of Judah. It thus became a story of shame that a deliverer of Israel who was given the spirit would keep a vow and offer an offering that Yahweh condemned.

The daughter requested (Judg 11:37-38) and Jephthah agreed that she might have a two-month reprieve when she and her friends might go to the hills and mourn her virginity; that is, that she would never fulfill her role as a wife and mother. At the end of the two months (v 39) she returned and Jephthah kept his vow. The story ends (v 40) with a liturgical note that for four days each year the women would lament the fate of Jephthah's daughter. This is the only place that the practice is mentioned.

What Happened to Jephthah's Daughter?

Early Jewish discussions of Jephthah condemned the vow as rash and the sacrifice as contrary to Torah. In the twelfth century the Jewish scholar Ibn Ezra suggested that the end of v 31 should read: ***it shall be (a gift) for Yahweh or I will sacrifice it as a burnt offering.*** Since sacrificing his daughter would be unacceptable, Ibn Ezra proposed that Jephthah then built a house where she resided as a perpetual virgin. The "survival" of the daughter came into Christian interpretation when it was adopted by Nicholas de Lyra (ca. 1270-1349). Since Jephthah is listed as one of the heroes of faith (Heb 11:32), it was thought inappropriate that he would actually commit human sacrifice. The survival interpretation eased the tension. For the next several centuries scholars debated the two interpretations. In the eighteenth and nineteenth centuries many commentators and preachers such as John Wesley, Jonathon Edwards, Adam Clarke, and Richard Watson accepted that the daughter was not killed but remained a virgin. In the twentieth century with the rise of historical criticism and an understanding of "progressive revelation," that God revealed his will over a period of time climaxing with the Incarnation; the human sacrifice interpretation again dominated scholarly opinions. (For a full discussion of the history of interpretation of the vow and sacrifice, see Gunn 2005, 133-69.)

2. The War with Ephraim (12:1-7)

BEHIND THE TEXT

This is the third account of Ephraim being called to war. It was an important tribe located in the hill country on the west side of the Jordan River. In Judges Ephraim also serves as a barometer of the social decline and disintegration of Israel. During the time of the earliest and most successful judges, it had responded to the call of Ehud and had won a great victory over the Moabites by seizing the fords of the Jordan River and blocking their escape (3:27-29). During the transitional phase of Gideon they were called to seize fords when the Midianites were attempting to escape after his initial victory (7:24-25). Although they were successful in capturing even the captains of the army, the Ephraimites were angry that Gideon had not called on them earlier. Gideon was able to diplomatically placate them and violence was avoided (8:1-3). In the third and most disastrous phase of the judges, beginning with Jephthah, the Ephraimites were angry with Jephthah because he had not called on them to fight. Jephthah was not able to placate them, and an intertribal war broke out. The Gileadites this time seized the fords and blocked the Ephraimites' escape. The result was that Ephraim suffered a humiliating defeat and the loss of 42,000 men. The enormity of the loss can be recognized when compared with the census figures given in Num 1:33 of 40,500 and 26:37 of 32,500. The social chaos represented by this intertribal war would continue to worsen until at the end of the book the tribe of Benjamin was almost wiped out (Olson 1998, 837).

IN THE TEXT

■ **1** Verse 1 begins with the blunt statement *the men of Ephraim were called out.* Who called them out is not given. Having crossed over the Jordan they went to Zaphon, located near Succoth and originally given to the tribe of Gad (Josh 13:27). However, Mahanaim was the southern border of the half of the tribe of Manasseh that settled east of the Jordan (Josh 13:30), and Zaphon is located north of it. It is likely that the tribal borders shifted at various times. Because Jephthah had not called them to war, and thus insulted their honor, they planned to punish him by burning down his house. His "house" had already been destroyed in that his only child had been sacrificed and he could not establish a house or dynasty. This will be in contrast to the prolific houses of the minor judges Ibzan and Abdon (vv 9, 14).

■ **2-3** Jephthah's response emphasized the danger he and his people were in. He stated that he had called to Ephraim but that *they did not save him* (from root *yāša'*, "to deliver, save") *from their (the Ammonites') hand* (v 2). When he saw (v 3) that they would not deliver/save (*yāša'*) him, he took his life in his own hands and fought the Ammonites. It was Yahweh who gave them into his hands. From a man who had tried diplomacy to avoid a war, this was not a diplomatic answer. First, he accused Ephraim of refusing to fight, and second, he claimed that the victory was from Yahweh. To fight against him would be to fight against Yahweh.

■ **4-6** Ephraim responded by insulting the Gileadites, accusing them of being *refugees* (*pĕlîṭê*) *from Ephraim and Manasseh* (v 4). The statement questioned the parental legitimacy of the Gileadites and reflected on Jephthah's own legitimacy (11:1). In the battle the tables were turned on the Ephraimites. The Gileadites seized the fords and the refugee (*pĕlîṭê*) Ephraimites were trapped. To identify the fleeing Ephraimites the Gileadites required them to pronounce the word "shibboleth," meaning an "ear of grain" or "stream." This would delight an audience, poking fun at the Ephraimites who were so inept that they could not reproduce the sound that they had just heard. The horrific loss of life was, however, tragic.

■ **7** Jephthah judged for only six brief years. There is no note that Israel enjoyed a period of rest or peace after his death. He was buried in one of the cities in Gilead, but we are not told which one.

3. Ibzan, Elon, and Abdon (12:8-15)

BEHIND THE TEXT

The violent story of Jephthah is bracketed by two sets of "minor" judges. The times of Tola and Jair provide an interlude of peace after the violent rule of Abimelech and before the battles of Jephthah. Similarly the peaceful times of Ibzan, Elon, and Abdon contrast with the violence of Jephthah and of the following story of Samson. No enemy had to be repelled. No battles were fought. Each judge is introduced with the set phrase, **after him.** The length of the three judges is less than half that of Tola and Jair, in keeping with the theme of a continual decline in the effectiveness of the judges. The five judges ruled for a total of seventy years, a round number meaning completion. The length of Shamgar's judgeship, the first of the minor judges, is not given (3:31).

IN THE TEXT

■ **8-10** Ibzan was from Bethlehem. There was a Bethlehem located in the tribe of Zebulun (Josh 19:15), but since the tribe is not mentioned and because Bethlehem of Judah is important in a following story (chs 19—21), the Judean one is probably intended. In contrast to Jephthah's lack of children, Ibzan had thirty sons and thirty daughters. He married his daughters to sons **outside** and took daughters from the **outside** for wives for his sons. The text does not state whether the outsiders were those from other Israelite clans or tribes, or from outside Israel. The reader is left to reflect on the spiritual and social decay that was taking place in Israel, and to wonder if Ibzan was contributing to that decay.

■ **11-12** Of Elon, whose name means "oak," we are only told that he was from Zebulun, that he judged Israel ten years, and that he was buried at Aijalon in Zebulun.

■ **13-15** Abdon was from Pirathon, a town in the hills of Ephraim that had formerly been held by the Amalekites. His wealth was evident in that he could provide his forty sons and thirty grandsons, again a total of seventy, with donkeys to ride upon.

FROM THE TEXT

1. Jephthah did not receive a commission from God to deliver the Gileadites, but from the elders of the tribe. Othniel and Ehud were both "raised up" by God (3:9, 15), but we are not told how they received their commissions. Did they chafe under the oppression and seize an opportuni-

ty to fight? Did God speak directly to them? Deborah as a prophet issued the commands of God to Barak (4:6). Only in the story of Gideon is a direct commission recorded (6:14). God worked in various ways to select deliverers. While God refused to raise up a deliverer (10:14) to face the Ammonites, that does not mean that the selection of Jephthah was illegitimate. Rather he chose to empower the leader the people selected by giving to him the spirit (11:29). God through his prevenient grace works through humans to accomplish his will. Caiaphas prophesied of Jesus' death even though he opposed Jesus' ministry (John 11:49-52). Some have natural ability, training, or position that God uses. Others appear to lack any qualifications for leadership. God is committed to work with both the abilities of humans and their decisions. However, while the Spirit empowers persons for the work of God, he does not restrain their decisions when in anger, hatred, or foolishness they use their positions and power to do evil.

2. Vows made to God should be taken seriously. The Teacher in Ecclesiastes warns against delaying to pay a vow. Better not to make a vow than not to fulfill it (Eccl 5:4-6). However, what if one, like Jephthah, makes a foolish vow? To raise such a question is to inquire of the nature of God himself. The God of Israel was not like the Canaanite gods. He did not accept a human sacrifice. Jephthah and his daughter both viewed Yahweh as similar in nature as a Canaanite god and thought that the vow had to be fulfilled. They were changing the Israelite religion into a Canaanite one, adding religious elements from that culture that were incompatible with the character of the God of Israel. In order for the message of the gospel to speak to the culture of the people, worship practices and methods of communication have to be adapted to reach the target audience. However, care has to be exercised in selecting which elements of the culture should be incorporated. Those that are incompatible with the message have to be rejected. The gospel is often in conflict with the values and religious practices of a culture. The disciples of Jesus often found themselves in trouble with the religious and civil authorities because their preaching conflicted with the religious ideas and practices commonly accepted. The task before the church is to communicate the gospel in a manner that belief and faithful obedience becomes a possibility, but also to maintain its distinctiveness so as to provide a message of liberation from the forces that have bound the people in sin.

3. The Spirit of God enabled Jephthah to gain a great victory over the Ammonites. Yet the writer indicates that the office of the judge was continuing its slide into disaster. While Jephthah was successful in deliver-

ing Israel from an oppression that lasted eighteen years, in contrast he judged Israel only six years. No note indicating that Israel enjoyed a period of peace is appended. His final military action ended with the slaughter of the Ephraimites. This charismatic warrior became a destructive force in Israel. Stone accurately notes, "Power alone, even God's power, without the accompanying grace of character, destroys" (1992, 341). God may appoint a leader, but that does not mean that God initiates or even condones all the actions of a leader. A leader of a church today has to be sensitive to the leadership of the Spirit. That guidance does not often come as a direct revelation. God uses various voices. Some of those voices include the needs of the larger community, such as when a natural disaster strikes, or it is mired in poverty, violence, or corruption; counsel from the congregation as a whole and its leaders specifically; and the wisdom of outside consultants. Mixed in with careful listening, the pastor must use his or her own wisdom and common sense. Self-centered leadership pushes its own agenda regardless of the harm it does to others. Good leaders listen carefully to hear the guidance of the Spirit. Searching out which voice the Spirit uses to communicate his will is difficult, but it will always be in accord with the proclamation of the Gospel and for the improving of the spiritual health of the congregation.

E. Samson (13:1—16:31)

OVERVIEW

Israel's last judge was Samson, and with his story the failure of leadership during this time period comes to a conclusion. Although Samson had tremendous strength and could accomplish superhuman exploits, his spiritual and political life were sorrowfully inadequate. He broke every vow to which he was committed. Not content to marry an Israelite woman, he continually sought alliances with the women of the uncircumcised Philistines. He never led a military campaign to liberate the tribes. He was ultimately ineffective in removing the Philistine yoke of oppression from Israel. As a result, his own tribe of Dan was forced to relocate due to the Philistine pressure (Judg 17—18).

Samson, the last judge, stands in contrast to Othniel (1:12-13; 3:7-11), Israel's first judge. Both were moved by the spirit, but Othniel was equipped to lead in battle and deliver Israel. Samson performed personal exploits, but only began to deliver Israel (13:5). Othniel had a proper Israelite marriage, to Achsah, the daughter of Caleb, but Samson refused to marry an Israelite and pursued Philistine women. Othniel judged Israel for forty peaceful years. Samson judged Israel half that long and never brought to the tribes a period of peace. Othniel represents the ideal of what a judge should be and do; Samson falls far short. As we work through the account of Samson's life, parallels with other judges as well as other biblical persons will be noted.

The concepts of knowing/not knowing and trickery help bind together the disparate stories about Samson. In ch 13 the angel/messenger of Yahweh revealed to the wife of Manoah that she would bear a son, but neither she nor her husband recognized who the messenger was until the end of the story. When Manoah asked him his name, the messenger refused to tell him. In ch 14 the word *nāgad*, "to reveal, make known" (BDB, 616-17), occurs twelve times. Samson made known to his parents that he wanted the woman of Timnah for his wife, but he did not tell them about the lion or the honey. In the story of the riddle (vv 12-19), *nāgad* appears nine times. In ch 15 the Philistines wanted to know who had burned their fields and in ch 16 Delilah pestered Samson to find out the secret of his strength. Knowing or not knowing is one of the themes that bind the stories together.

Samson is also portrayed as a trickster who tricked others and who was tricked. He tricked the companions at the feast with his riddle, but they tricked him by pressuring his wife to find the answer. When his wife was given to another, he then "tricked" the Philistines when he burned their fields. He surrendered peacefully to his kinsmen and then slaughtered the Philistines. Delilah tricked him into revealing the secret of his strength, and finally Samson tricked the Philistines by pulling down the pillars that supported the temple and killing many. As the stories were told in ancient Israel, they would have been highly entertaining. The hero of Israel always got the best of his Philistine enemies, even in his death. As the stories function in the larger context of the book, Samson becomes an antihero who breaks his vows to God, fails to deliver Israel, and dies in a desperate act of revenge for the loss of his sight (16:28). Yet the writer of Hebrews still listed Samson as one of the heroes of faith (Heb 11:32). He was used of God to begin the deliverance of Israel from the oppression of the Philistines. He was empowered by the spirit to defeat his enemies. God did hear his prayers for help in times of desperate need. The hero of the story thus becomes a gracious God who enabled an imperfect person to accomplish his will.

1. The Birth of Samson (13:1-25)

BEHIND THE TEXT

The story of Samson is bracketed with several editorial notes. The first in 13:1 identifies the nature of Israel's sin and their oppression. The normal cycle of sin, oppression, crying out to God, and deliverance is broken. Israel does not cry out to God and people are not delivered. Two closing notes appear, one at 15:20 and the other at 16:31. Chapter 15 ends positively. Samson had won a great victory over the Philistines, and God had answered his prayer to satisfy his thirst. The editorial note concludes the account by stating that Samson judged Israel for twenty years, but it lacks a description of a period of rest. The first Deuteronomic edition probably ended with this verse. Chapter 16, which also ends with a notice that Samson judged for twenty years, was added as part of the last editorial addition. The addition changes the image of Samson from a local hero to that of a tragic figure who was betrayed into the hands of his enemies. This image is in keeping with the overarching theme of the book, which describes the descent of Israel into social and moral anarchy because of their failure to be obedient to the commands of God.

The life of Samson in microcosm reflects the disintegration of the nation itself. Chapter 14 describes how Samson broke the Nazirite vow concerning not touching a dead carcass (Num 6:1-8). During the wedding feast he drank wine (Judg 14:10). The Hebrew word for "feast" is often associated with drunkenness. In ch 16 the vow concerning the cutting of his hair was violated when Delilah had his locks shorn. The narrator's note tells the reader that when Samson awoke he was unaware that God had departed from him. Yet God heard his final prayer and the last judge was permitted to die a heroic but tragic death. The story leads the reader to conclude that the charismatic leadership of the judges ended in failure and that another type of leadership would be necessary if Israel was to survive (Stone 1987, 369-72).

IN THE TEXT

■ 1 The chapter opens with the standard notice that *the Israelites again did the evil in the eyes of Yahweh* (v 1) and that he gave them into the hands of their enemies, in this instance the Philistines.

Who Were the Philistines?

The Philistines were part of a larger people movement that came out of the Aegean area during the late thirteenth century. The movement was composed of a number of different tribes or groups that invaded different parts of the eastern Aegean and Mediterranean. Some attacked the area now known as western and central Turkey, destroying not only the city of Troy but also Hattusha, the capital of the Hittites, effectively bringing that empire to an end. Others attacked along the coastline of the eastern Mediterranean, and several groups combined forces to attempt an unsuccessful invasion of Egypt (ca. 1175 B.C.). One of the latter groups, the Philistines, then conquered and occupied the cities of Gaza, Ashkelon, Ashdod, Ekron, and Gath. The Philistines soon adopted much of the Canaanite culture, worshipping gods such as Dagon, the god of grain, and Baal, the storm god. However, they maintained some of their older cultural forms, particularly leaving their males uncircumcised. In Judges and Samuel they are referred to derisively as the uncircumcised Philistines. They had a technological advantage over the Israelites in that they maintained a monopoly for working with iron (1 Sam 13:19-21) and they used chariots in battle. Although each of the cities was ruled independently, the Philistines were able to cooperate in battle. These advantages made them a formidable foe against the Israelites.

Shamgar had earlier fought the Philistines (3:30). They were also mentioned along with the Ammonites as oppressing Israel during the time of Jephthah (10:7). What is missing in the note is the cry of Israel to God.

■ **2-14** Manoah's wife was barren, like Sarah (Gen 11:30), Rebekah (Gen 25:21), Rachel (Gen 29:31), and Hannah (1 Sam 2:5). The appearance of a special messenger of God to announce that a child would be born signified that the child would in some manner be special (see Gen 18:10; Luke 1:13, 31). The angel/messenger of Yahweh was a member of the heavenly court and represented God himself. The messenger informed the unnamed wife of Manoah that she would give birth to a son and that she had to avoid drinking wine or strong drink (šēkār) and unclean foods (Judg 13:4). The strong drink (šēkār) was probably beer, as in ancient times they did not have distilled liquors (Boling 1975, 219). It was not until the Middle Ages that the distilling of various grains, vegetables, and fruits to produce liquors became widespread. The child was to be a **Nazirite** from birth (v 7; see Num 6:1-8). He was to abstain from any food or drink derived from grapes, to avoid touching a dead body, and was not to cut his hair. His task (Judg 13:5) was to begin to deliver Israel from the Philistines. Unlike the other judges, he would never fully deliver Israel or bring a time of rest/peace to them. Samuel was also a Nazirite his whole life (1 Sam 1:22) and fought the Philistines (1 Sam 7:10-11). Neither was wholly successful, and it was left for King David to pacify the Philistine threat (2 Sam 5:17-25). The inability of the charismatic leaders Samson and Samuel to deliver Israel from the Philistines portrayed the crises of leadership that later led to the establishment of the monarchy.

There is a mystery as to the identity of the visitor. The wife told her husband that she had been visited by *a man of God* whose appearance was *like an angel/messenger of God* (v 6). She then related the purpose of his visit, to inform her of the birth of a son and to make plain the requirements she had to observe. Manoah's response (v 8) was to pray to God asking for *the man of God* to return. God heard the prayer and sent the messenger again to the woman who hurriedly went and told her husband. Both appearances were to the woman. The husband was absent. To Manoah's request for information about what manner of life the lad (*naʿar*) would live and what he would do, the messenger referred to the information already given to the wife. While the wife is unnamed, she is the central character in the story. The messenger appeared both times to her while she was alone. The announcement of the birth of a son, the requirements for her time of pregnancy, and the Nazirite status of the son were revealed to her, not her husband. Manoah was given the information by his wife.

■ **15-23** Manoah, like Abraham (Gen 18:3-5), offered hospitality to the messenger, a feast of a young goat (see Judg 15:1). Oddly the messenger refused the offer, a serious breach of hospitality, but suggested that Manoah prepare the animal as an offering to God. The narrator then added (13:16) that Manoah at this point in the story did not know who the messenger was. This is one of the subthemes of the chapter. Neither the wife nor the husband knew who the messenger was, although both had some understanding that he was sent from God. Manoah had already (v 12) asked about the lifestyle and deeds of the son, but the messenger only repeated what he had told the wife. Then Manoah asked the name of the messenger (v 17). The request was refused (v 18) as the name was "too wonderful" (NRSV; adjective *pilʾi* from the root *plʿ*, occurs only here and in Ps 139:6) for him, meaning that he would not understand it. Manoah (Judg 13:19) placed the offering of the kid and grain upon a rock, offering it to **Yahweh who does wonders** (*mapĕliʾ*, a participle form of *plʿ*) (following LXX as MT is awkward). Note the play on the word "wonders" (from the root *plʿ*) in vv 18-19. The messenger's name was too wonderful, as he was the representative of Yahweh who performed wonders. Only when the messenger ascended to heaven in the flame of the offering did both the husband and the wife recognize the visitor as the angel/messenger of Yahweh (vv 20-21).

Manoah was frightened and exclaimed to his wife, **Certainly we are going to die, for we have seen God!** (v 22). It was a common belief that those who saw a divine being whose glory was not somehow cloaked would be destroyed. Moses had to be sheltered when God passed by (Exod 33:20-

23). Isaiah feared that he would die when he had a vision of God in the temple (Isa 6:5). In this whole scene it is the unnamed wife who is more prominent. It was to her the messenger appeared twice, and it was she who received the instructions. She was the one who understood better who the messenger was, a man of God whose appearance was like the angel of Yahweh (Judg 13:6). She showed much more practical sense than her husband and gave him the wise response that God would not have accepted their sacrifice nor have informed them about the things to come, if he had intended to kill them (v 23).

■ **24-25** When the child was born (v 24) he was named Samson (*šamšŏn*), which derives from the word for the sun (*šemeš*). The LXX transliterates his name as *sampsōn*. With such a name an ominous chord sounds. The one who was "sunny" would end his days in darkness (16:21). In what manner the child was blessed by God we are not told, except that he grew. This may refer to him growing large and powerful. **And the spirit of Yahweh began to stir [disturb] him** (v 25) (see comment on 3:10, p. 66, for "spirit" as the power of Yahweh). The word *pāʿam*, translated in this verse as **stir**, only occurs five times in the OT. In Gen 41:8 Pharaoh was disturbed or troubled by a dream, as was also Nebuchadnezzar in Dan 2:1 and 3. In Ps 77:4 (v 5 in Hebrew) the psalmist was also troubled. In some way the spirit agitated Samson. The comment indicates that God was working with him as he grew.

Zorah (v 25) was located about 15 miles, 25 km, west of Jerusalem and 2 km north of Beth-shemesh. **Eshtaol** was located a short distance to the east. Both were located in the Sorek valley, a fertile area in the northern Shephelah. Samson and his father were buried in the area (16:31), and from it the Danites began their migration to the north (18:2).

FROM THE TEXT

1. The Bible portrays God as using various means and times to call persons to do his will. Abraham was already mature when God called him to leave his home and journey to an unknown land (Gen 12:1-3). Moses was a shepherd when he saw the burning tree on the mountain of God (Exod 3:1-6). Amos was also a shepherd when God told him to go prophesy in Israel (Amos 7:14-15). Jeremiah had not been conceived when God chose him to be a prophet (Jer 1:5). Paul was a persecutor of the church when he had his Damascus vision (Acts 9:1-8). Why God chooses specific individuals for specific tasks is a mystery. Why does the God of the universe, Creator of all, choose as his own a specific person or even one nation out of all his creation? Why Abraham or Jacob or Isaiah or Paul? Yet he does. The issue is formulated by theologians as the problem of particu-

larity vs. universality. This is one of the three issues that Bernard Anderson, following Fackenheim, identified as "dialectical contradictions." The second is stated as the transcendence of God vs. his immanence or closeness. How can the Sovereign God who created the universe and whose existence is different from all his creatures be present in the lives of his people? The third concerns the sovereignty of God vs. human freedom. If God is absolute Sovereign of the universe, how can humans be free to choose whether or not to obey him (1999, 77-78)? It is difficult in each of the issues to achieve a balance, and a theologian usually ends up emphasizing one side of an issue to the neglect of the other.

God chose Samson before he was conceived to be a judge who would begin to deliver Israel. His spirit came upon Samson in order to prepare him for his calling. However, Samson would not be the "obedient servant" who like Joshua fully obeyed God. He was more of a rogue whom God used. The call of God does not violate the person's free will. One is still free to choose to respond or not to the call of God. In the mystery of human freedom, however, these are not one's only choices. Too often like Samson a person responds to God, but then perverts the call for one's own purposes. Hananiah (Jer 28:1-17) may have been called by God to be a prophet, but he bowed to public opinion and preached what was popular rather than what God wanted. The temptation to pervert a call, even for so-called good reasons, is a constant pressure on those who are called by God into ministry. In the church, the laity rightly demands that the clergy live by the highest moral and ethical standards, but they also should support their leaders by fostering an atmosphere of acceptance and obedience to the proclaimed word of God. There should be a freedom to proclaim faithfully the message of God, but not harshly. The true shepherd always has a heart of compassion for those in his care.

2. Manoah and his wife responded with joy over the visitor's announcement of the birth of a son, and with fear when they realized that the visitor was the angel of the Lord. From the beginning they were aware that he was sent from God. There was no resistance to his message; only a desire for clarification of the lifestyle the child was to follow. Manoah offered hospitality as part of the custom of the day. The visitor chose to use the offer as a means of directing them to worship God. Rarely today do we respond in fear when attending a worship service. We have rightly heard Jesus' message of forgiveness extended by a loving Father. Unfortunately, too often our familiarity with the rituals of the church has bred in us complacency about worship. In contrast, if we would have the opportunity to meet a high public official such as a governor, a congressman, or

the president, we would probably show more respect and excitement. The casual attitude of the people in Malachi's day drove him to wish that someone would shut the doors of the temple so that they could not carry on in the same careless way (1:10). God does not expect us to approach him in cringing fear, but respect and reverence should characterize our times of worship.

2. Samson's Conflict with the Philistines (14:1—15:20)

BEHIND THE TEXT

The beginning of ch 14 leaps ahead to several years later when Samson was of an age to marry. He was attracted to a Philistine woman in Timnah (v 1), a town in the Sorek valley about 5 miles (9 km) west of Bethshemesh. Its site, Tell el-Batashi, has been excavated and a large Philistine town from Iron I was discovered (Kotter 1997, ABD-CD). The archaeological evidence also indicates that Timnah was not destroyed by the Philistines, as was nearby Ekron. The town was populated by a Philistine ruling class plus a large mixture of Canaanites and possibly Israelites. This diversity of population explains why Samson could easily enter the town and negotiate for a Philistine wife (Shanks 2008, 84).

Several overarching themes are either continued or introduced in this chapter. The theme of "revealing/making known" (*nāgad*) is further developed. Samson shared the honey with his parents, but he did not reveal to them where it came from. Samson proposed a riddle to the wedding guests that they did not know. He revealed the secret to his wife who then revealed it to the guests. Samson becomes the "trickster" in this chapter. He tricked the guests with his riddle and they tricked him by getting the answer from his wife. In response Samson tricked the Philistines by slaying thirty men to get their garments and by later burning their fields. Finally, Samson wanted the woman from Timnah because **she was right in his eyes** (v 3). This theme will be further developed until it becomes the concluding remark of the book, **every man did what was right in his own eyes** (21:25).

IN THE TEXT

■ **1-9** Samson requested that his parents arrange for him a marriage with the Philistine woman. They protested asking if he could not find a suitable Israelite woman instead of a woman of the uncircumcised Philistines. Samson responded (v 3) specifically to his father that he wanted her **because** *she was right in his eyes* (v 3). The editorial note (v 4) informs the reader that the parents were unaware that God would use the situation to enable Samson to act against the Philistines. It also states that **at that time the Philistines ruled** (*māšal*, the same term used when Gideon was offered rule, 8:22) **over Israel.**

Samson's request illustrated Israel's continued attraction for intermarriage with the people of the land. Such marriages ensnared them in the sin of worshipping other gods (3:6). Yet each time Israel's last judge desired a woman, it was always with a Philistine, never an Israelite. Two reasons are given as to why Samson wanted to marry the woman from Timnah. First, she was *right in his eyes,* a phrase that later characterized the spiritual and social anarchy that gripped Israel when *each man did what was right in his own eyes* (21:25; contrast Deut 12:8). Second, God was using the incident for his own purpose. God did not cause Samson to desire the woman of Timnah, but used that choice for his own purposes, to begin to bring about Israel's deliverance from the Philistines' oppressive rule.

Samson with his mother and father went to Timnah (v 5), probably to negotiate a marriage with the father of the woman. Evidently Samson had separated himself from his parents when he met a young lion. The writer notes that the incident occurred at a vineyard. What was Samson, a Nazirite, doing in a vineyard? The reader is alerted that something is not quite right. Samson was in an area he should have avoided.

The spirit of Yahweh rushed (*ṣālaḥ*, appears here and in v 19 and 15:14) upon Samson (v 6) and empowered him to kill the lion easily. The writer emphasized the ease with which Samson disposed of the lion by comparing his action to that of killing a kid, or young goat, and by noting that he had no weapon in his hand. On a more ominous note, we read that he also kept his kill a secret from his parents. In v 7 the verbs switch to the singular, indicating that it was Samson rather than his parents who took the lead in the negotiations. The verse closes with the comment that *she was right in Samson's eyes,* thus emphasizing as in v 3 that he was making a willful choice.

When Samson went down later **to take her** (the woman; v 8), a phrase commonly used to indicate marriage, he saw that the carcass of the lion had become the nest of bees. He scraped out the honey and ate it (v 9). Samson thus violated his Nazirite oath not to touch a dead carcass (Num 6:1-8). Since the honey came from the carcass of the dead lion, it was also ceremonially unclean. When Samson gave the honey to his mother and father, he was also defiling them (Lev 11:24-25, 39-40). For good reason then he did not tell them from where he got the honey.

■ **10-20** The beginning of v 10 is a separate note that the father of Samson *went down to the woman,* probably to conclude the marriage negotiations. The phrase *went down* indicates elevation, as Zorah was higher in elevation than Timnah.

Normally the wedding celebration was held at the home of the parents of the groom, not the bride. Yet Samson held a wedding feast or festival (*mišṭê*) that lasted seven days. The word *mišṭe* is also used to indicate occasions of drinking wine and even drunkenness (Isa 5:12; 25:6; Jer 51:39). The drinking of wine was a second violation of Samson's Nazirite vow. There are some problems understanding Judg 14:11. First, the Hebrew reads, *when they saw him,* but the LXX has, *when they feared him.* The Hebrew words for "see" (*rāʾāh*) and "fear" (*yārēʾ*) are similar and can be misread. Who is "they," the subject of the phrase? Is it the Philistines? Were they afraid of Samson and wanted a group of men to be with him in case things got out of hand? Is it the family? Since Samson seems to have been alone (did no Israelite want to attend this feast celebrating the marriage of an Israelite man with a Philistine woman?), did the family of the bride decide to invite the men to be companions of the groom? The number thirty is a round number, possibly signifying an honorable position. David had a select group of warriors named the Thirty, of which there were actually thirty-seven (2 Sam 23:18-39). The number thirty will play a role in the story.

During the feast Samson set forth (*ḥûd*) a riddle (*ḥîdâ*); he riddled a riddle for them (v 12). Samson proposed that the wager would be for thirty linen cloaks or outer wrappers and thirty changes of clothing or normal attire (vv 12-13). The practice of proposing riddles during a weeklong festival was a regular activity. Samson's riddle was so difficult that the men were unable to solve it (v 14). On the "seventh day" (MT) the men approached the *wife of Samson* (v 15). The LXX reads here "on the fourth day." This seems better for we are told in v 17 that the wife wept before him for seven days, probably meaning until the seventh day. Whatever the discrepancies, they are minor. The men demanded that she entice (*patî,* see also 16:5) him to learn his riddle or they would burn her and her father's house (v 15). She took the threat seriously and tried to trick Samson into telling her. The *wife of Samson* wept and accused him of hating her, not loving her (v 16). Samson responded by stating that he had not even told his parents, so why would he tell her. Samson placed the love of his mother and father above that of his wife. The irony was that he could not tell them. He would have revealed that he had broken his vow not to touch a dead carcass and that he had given them unclean food. She continued to weep before him; hardly a fitting attitude for one who was being married. Finally, on the seventh day he told her, and then she told the men (v 17). Before the sun set on the final day of the feast, the men answered Samson with another riddle, **What is sweeter than honey and what is stronger than a lion?** (v 18). The obvious answer to this riddle is love, but in the context of Samson's riddle, it was a telling answer. Samson had been tricked, and he knew that his wife had betrayed him. She accused him of not loving her, but it was she whose love for her father was stronger than her love for her husband. Neither of the two was willing to love the other more than their respective families. Family ties in the cultures of the Middle East were, and still are today, very strong. Yet even in that culture the statement in Gen 2:24 should have been a guiding principle: **For this reason a man will leave his father and mother and cling to his wife, and they shall become one flesh.**

In anger, but also driven by the spirit of Yahweh, Samson left the feast and went to Ashkelon, a Philistine town on the coast (v 19). He killed thirty men and took their garments to pay his debt. His thirty Philistine companions were paid at the cost of the death of thirty of their countrymen. Samson did not stay at the house of the woman's father, but in anger went to the house of his father. As a consequence, the father gave in marriage the **wife of Samson** to his friend (v 20), or what we would call at the wedding his "best man."

■ **15:1-8** After some days Samson decided to reconcile with his wife and took a present of a young goat to her (v 1). It was the time of the wheat harvest, May to June. In Israelite custom normally the wife would be taken to the home of the groom, which often was the home of his parents. Three or four generations would live together in the same house. A different custom was being followed in this story. The husband visited the wife at the home of her father. When Samson went to visit her, she was still at her father's house; she did not go to the home of her new husband, Samson's best man. The father refused to allow Samson to enter her room. He defended his action by pleading that he thought that Samson had divorced her. The Hebrew expression is **I said surely hating you hated her** (v 2). The word **hate** used in 14:16 describes emotions, but here it functions as a technical term for divorce. If he thought that Samson was only displeased with his wife, and then gave her to another, she would be guilty of adultery. His explanation, at least in his own mind, but not in that of Samson, justified his action. In an attempt to placate Samson, the father offered him his younger, more beautiful daughter in marriage. Samson was not interested in the younger daughter and told **them** (father and daughter? servants? husband?) that he would be guiltless when he did harm to the Philistines (v 3). His anger was focused not against the father, but indiscriminately against the Philistines. His actions point back to the editor's comment in 14:4 that God would use the situation as a pretext for Samson to act against the Philistines.

The animal (šûʿālîm) Samson caught is often translated fox, but more likely was a jackal (v 4). Foxes are solitary animals and are not as numerous in the area as are jackals (Soggin 1981, 246). The number three hundred is quite high. It is ten times the number of his wedding "friends." Three and ten are common numbers in the Bible. Multiplying a number by ten is to bring it to completion. Another function of the number is to draw a comparison between Samson's act of revenge with the jackals and Gideon's victory against the Midianites with his three hundred men (7:8). Samson released the jackals into the fields of grain. Since there were both standing grain and stacks of sheaves (v 5), evidently the harvesting of the wheat was in process. When the Philistines asked who burned the fields, "they" told them that Samson did it because his father-in-law had given his wife to his best friend (v 6). The anonymous "they" occurs several times in the story; those who barred Samson's entry to his wife (v 3), here those who informed the Philistines, and in v 8 the unidentified Philistines he killed. By calling the woman "Samson's wife" the informers rejected the father's justification for giving her to another man. Samson was justified in his reaction, at least in their eyes. The Philistines did not try to capture Samson, but took their revenge out on his wife and father-in-law. What the guests threatened (14:15) the Philistines did; burned both her and her father.

Revenge calls for revenge; and the cycle continued. Because the Philistines killed his wife, Samson decided that he was guiltless in taking revenge on them (v 7). He also thought that his actions were so justified that when he finished, the matter would be at an end. The phrase **he struck them hip and thigh** (v 8) is odd. While its meaning is obscure to us, it probably was a common expression of that day to mean that he delivered a devastating defeat against his foes. The location of the **rock of Etam** is unknown. The area has a number of caves in which a person could stay. There were two towns in Judah that were named Etam, but they were too far away. However, its location was evidently in the territory of Judah as the next story involves the Judeans, not Samson's tribe of Dan.

■ **9-17** The Philistines were not content to let Samson's attack end the affair. They moved against Judah at Lehi (v 9). The location of the town is not known. The name Lehi (leḥî) means "cheek" or "jawbone." It forms a pun with the use of the donkey's jawbone (lĕḥî) (v 15). The Judeans quickly submitted to the Philistines' demand for Samson and took three thousand men to the rock of Etam to capture him (v 11). The thirty that had grown to three hundred had now become three thousand. Instead of following Samson in revolt, they were willing to accept Philistine rule and to hand over to them a judge. The Judeans who were the first to take control of their allotted territory (1:3-21) were reduced to servitude, quickly complying with the orders of their Philistine overlords. Samson requested and received assurances that the Judeans themselves would not harm him (v 12). However, they did bind him. The fact that they used new ropes heightens the miracle of his escape. They were not old ones that might have been frayed or rotten. When the Philistines saw Samson being delivered to them bound, they raised a great shout of triumph (v 14). Yet their rejoicing was short-lived. For the second time **the spirit of Yahweh rushed upon him** (v 14). The new ropes became like burned cords of flax, melting off his hands. Using the fresh jawbone of a donkey, not an old and brittle one that might crumble, Samson slaughtered the Philistines (v 15). The term '*elep* is often translated "a thousand." It can designate a military unit of a smaller number. Boling translates it "a contingent" (1975, 237). When the slaughter was at an end, he recited a short poem to boast of his victory. It plays on the word *hămôr*, which can be translated as donkey or heap (BDB, 331).

> *With the jaw bone of a donkey,*
> *heap upon heaps;*
> *With the jaw bone of a donkey,*
> *I have killed a thousand men.* (V 16)

Samson boasted of his victory; not that of God's triumph whose spirit empowered him. The place was then called **Ramath-lehi,** or hill of the jawbone (v 17). Samson achieved a victory like that of Shamgar who killed six hundred Philistines (3:31). However, the writer noted that Shamgar delivered Israel. Regardless of his great strength, Samson's victories never delivered Israel from the hands of her enemies.

■ **18-20** Samson had a great thirst, so great that he thought that he might die (v 18). One is reminded of Esau who feared he would die of hunger. He sold his birthright to Jacob for food (Gen 25:29-34). Samson instead cried out to Yahweh for help. What good was the great victory if he then died of thirst or fell into the hands of the Philistines, **the uncircumcised** (v 18)? In response, God split open a hollow place in the rock at Lehi. God had in the wilderness brought forth for Moses and all Israel water from a rock (Exod 17:6). He again graciously provided for the needs of his servant. The place then was called **En-hakkore,** or **Spring of the One who Called.** The chapter closes with the note that Samson judged Israel for twenty years (v 20). What is missing is the note that he brought Israel a time of rest from its enemies.

FROM THE TEXT

1. Revenge is an ugly word. In the mind of the offended it is a matter of justice; the victim balancing the scales by getting even with the perpetrator. However, the scales are never evenly balanced. Revenge calls for revenge, too often in a seemingly never-ending and often escalating cycle. Samson sought revenge against the Philistines for the insult he had suffered. In turn the Philistine not only killed his wife and father-in-law but also pursued Samson himself.

Justice may be attained by appealing to a third party. If the offense involves the breaking of the law, the victim can turn to the police for protection and help. If it is a personal offense between Christians, we should be able to ask some of the older, respected members of the church to help us achieve reconciliation.

What is the motivation for revenge? Is it a matter of justice? Righting a wrong? Or is it more a matter of dominance and control? What is to be gained by revenge? All we do is confirm that the other person is an enemy. In personal matters we should heed the words of Paul, who counsels us to let God be the one to bring justice while we return good for evil (Rom 12:19-21). In so doing perhaps we can turn an enemy into a brother or sister in Christ.

2. Judah had accepted the oppression of the Philistines. When the Philistines demanded that they hand over Samson, they quickly complied. There was no debate on what was the right course of action. Evidently resistance was viewed as futile. Even when a judge who possessed extraordinary powers and upon whom the spirit moved was in their midst, the people were more interested in pleasing their masters than seeking freedom. When Samson slaughtered the contingent of troops sent to capture him, no help came from Judah. There are times when evil is so powerful that it is wise to keep silent (Amos 5:13). There are risks to opposing evil. Neighborhood drug dealers are armed. Local gangs react violently to those who stand up against them. If good people do nothing, how will the violence be stopped? It is a difficult decision to decide to oppose evil. The risk is great. Yet God does not want evil to triumph. He was willing to risk his son in the battle against evil. The church is called to be a positive force in the midst of an evil world. By so doing it offers hope to those who are oppressed. When individuals are moved by God to lead the fight, the corporate body must find the courage to respond. It is difficult and sometimes dangerous. Yet to accept the rule of evil when it might be opposed is to lose not only one's freedom but possibly also the next generation to the power of evil.

3. Samson's Final Exploits (16:1-31)

BEHIND THE TEXT

The final chapter of Samson's life describes his involvement with two women, one a Philistine prostitute in the town of Gaza and the other a woman named Delilah. We are not explicitly told that Delilah was ethnically a Philistine, but her name is not Israelite and the lords of the Philistines were able to bribe her into betraying him. It seems reasonable to conclude that she was Philistine, or at the least a non-Israelite. The account of Samson's exploits at Gaza is told briefly in three verses. The rest of the chapter revolves around Samson's involvement with Delilah and its consequences, including his death.

The story of Samson and Delilah has been told in a number of formats: Milton's poem *Samson Agonistes* (1671), Handel's oratorio *Samson* (1741), numerous paintings, and DeMille's motion picture *Samson and Delilah* (1949). Delilah has been portrayed as greedy, sensuous, deceitful, demonic, evil, licentious, traitorous, and one of the "bad women of the Bible" (Gunn 2005, 211-22). Samson appears as lustful, a simpleton, corrupt, driven by passion, and lacking good sense. This story brings to a close Samson's exploits, both physical and sexual. While in his death he destroyed many of Israel's enemies, the story closes with the Philistines still in control. Not until David defeated them twice in the Valley of Rephaim (2 Sam 5:17-25) was Israel free from Philistine domination.

Even though Samson was unable to deliver Israel, he was not deserted by God. After being captured by the Philistines, his eyes were gouged out and he was forced to grind grain like a woman (Judg 16:21). He had fallen into the depths of slavery and was mocked by his captors. Yet God still answered his prayers. He had been commissioned by God to begin to deliver Israel (13:5), and the circumstances of his life were used by God as excuses to afflict the Philistines (14:4). Although he did not bring a period of rest to Israel, he was honored by his family in burial (16:31) as one who judged Israel for twenty years (15:20; 16:31).

IN THE TEXT

■ **1-3** Samson did not fear to enter Gaza, a city in the heart of Philistine territory. Having lost his wife, he pursued his pleasure with a Philistine prostitute (v 1). His enemies decided to wait until the morning to kill him (v 2). However, he tricked them by leaving in the middle of the night. The barred gates were no barrier to him. By his own great strength (there is no mention of the spirit in this story) he picked the gates up out of their sockets and carried them away (v 3). The doors turned in sockets hollowed out of the stone entryway. They could be lifted up and then pulled out. He carried them about 40 miles to Hebron, the central city of the tribe of Judah. With the gates removed, the city of Gaza would be vulnerable to attack. There was no response from Judah; no attempt to break the oppressive rule of the Philistines. Judah is once again seen as impotent; far different from the Judah of 1:3-19.

■ **4-22** The first part of the story (vv 4-9) begins simply, ***and it was after this,*** tying it to Samson's previous exploits at Gaza. Samson loved a woman from the Valley of Sorek whose name was Delilah (v 4). We are not told if she was a Philistine like Samson's previous women, or a Canaanite, but it is unlikely that she was an Israelite. The Valley of Sorek was part of the water system that ran west from the Jerusalem area to the Shephelah. It was a fertile area where the tribe of Dan settled, but it was much desired by the Philistines. Eventually the tribe of Dan was forced to relocate (ch 18) (Ferris 1997, ABD-CD). The **rulers** (*seren,* a term used only to describe the Philistine rulers and sometimes translated "tyrants") ***of the Philistines*** approached Delilah with an enormous bribe of eleven hundred pieces of silver each (v 5). If all five lords made the offer, this would be fifty-five hundred pieces of silver, a highly inflated figure that indicated the lengths to which the rulers were willing to go to capture Samson. She, like Samson's wife, was to **entice** (*pati,* see also 14:15) him to tell her the secret of his great strength so that they might ***overpower him, and bind him, and afflict/imprison him*** (v 5).

Delilah made a direct approach when she asked him to **tell** or **make known** (*nāgad*) to her his great strength (v 6). Samson first replied that if he was bound by seven new bow strings he would become like other men (v 7). She had the rulers send her the new strings. She had men lie in hiding in an inner room of the house while she bound Samson (v 8). Then she told him that the Philistines had come for him. He broke the strings easily and went out to meet the threat (v 9).

Delilah's second attempt (v 10) began with an accusation that Samson had deceived (*tālal,* also vv 13 and 15; Gen 31:7; Exod 8:25 [Eng v 29]; Jer 9:4; Isa 44:20; Job 13:9) and lied to her. She pleaded with him to make known (*nāgad*) to her how he could be bound. He responded by saying that if he was bound with seven new ropes he would become like other men (Judg 16:11). The reader already knows that Samson deceived Delilah again. The Judeans had earlier bound him with new ropes to hand him over to the Philistines, and he had easily broken them (15:13-14).

When she warned him that the Philistines were there to capture him, he again broke the ropes as if they were threads (v 12).

Again Delilah accused Samson of deceiving and lying to her (v 13), which of course, he had. This time, Samson got closer to the truth as his answer involved his hair. She was to weave his seven locks of hair into a loom and fasten them with a pin. The Hebrew in v 13 reads: *If you weave the seven locks of my head with a web.* The LXX adds, *and fasten it with a pin to the wall.* For the beginning of v 14 the LXX also adds, *and he fell asleep and she wove the seven locks of his head with a web.* Since these additions supply information assumed in the story and make for smoother reading, most translations follow the LXX and include them.

Delilah continued pressuring Samson, protesting that while he told her that he loved her, *your heart* (*lēb*) *is not with me* (v 15). Over a period of time she continued to *pressure* him (*ṣûq*, see also 14:17 where the same word is used to describe Samson's wife's attempt to learn the secret of his riddle). She **urged** him (*'ālaṣ*) until his life was **worn down** (*qāṣar*) to death. The three Hebrew words noted here all contain the consonant *ṣ* or *ṣādê*, normally pronounced with a *ts* sound. The writer used alliteration to emphasize the distress Delilah placed on Samson.

Verse 17 begins **and he made known** (*nāgad*) **to her all his heart** (*lēb*). The statement plays on the word "heart" from v 15 and "make known," which has been a continuing theme throughout the Samson story. Samson was worn down. He told Delilah that from the womb of his mother he had been consecrated as a Nazirite and his hair had never been cut. If it was cut, then he would be as weak as other men. This was the only vow as a Nazirite that he had not broken. He foolishly placed his life into the hands of Delilah. Unfortunately Samson did not know what the reader had been told. She was motivated not by love, but by greed. A large reward was promised to her by the Philistine lords (v 5). Also, Samson had not learned from the experience with his wife. He was a pawn in the hands of women he desired. Their continual pressure had led him to tell his secrets, and they in turn told them to his enemies. His passion for his lovers overrode his good sense.

Delilah realized that Samson had told her **all his heart** (v 18), that is, he had revealed everything.

Biblical Use of the Word "Heart"

For people in the ANE the heart was the center of the person, and thus where the mind and will came together to make decisions. Rarely did they think of it as the seat of the emotions. They did not understand the function of the brain. When a person in Egypt was embalmed, the embalmers threw away the brain but embalmed the heart.

She sent word to the Philistine lords to come up to take Samson. The verse ends with the words, **they came up with the silver in their hands** (v 18). They were prepared to give the money for Samson. Delilah was greedy for the money. They were greedy for Samson.

She made Samson go to sleep on her knees and then called to a man to come to her (v 19). Why the man was called is a problem. The MT reads **and she cut the seven locks of his head.** Most translations follow a few Hebrew manuscripts (which read **and he cut the seven locks of his head**) and the LXX (which reads **and she called the barber and he cut the seven locks of his head**). Then **she began to afflict him** (v 19). In some way she was testing to see if his strength had left him, but it is not clear exactly what she did. She then said to Samson that the Philistines were there (v 20). He arose to go and meet them, thinking that he would **shake** himself (*nāʿar*) and vanquish them as before. The writer then noted, not that Samson did not know that his strength had departed from him, but that he did not know that **Yahweh had departed from upon him** (v 20). His hair was the symbol of his vows to God. His strength came from God himself. When the last of the Nazirite vows was broken, then God no longer empowered him with abnormal strength.

The Philistines seized Samson and gouged out his eyes (v 21). Then they took him back to Gaza, the city from where he had previously removed the gates (v 3). He was placed in shackles of bronze and in the prison was forced to grind grain. The last was a further humiliation, as that was work normally done by women. With his capture, Delilah is no longer mentioned in the story. This section of the story ends with a short note that foreshadows the future. **The hair of his head began to grow abundantly after it had been shaved** (v 22).

■ **23-31** The scene shifts to a religious festival in the city of Gaza where the Philistines celebrated the capture of Samson. The city where men waited in vain to kill Samson would become the place of his death. Three times we are told that the lords of the Philistines were present (vv 23, 27, and 30). This emphasizes both the political importance of the festival and the completeness of Samson's revenge. In a sense of poetic justice, all the lords who had bribed Delilah (v 5) were killed. The text emphasizes that this was a great festival where they sacrificed to their god Dagon. They rejoiced before this god because Samson had been delivered to them. The implication was that since Dagon had made Samson their prisoner, he was greater than the God of Samson who had enabled him to do such great exploits.

The God Dagon

The god Dagon was worshipped throughout the Mesopotamian and Canaanite areas. He is mentioned in texts as early as the end of the third millennium. In texts of the Canaanite city of Ugarit he is mentioned as the father of the rain god Baal Hadad. One of the two most prominent temples of the city was his; the other was Baal's. We do not know his exact function. Jerome (fourth century A.D.) and early rabbinic interpreters associated him with fish, but that identification has generally been rejected. His name appears in Hebrew to be in some way associated with grain, probably wheat. In this passage and in the stories about the ark of the covenant (1 Sam 5:1-5), he is a national god of the Philistines (McKenzie 2007, 3-4).

The lords (v 23) and the people (v 24) rejoiced at Samson's capture. The people praised their god singing, **Our god has given into our hand our enemy, the destroyer of our land and the one who has slain many of us** (v 24). At some point during the festival (v 25), **when their hearts were merry,** they wanted to have Samson brought out to entertain them. It is possible that they were feeling fine not only due to the collective rejoicing but also from the effects of drinking wine. They wanted to **make sport** (śāḥaq) of Samson; that is, publically humiliate him by making him "dance" before them. The word carries sexual nuances, which indicate "the feminization of the hero" (Niditch 2008, 171). They brought him from the prison and **he made sport** (ṣāḥaq) **before them,** perhaps stumbled around in his blindness (v 25).

Hebrew Terms for Making Sport

Note the slight difference in the spelling of the two words, śāḥaq and ṣāḥaq. They are synonyms and vary only slightly in pronunciation. The words probably originated during a period when the story circulated orally and reflect the storytellers' art of shifting the sounds to entertain the audience.

Samson asked the young man (naʿar) who held his hand to let him touch the pillars that supported the temple roof (v 26). This type of construction was widely known in Canaan. Excavations of the cities of Lachish and Beth-shean found similarly constructed temples where two central columns in the main hall supported the structure (Ussiskin 1987, online basarchive.org). The removal of the pillars would have led to the collapse of the building. The temple in Gaza was filled with prominent men and women of the city as well as the lords of the Philistines (v 27). Those who had bribed Delilah to betray Samson would die with him. The note that three thousand men and women were on the roof viewing Samson's humiliation is hard to understand. The temples were generally roofed and without an open central court. The two central columns supported the roof. How the spectators would have been able to see the activities inside the temple is a puzzle. The number three thousand (his thirty "friends" times ten, times ten), however, functions to increase the scope of Samson's victory over the Philistines and give him the honor of being a hero and noted judge.

In the midst of his humiliation Samson called upon Yahweh, the God of Israel (v 28). He asked for revenge against the Philistines in return for the loss of his eyes. Then grasping a pillar in each arm, he made his final request; that he might die with the Philistines. God heard his prayer and his strength returned. The temple collapsed, killing all in it, including Samson himself. The story ends with the note that his brothers and his father's extended family brought back his body and buried it in his father's tomb (v 31; also Gideon, 8:32). Thus he was given a hero's death and burial (Niditch 2008, 172). The story closes with the note that he judged Israel for twenty years.

FROM THE TEXT

1. The writer of Hebrews includes Samson, along with Jephthah, Barak, and Gideon, in the list of heroes of the faith (11:32). Samson is certainly not a model of devotion and piety. He broke his Nazirite vows. He pursued Philistine women, including a prostitute. He killed and murdered many of Israel's enemies but was never successful in delivering Israel from Philistine domination. The writer of Hebrews was encouraging the early Christians by emphasizing the positive characteristics of the judges, how they accomplished their God-ordained mission in the face of overwhelming odds; not justifying their moral or ethical lapses. The writer did not condone Samson's visit to the prostitute or the breach of his vows. He was a leader moved by God's power that enabled him to participate in God's plan to deliver Israel. He was not granted immunity to temptation or human fallibility (Martin 2008, 1-16). The church continually faces the problem of leaders who are morally and ethically flawed. At times their sin is overlooked and counted as a normal human failing. Others are demonized and driven out of their positions of leadership. We struggle to find ways to reach out redemptively to encourage repentance and to find means of restoration. The tragedy of sin should not be glossed over, nor should God's offer of forgiveness and cleansing be minimized. The moral failures of leaders affect the entire congregation. The lives of those directly involved are deeply scarred. Others are disillusioned. Some are disheart-

ened and give up the faith. Wisdom must be used not to enlarge the damage. Yet, the entire congregation needs to be involved in the healing process. The sufferings of the people are not just psychological and emotional; although these elements must not be overlooked. Ultimately they are theological and spiritual. We must depend on God to bring healing and reconciliation to the individuals and the congregation.

2. The spirit of God moved upon Samson more than any other judge. Yet no other judge had so many moral failings. Does God continue to use sinners to accomplish his will? The Bible makes a distinction between common human failings or unintentional sin and intentional or high-handed sins (Num 15:27-31). All of humanity is involved in unintentional sins, but by God's grace we need not be enslaved to sin and driven to flout God's commands (Rom 6:12-14). Samson was continually moved by the power of God, even though he broke his vows. At this point Samson reflected the pattern of Israel's disobedience in the entire book. Israel intermarried with the people of the land and were led into idolatry through the influence of their marriage partners. When they became oppressed, they cried out to God for deliverance. God then raised up a judge to save them. The spirit was not always the agent who empowered Samson (Judg 15:4; 16:1-3, 9, 12, 14). He was a man of exceptional strength who was able to accomplish amazing feats apart from the movement of the power of God. More importantly, he was used by God as a deliverer of Israel to fight the Philistines (14:19; 15:14). He had been captured by the Philistines and was still their slave when he cried out to God. God heard and answered Samson's last prayer. In his last act of revenge Samson killed more Philistines than during his entire life (16:30). God is free to use whomever he chooses to accomplish his will. Even Caiaphas the high priest who counseled others that Jesus must be put to death spoke as a prophet (John 11:49-51). It is a mystery why God will continue to work through those who willingly disobey God. We want to think that God works only with those who are spiritually prepared and morally pure. However, God is not limited by our categories of justice and moral rectitude. His instruments, though often flawed, may yet be empowered by him to accomplish his purposes. This is not a defense of immoral leadership. Discipline must be maintained. But we must not discount that which has been accomplished by God who works through human agents. The people of God are called to praise and give thanks for the saving works of God, however he chooses to accomplish them.

3. How tragic are the words, **he did know that Yahweh had departed from him** (Judg 16:20). God is patient and long-suffering with his people,

but there is a point when even he says, "Enough!" He withdraws and allows the sinner to reap the harvest of his or her own sins. Samson was captured by his enemies, blinded, and made to grind grain like a woman. Will God hear the prayer of a sinner? He heard Samson's. God does not wish that any will perish, but is long-suffering (2 Pet 3:9). He keeps open the door of reconciliation through repentance. The sinner need not despair. The righteous should not presume. We are all called to cast ourselves wholly upon the mercy of our gracious Lord and Savior.

III. FAILURE COMPLETE (17:1—21:25)

OVERVIEW

The final five chapters of the book contain two narratives, the relocation of the tribe of Dan (chs 17—18) and the war against the tribe of Benjamin (chs 19—21). These chapters along with the first introduction of the book (1:1—2:5) come from the hands of the final editors (see Introduction) who worked in the late seventh or early sixth century. The downward spiral toward spiritual bankruptcy and social disintegration comes to completion in these narratives. The tribe of Dan, the last tribe to be given an allotment of territory (Josh 19:40-48), was unable to take possession of its inheritance. According to Judg 1:34, they were driven back into the hill country by the Amorites, a collective term used to designate the various groups of inhabitants of the land. Since they were not strong enough to take their inheritance, they decided to relocate to the north. They were given no authorization by God, through a prophet or an angel or a leader, to relocate. The people they destroyed are described three times as peaceful, living quietly and unsuspectingly. In the process of the journey northward a band of Danite soldiers robbed Micah of his household gods in order to establish an illegitimate worship center for the tribe. This act foreshadowed Jeroboam's establishment of an idolatrous worship center with a golden calf image at the high place of Dan (1 Kgs 12:28-30). The reason why Israel was taken into captivity by the Assyrians in 722 B.C., according to DH, was because of its idolatry and failure to worship Yahweh exclusively. The book of Judges traces the roots of the tribe of Dan's spiritual corruption back to the very beginnings of the city of Dan.

The last three chapters chronicle the near destruction of the tribe of Benjamin. A Levite's concubine was sexually abused and killed in the city of Gibeah by men from the tribe of Benjamin. The people of the other tribes demanded that the men be given over for judgment, but the Benjamites refused. The tribes then decided that in order to restore justice an army should be raised for the purpose of exterminating the whole tribe of Benjamin. The first two battles went badly for the coalition of tribes. The tide turned against Benjamin during the third battle and all but six hundred men were killed. The final chapter discloses how wives were secured for the survivors through kidnapping women and forcing them into marriages. The book ends by noting that no king reigned in Israel in those days and that the people did what was right in their own eyes. This was not how God had commanded them to live.

The narratives may have been a late editorial addition to the book, but they contain a number of literary references that unite them to the book as a whole, as well as to each other. Samson was from the tribe of Dan, and the following story describes the relocation of Dan. The eleven hundred pieces of silver that Micah stole from his mother (17:2) is the same amount that each of the lords of the Philistines paid Delilah (16:5). Schneider suggests that since the two stories are placed together and that the amount of money is the same, the reader should recognize that Micah's mother was Delilah. The silver was part of her payment for betraying Samson. In the story Micah's father is never named, leaving it to the reader to surmise that he was Samson's son (2000, 232). The phrase **every man did what was right in his own eyes** (17:6 and 21:25) is similar to the note that the Philistine woman Samson wanted to marry was right in his eyes (16:12, 28). It is also a variation of the refrain that **Israel did evil in the eyes of Yahweh** (2:11; 3:7, 12; 4:1; 6:1; 10:6; 13:1). The Deuteronomistic editing of the book can be seen in these phrases, as they also appear a number of times in Deuteronomy. Moses warned Israel not to do what was right in their own eyes (Deut 12:8) or what was evil in the eyes of Yahweh (Deut 4:19, 25; 17:2; 31:29), but encouraged them to do what was right in the eyes of Yahweh (Deut 6:18; 12:18; 13:19; 21:9). Another indication of the unity of the book is seen in the lead that Judah takes. In Judg 1:2 when Israel inquired who was to take the lead in conquering the land, God responded by selecting Judah. Judah was also selected by God to lead the tribes in the war against Benjamin (20:18). So in both the beginning and the end, Judah was the lead tribe.

The two stories also share literary ties. In the first story a Levite moved from Bethlehem to the hill country of Ephraim. In the second a

Levite traveled from the hill country of Ephraim seeking his concubine who had returned to her father's house in Bethlehem. The refrain *in those days there was no king in Israel* occurs only in these stories (17:6; 18:1; 19:1; 21:25). Both stories center on the larger issues of worship and war. Dan confiscated the idols of Micah's household to establish their own worship center. They then destroyed a peaceful city and renamed it after their ancestor Dan. The Levite who presided over the new city's worship center was Jonathan, the grandson of Moses. When the tribes went to war with Benjamin, they sought Yahweh's advice at the shrine at Bethel as to who should lead the attack. After each defeat they went back to Bethel and prayed and fasted before Yahweh. At the time the high priest Phinehas, the grandson of Aaron, presided at the shrine of Bethel. Jeroboam I would later set up a golden calf in each of the shrines (1 Kgs 12:28-33), an act that earned him a severe judgment as pronounced by the prophet Ahijah (1 Kgs 14:6-16).

A. Relocation of Dan (17:1—18:31)

1. Micah and the Levite (17:1-13)

BEHIND THE TEXT

The main characters in this section of the story are Micah and the Levite. Micah is more prominent as he stole the silver, restored it, made an idol, established a shrine, and hired the Levite. Micah's mother and son are minor characters. The mother with her eleven hundred pieces of silver form a transition from the Samson stories to this one. God is mentioned but is not an actor in the scene.

The story opens with the account of the theft of eleven hundred pieces of silver. As noted above, this amount links this story with the story of Samson and Delilah, as she received the same amount from each of the lords of the Philistines for betraying Samson. The use of the silver to make a cast idol was a clear violation of the Ten Commandments. Israel during the time of the judges was allowed to worship at various religious centers as one central location, for a temple had not yet been chosen by God (Deut 12:5-7). There is a discussion among scholars about whether or not the second commandment, which prohibits the making of idols, was actively enforced at the time of the judges. The Deuteronomic History (see Introduction) was written from the standpoint that the terms of the covenant made at Mount Sinai (Exod 19—24) were fully known from the time of Moses. The stories, however, recount how the people repeatedly turned to the worship of idols. Archaeologists have also found evidence that the Israelites at this time made idols (Mazar 1983, online) and worshipped the Canaanite gods (Lemaire 1984, online). This is a technical question about the actual worship practices of the Israelites as distinguished from what later was written as required. It is possible that Micah and his mother believed that the making of an idol was a permissible custom. However, at the time of the writing of the book, the writer was implying that the actions were improper and the audience would have understood them as a clear violation of the commandments of God. Thus the entire episode was then viewed and should now be read as another incident in the history of Israel's violation of the covenant.

The time of the story is set after the death of Samson who was of the tribe of Dan; specifically, at the time of the migration of that tribe. The Danites were unable to secure a permanent inheritance because the indigenous peoples were too powerful for them (1:34-36). The enemy of Samson was the Philistines, a people who had migrated from the Aegean area and settled on the eastern coast of the Mediterranean early in the twelfth century. While the stories of the judges are set in a chronologically sequential framework, there are indications that there may be some movement back and forth historically (see the discussion on chronology in the Introduction). In the story of the war against Benjamin, Phinehas was serving at Bethel as high priest. He was the grandson of Aaron (Exod 6:25) and served as a priest during the time of Joshua (Josh 22:13, 31, 32). This note about Phinehas would place the story of the war with Benjamin at an early time in the period of the judges. Thus it is difficult to give exact dates for the settings of the stories.

IN THE TEXT

■ **1-6** The first section of the chapter describes the origin of Micah's household shrine (vv 1-6). The first four verses, which explain why a silver idol was made, are framed by the fuller spelling of Micah's name. Both v 1 and 4 end with *mîkāyĕhû*, which means **Who is like Yahweh?** The obvious answer is that a silver idol was not like Yahweh and thus was an illegitimate representation. The section closes with two additional comments. Micah's son was installed as a priest of the household shrine (v 5). An editorial note (v 6) explains that the people did whatever they wanted to do, for in those days there was no king.

The narrative begins with a standard introduction, **and there was a man** (v 1). This is followed by giving his name and place of residence, the hills of Ephraim located in the central hill country north of Jerusalem. The names of his father and tribe are missing. Was he of the tribe of Ephraim, or as Schneider suggests (see above) was he the son of Samson and thus a Danite? Eleven hundred pieces of silver had been stolen from his mother (Delilah?), and she had cursed the thief. When Micah confessed and restored the money she blessed him in the name of Yahweh, thus countering the curse. She had given her son a Yahwistic name and called upon Yahweh to bless him. These actions indicate that the narrator accepted that the household was Israelite and, however much they strayed from proper worship as given in the Law, they were worshippers of Yahweh, not Canaanite gods. In v 3 the mother declared that the silver was consecrated to Yahweh but gave her son only two hundred pieces of silver (v 4) for the purpose of making an idol (*pesel*) and a molten image (*masēkâ*). The expression may be a hendiadys, two terms connected by the word "and" used to indicate one thing. In v 4 the verb used with them is singular (Boling 1975, 256). Idols were commonly made by carving a figure out of wood (*pesel*?) and then covering it with a layer of metal foil (*masēkâ*?), bronze, silver, or gold (Niditch 2008, 181). The image probably was not thought of as a physical representation of a god, in this case Yahweh, but as a pedestal for the invisible God and thus an aid to the worshipper in focusing his or her devotion. Yahweh was enthroned upon the cherubim in the temple in Jerusalem. In v 5 we are told that Micah (*mîkâ*, regular spelling of his name used in all other occurrences) had a household shrine dedicated to God (*'elōhîm*), which also contained an ephod (note how Gideon led Israel astray, 8:27) and teraphim, idols of varying sizes used in worship (Gen 31:19, 34-35; 2 Kgs 23:24). He also installed (***filled the hand***) of one of his sons as a priest of the shrine. The editorial note in v 6 makes a negative evaluation of Micah's action. He did what was right in his own eyes as there was no king in Israel. The note might have been added during the time of Josiah as an encouragement to the king to establish proper worship in Judah by carrying out his reforms and purging the land of false worship (2 Kgs 23:1-24).

■ **7-13** Verse 7 begins in the same manner as v 1, ***and there was a young man,*** thus tying the two sections together. The term ***young man*** (*naʿar*) occurs five times in the story (17:7, 11, 12; 18:3, 5) to emphasize his youthfulness.

Hebrew Term for Young Person

Naʿar is used to refer to a servant (19:3, 9, 11, 19), an armor bearer (7:10, 11; 8:20), a young man or soldier (8:20), a boy (8:14; 13:24; 16:26), a young woman of marriageable age (19:3, 4, 5, 6), or even an unborn child (13:5, 7, 8, 12).

He lacked the wisdom of age and seized his opportunities as they arose without considering their appropriateness as judged by the standards of the covenant, which as a Levite he was to uphold. The young man was from Bethlehem of Judah and **was residing there** (*gār šām*, a play on the name of his father Gershom [*gēršōm*] who is not revealed until 18:30). He left Bethlehem to seek another place to live and came to the house of Micah in the hill country of Ephraim. Micah (17:10) offered him the position of family priest and set forth his wages as ten pieces of silver, plus his clothing and food. Micah said that the Levite would be **his father and priest,** a standard phrase to indicate his spiritual position in the household (see 18:19). The young man agreed and Micah installed him (**filled the hand**) as priest of his household. The relationship between the two men is emphasized in 17:11; Micah treated him as **one of his sons.** Micah considered himself fortunate (v 13) because he thought that Yahweh would do him good because he had a Levite for a priest. A Levite was considered a holy person who would be better able to bring the blessings of God upon the household.

2. New Home for the Tribe of Dan (18:1-31)

BEHIND THE TEXT

In this section the main characters are the five spies who are never named and who always act as a single character, and the Levite whose name is revealed at the end of the story. The minor characters include Micah who only appears at the end, the Danites who act as a whole to commission the five and later receive their report, the six hundred Danite warriors with their little ones, the men of Micah's village, and the people of Laish who were slaughtered. The story moves elliptically between the area around Zorah and Eshtaol to that of Laish, with the house of Micah forming a midpoint. The five asked the Levite to inquire of God about their mission. The Levite gave them a favorable response, but God himself is missing from the story.

The early chapters of the book have already alerted the reader to the desperate situation of the tribe of Dan. The tribe was unable to take possession of the territory allotted to it, for the inhabitants were too strong for them. They were driven out of the plains of the Shephelah and back into the hill country (1:34). In the final section of the introduction (2:1-5) the angel of Yahweh announced to Israel that because they had refused to obey God, he would no longer drive out the inhabitants of the land. The conquest had theologically come to an end. In the Song of Deborah, Dan was described as located near the sea (5:17). The Philistines, whom Samson fought, were part of a larger group who had begun their migration from the Aegean area in the mid-thirteenth century. After a failed attempt to invade Egypt in the early twelfth century, the Philistines settled on the southwestern shore of the land. Gaza and Ashkelon were two of their more prominent cities with access to the sea. Possibly the Danites found employment working on their ships.

The story of the relocation of Dan, along with the other concluding narratives, is part of the latest edition of the book. However, the incident itself probably took place earlier in the time of the judges. Its placement in the book functions to describe the continuing spiritual deterioration of the nation. The tribe destroyed a peaceful people and established an idolatrous worship center that continued until the people were taken into exile by the Assyrians (721 B.C.). While no open condemnation is given by either God or the narrator, the open violation of the commandment against bringing images of gods into their houses (Deut 7:25-26) conveys its own unspoken censure.

There are few textual problems in the account. There are, however, some verses that provide challenges to translators. Idiomatic expressions, such as appear in Judg 18:3, 6, and 8, are always difficult to translate into another language. Also, the complex of compact descriptions of the residents of Laish (vv 7, 10, 27) presents a challenge. These will be dealt with in more detail in the next section.

IN THE TEXT

■ **1-7** The opening note that there was no king at that time (see 17:6) links the two stories. The Danites, like Micah, did as they desired. In Josh 19:40-48 Dan was allotted a territory to the west of the Judean hills in the plain or Shephelah. Because the Amorites (1:34), and later the Philistines, were too powerful, the tribe was unable to possess their inheritance. Five valiant men (18:2) from their clan were sent **to walk the land and investigate it** with the implied intent of finding a place to which the tribe could relocate. Their mission was similar to the twelve sent by Moses from the wilderness into the southern part of the land (Num 13:17-20). The five stayed at the house of Micah in the hill country of Ephraim. **When they heard the voice of the young Levite, they recognized him** (Judg 18:3). The accent of the young man from the southern area of Judah was like their own, which was distinct from the tribes of the north (Boling 1975, 263). There followed a series of short questions inquiring about how he got there and what he was doing there. The questions are in idiomatic expressions (**who caused you to come here, and what are you doing in this, and** *what to you here?*), which are clear in intent but awkward to translate literally. The Levite's response (v 4) compresses the details but emphasizes the facts that Micah had hired him and that the Levite was his priest. The shortness of the answer highlights the mercenary aspect of the arrangement. The Levite viewed his position as a job for which he was well paid while Micah looked upon him as one of his sons (17:11).

The Danites asked him (18:5) to inquire of God (*'elōhîm*, not Yahweh) that they might know if he would prosper their journey. He responded (v 6) that they should go in peace (*šālôm*), **for Yahweh is in front of your journey**, an idiomatic expression that means that he would be with them. The five (v 7) journeyed north to Laish, present-day Tell Dan, which lies at the headwaters of the Jordan River. The area has abundant water, and the fertile land is good for farming. The verse is packed with descriptive terms. The inhabitants lived with a confident attitude in the **manner** or **customs** (*mišpāṭ*) of the Sidonians, Phoenicians whose city was located about 20 miles north of Tyre on the coast of the Mediterranean Sea. They lived undisturbed and trusting or unsuspecting. Soggin notes that the next phrase is difficult either because it is corrupt or it contains technical terms we do not know. He paraphrases it as, "in that region with its rich produce they lacked nothing" (1981, 271-72). Niditch translates it more literally, "not plotting a thing in the land, possessing restraint" (2008, 174). Boling has, "without anyone perverting anything in the territory or usurping coercive power" (1975, 260). The city was located far from Sidon in the west. The concluding phrase reads, **and there were no dealings with humans** (*'ādām*). Boling notes that the phrase is almost unintelligible and that the LXX, Old Latin, and Syriac versions read the last word as *'ărām* or Syria whose leading city was Damascus. The Hebrew *d* and *r* were sometimes confused (1975, 263). The change would pair Sidon in the west with Syria/Damascus in the east, indicating that Laish was isolated from all help. The verse emphasizes that the people of Laish dwelt peacefully without fear of enemies and isolated from their neighbors.

■ **8-10** The five returned to their kin at Zorah and Eshtaol. Samson and his father Manoah were buried in the area between the two towns (16:31). The kinsmen inquired, **What you?** meaning **What did you find?** The five reported (18:9) that the land was very good; the same judgment God pronounced about creation (Gen 1:31). They urged their kinsmen not to delay but to go immediately **to take possession of the land** (*lārešet 'et-hā'āreṣ*, the same phrase that appears in Judg 2:6 for the conquest). They described (18:10) the people as trusting and the land as spacious and bountiful, adding that God had given it into their hand.

■ **11-26** The six hundred men equipped for war were from a clan, not the tribe of Dan. We are not told if these were the only volunteers or whether it was decided that these would be enough to take the city and that all the men from the tribe were not needed. When the troops camped in Judah (v 12), the place became known as the **Camp of Dan.** Their next recorded stop was in the hills of Ephraim, north of Judah, at the house of Micah. The original five told the others (v 14) about the worship center in the house of Micah. The verse ends with the ominous question addressed to the six hundred, **and now consider what should you do?** They first went to the house of the young Levite and asked about his welfare (šālôm), a standard form of greeting. The six hundred men who were equipped for war remained at the gate. The houses of small settlements were built in a circle with the back walls of the houses forming a defensive wall around the village. This provided a degree of protection from wild animals and small raiding parties. There would be a gate to the complex. During the day the men of the houses would be working in the fields around the village.

Through repetition the text emphasizes several points. It was the five men who originally investigated the land who took the lead in the incident (vv 14 and 17). The six hundred are described as equipped for war (vv 11, 16, 17) and thus very intimidating. The taking of the worship objects is described three times (vv 17, 18, and 20). In v 20 it was the Levite himself who gathered up the ephod, teraphim, and idol. The act of establishing an illegitimate worship center for the tribe of Dan was a conscious and deliberate act.

When the Levite recognized what the men were doing, he protested (v 18). He was told to be quiet and keep his mouth shut; literally, **place your hand over your mouth.** He was then invited (v 19) to go with them and become **father and priest** (see 17:10) for the tribe, which would be better for him than serving just a house. The Levite had indicated earlier (v 4) that his motivation for serving was basically monetary, and so it was no surprise that he accepted the offer (v 20). He then gathered the ephod, teraphim, and idol and **went in the midst of the people** for protection from his former employer Micah.

The men then placed **the little ones** (or children) plus the cattle and valuables in the front (v 21), obviously expecting trouble from Micah and his neighbors. When Micah and the other men heard what happened, probably from the women, they went after the Danites, literally **sons of Dan.** When they caught up to the Danites (v 24), Micah complained, **you have taken the gods which I made and my priest.** The Danites warned Micah not to let his **voice be heard** among them **lest men bitter of life** attack and kill him and his men (v 25). The warriors were described as **bitter** *of life/soul* (*nepeš*), meaning that they felt that they had been badly treated in life (the reason why they were relocating) and had nothing to lose. They would retaliate quickly and think nothing about killing them. When Micah saw (v 26) that the Danites were so numerous and that he could not win in a fight, he and his men returned to their village.

■ **27-31** The first part of v 27 summarizes the previous events; they took the things Micah had made and his priest. The second half moves the story forward. They come to Laish. The text repeats that the people lived quietly and were trusting. They were not aggressive toward the Israelites nor were they oppressing them. Yet the Danites slaughtered the people and burned the city. Verse 28 emphasizes their helplessness before the Danites. There was no deliverer, such as a judge, to help them as they lived far from both Sidon and Damascus (see v 7). They rebuilt the city and named it Dan after their forefather. The valley of **Beth-rehob** extended northward into Syria unto just south of Nebo-hamoth. It was the most northern extent of the search by the spies Moses sent out (Num 13:21) (Luker 2006, 445).

The Danites established a worship center with the idol that they had taken from Micah (v 30). For the first time the name of the priest is given, Jonathan the son of Gershom, the son of either Moses (*mšh*) or Manasseh (*mnšh*). The difference in spelling is one letter—"n" in Hebrew. Gershom was the son of Moses (Exod 2:22), not Manasseh. Also, the letter "n" in the name is raised, indicating that it was inserted later. It is likely that a scribe did not think it appropriate to have a grandson of Moses serving as a priest at a shrine with an idol; so he changed the spelling to Manasseh. The priestly family of Jonathan served the tribe of Dan until the Assyrians took the northern tribes into captivity in 722 B.C. The final note (v 31) states that the tribe of Dan continued to use the idol that Micah made during the years when the tabernacle was at Shiloh (1 Sam 1:3). The mention of Shiloh serves the function of linking the migration of Dan to the last incident of the book.

At the end of the story of Judges, to provide wives for the remaining Benjamites, the elders of Israel gave the Benjamites permission to kidnap the young women of Shiloh who were dancing in the vineyards in celebration of the harvest (Judg 21:21). The idolatrous shrine at Dan was a violation of God's commandments, and kidnapping of the women was another expression of people doing what was right in their own eyes (v 25*b*), not what was right in God's eyes.

FROM THE TEXT

1. The Danites took the idols from Micah because they had the power to do so. Six hundred armed men of war who were spoiling for a fight

made for an intimidating presence. Micah could do nothing but accept his losses. Does might make right? The use of power, whether it be military, political, corporate, or personal, is always subject to abuse. When is intimidation by police officers necessary to maintain order or an abusive action designed to frighten citizens? When is raising taxes a legitimate part of the legislative process to pay for needed social obligations such as roads and schools or a crushing burden on an oppressed society? Are work regulations established to enhance the working environment by making it safer and more pleasant or to manipulate the workers for the benefit of the company profits? Even in churches leaders too often manipulate workers and volunteers to protect their own positions or personal prestige. Power in itself is not an evil. It can be used for good. A parent has to discipline a child and set boundaries for the child's own good, even if the child does not understand. A leader can use power to support his colleagues and subordinates. A politician can work for a just society. A Christian is guided by the commandments of Jesus: love God and love your neighbors. Having power is an opportunity to demonstrate love for both.

2. Micah made images as part of his household shrine. According to the text they were dedicated to the worship of Israel's God Yahweh. While there is no explicit word of condemnation in the story, from the theological position of the book the act was a clear violation of the second commandment (Exod 20:23; Deut 5:8). The Deuteronomic compilers and editors (see the Introduction) so understood the commandment and were demonstrating to the readers that the worship of idols violated their covenant with God.

18:1-31

During the Middle Ages the churches were often adorned with religious paintings and statues. The common people were illiterate, and the artistic presentations were used to tell the biblical stories and the gospel. However, during the Reformation one of the points of contention between the Roman Catholics and the Protestants was the veneration of saints, particularly the use of statues in the church to help worshippers focus their prayers and devotion (see Gunn's discussion, 2005, 234-37). James Arminius (1560-1609) argued against Cardinal Bellamine's distinction that an idol represented something false, while an image represented something real and was therefore a legitimate aid to worship. Arminius refuted Bellamine's argument by citing the story of Micah as an example of idolatrous worship even if dedicated to God (1956, 1:655-56).

Today criticizing another's worship patterns is condemned as intolerant. If one spoke forcefully against the presence of statues in a church, he or she would be labeled as a narrow-minded demagogue. Catholic churches are adorned with stained-glass windows and statues of biblical characters and saints. Churches of other denominations also have stained-glass windows depicting biblical characters and venerated persons. Even in Evangelical churches popular paintings of Christ, oftentimes of dubious artistic value, decorate the sanctuaries. Few maintain a strict code of banning any artistic representation of a person, be that of Christ or a saint, in a house of worship. Most justify their inclusion as aids to the worship of God. They help worshippers focus their prayers and devotion on the deity represented. At what point does the worship of a person or a congregation or even a church become idolatrous? One of my colleagues in graduate school was a nun from Canada. Her order sent missionaries to South America. In the churches there a custom arose to purchase and dedicate a chalice in memory of a dead loved one. On the anniversary of the person's death, the family gathered around the chalice and offered prayers. One of the tasks of the missionaries was to return the chalice diplomatically, so as not to offend the family. The use of the chalice to focus their worship of the ancestor, she said, was idolatrous and the chalice needed to be removed from the church. What is the proper use of art in the church? When does it become, even with the best of intention, an act of idolatry?

3. In these stories God is mentioned, but he never acts. The main characters made their own decisions and carried out their plans without divine participation. Only once was his guidance sought. Otherwise, he is absent from the scenes. We theologically take for granted that God is always present, but life is most often lived with him in the background, seemingly absent. God has empowered us to make decisions concerning the course of our lives; sometimes major decisions and regularly minor ones. At times his Spirit may give specific instructions. These may range from which church to attend, to whether or not to accept a marriage proposal, to what is the next step in the career. We often ask God for guidance in decision making. However, the Spirit is free to respond or not. We cannot force him to tell us what to do. When he does not respond, we feel confused and maybe even angry. We seem to be on our own, deserted by God. Perhaps we should interpret these occasions as ones in which God trusts us to make the right decision ourselves; particularly when we have several options, each of which is morally and ethically right. When God allows us to make the choice, he is expressing confidence in our commitment to him and in our ability to choose wisely. He is sovereign enough to work his will whichever choice we make.

There is a delicate balance here between the sovereignty of God and human freedom. God's sovereignty is often equated with his power. He has created all things and rules all things. Yet in Christ Jesus we see that his sovereignty is governed by his love. He uses his power for the good of those he calls to be his people. When we choose to defy God, as Israel did repeatedly during the time of the judges, we open ourselves to destructive forces. Yet God is still sovereign and uses those experiences to call us back to obedience and life. Joseph's brothers sold him into slavery. When his father Jacob died, his brothers came seeking forgiveness, for as ruler he had the power to wreak a horrible revenge. Instead, he recognized that God as sovereign was able to use their evil deed to preserve the family (Gen 50:19-20).

We would like for God to tell us openly what in every situation we are to do. In Scripture God has given instructions that guide us in most of our decision making. We are to be honest in our dealings with others. Speak the truth in love. Be loyal to our marriage vows. There are times though when we are unsure, when no direct answer is given. The test of our faith comes in those times when God seems absent. Can we trust that as we make decisions, God will be in the decisions? Human freedom is a powerful privilege and responsibility. We must use it wisely to do the will of God even in difficult circumstances. It is when we are faithful in the difficult times that we exhibit what it means to be truly human; a redeemed people created in the image of God.

B. War Within Israel (19:1—21:25)

OVERVIEW

The last three chapters of the book of Judges begin with the murder of a woman and end with the kidnapping and forced marriage of six hundred women. In the book the treatment of women typifies the moral and spiritual health of the nation. At the beginning when Judah obeyed God and took possession of its inheritance, Achsah acted forcibly to persuade her father, Caleb, to give to her and her husband springs of water (1:14-15). Deborah was revered as a judge and as God's representative issued commands to Barak (4:4-6). As Israel turned repeatedly away from the path God had marked for them, Jephthah sacrificed his daughter (11:34-40), and the Levite's concubine was sexually abused until she died (19:25-26). Israel had fallen from honoring their women to treating them like chattel.

There are several references that tie this section to earlier parts of the book. In the previous story (chs 17—19) the Levite Jonathan moved from Bethlehem of Judah to the hill country of Ephraim. In ch 19 a Levite who lived in the hill country of Ephraim took a concubine from Bethlehem of Judah. The only time women are mentioned riding upon a donkey are when the concubine was placed on a donkey after she had been abused and when Achsah descended from a donkey to make her request to her father. In ch 1 when the tribes inquired of God which tribe should begin the conquest, God chose Judah. In ch 20 when the tribes inquired which tribe should lead the attack on Benjamin, again God chose Judah. The story of how Benjamin was nearly destroyed is part of the David-Saul polemic of the book. David was a descendant of the tribe of Judah, which led the battle, and Saul of the tribe of Benjamin. Also, the crime against the Levite's concubine was committed at Gibeah, which later became the city of Saul (1 Sam 11:4; 14:2; 22:6; 23:19; 26:1). The place of a terrible crime was the royal residence of Israel's first king who disobeyed God and thus lost his crown, his dynasty, and his life. The theme of keeping a foolish vow appears again. Earlier Jephthah had foolishly kept his vow and sacrificed his daughter. The people had vowed not to give any of their daughters in marriage to the men of Benjamin, but after the war lamented that one of the tribes would be lost if wives were not found for the six hundred surviving Benjamites. The men of the town Jabesh-gilead, which was situated in the area east of the Jordan River and part of the inheritance of Manasseh, had not joined in the fight. An army was sent to destroy all the inhabitants of the Israelite town, except for four hundred young women who were then given to the surviving Benjamites (21:1-12). Then the whole nation of Israel foolishly kept its vow and slaughtered a whole town. Later Saul saved the same town from destruction by the Ammonites (1 Sam 11:1-11).

1. The Levite and His Concubine (19:1-30)

BEHIND THE TEXT

Translations vary on the reading of v 2, ***his concubine committed fornication against him,*** following the MT, or ***his concubine became angry with him,*** following the LXX, Codex Alexandrinus (LXX^A). Codex Vaticanus (LXX^B) reads ***his concubine went away from him.*** The Latin Vulgate follows this reading. The Greek verb *poreuō* ("to go") is similar to the verb *porneuō* ("to fornicate") (Niditch 2008, 189). The confusion of the two words may have led to this latter reading.

Each of the textual traditions has had its followers in Jewish and Christian interpretations. (See Gunn 2005, 244-75, for a fuller discussion of the history of the interpretation of these chapters.) Those who followed the MT have suggested a couple of lines of interpretation. First, the woman was in some way displeased with the Levite and chose a lover and then left both to return to her father's house. Others proposed that being somehow displeased with her husband she returned to her father's house. Her act of fornication was not a sexual liaison but her leaving her husband (Niditch 2008, 191-92). Josephus, following LXX^A, explained that her anger was due to their constant quarreling, which disgusted her. Early Jewish sources criticized the husband's (supposed) harsh treatment of his wife, which was the reason for her running away (Gunn 2005, 244-45). The discussion to follow will follow the MT, which fits better the chapter's theme of sexual conflict.

The three main characters are the Levite, his wife/concubine, and the old man who invited them to stay in his home. The minor characters are the Levite's young servant, the woman's father, and the men who assaulted the woman. None are given a name. They move anonymously across the stage, play their parts, and depart. Only the Levite will be heard from in the next chapter, and then he falls silent. They are part of a larger drama that leads finally to war. While the characters are not named, several are given double titles or appellations (see 4:4 for the string of titles given to Deborah). Verse 1 reads, **And there was a man, a Levite . . . and he took to himself a wife, a concubine** (see also v 27). The father in vv 4 and 9 is called **his father-in-law, the father of the young girl.** Otherwise he is simply **the father of the young girl.** The man of Gibeah who invited them to his house is referred to as **an/the old man** (vv 16, 17, 20) except in v 22 where the men speak to **the old man, master of the house,** and v 23 where he is **the man, master of the house.** The giving of longer titles helps clarify who does what, except when v 25 reads, **And the man seized his concubine.** Commentators have been undecided as to which man is referred to, the Levite or the host. However, the host is always given the longer title "the old man" or "the master of the house." Only the Levite is ever referred to simply as "the man."

The setting of the story shifts from the home of the Levite in the hill country of Ephraim to Bethlehem to Gibeah and then back to the home of the Levite. Woven into the different settings is the theme of hospitality. The father joyously and elaborately entertained the Levite, urging him to lengthen his stay. In contrast to the warm welcome given in the Judean town of Bethlehem, no one in the Benjamite town of Gibeah extended to the travelers hospitality. Only an old man who originally was from the hills of Ephraim took them in. Then a lawless gang from Gibeah breached the rules of hospitality by threatening the Levite and abusing his concubine. Bracketing the theme of hospitality is that of sexuality. The story begins with the note that the woman committed fornication, either by taking a lover or deserting her husband and returning to the house of her father. At the end of the story she is sexually abused by the men of Gibeah. When their actions were made known to all the Israelites, there was intense reaction to the violent sexual abuse inflicted upon the woman.

There is a debate as to the location of Gibeah (*gibʿâ*, which means "hill"). Edward Robinson in 1841 identified Gibeah with modern Jaba, a hill located a little over 5 miles (9 km) northeast of Jerusalem, but later changed his mind and suggested that it was Tell el-Ful about 3 miles (5 km) north of Jerusalem. W. F. Albright's excavations (1922-23) at Tell el-Ful appeared to confirm Robinson's second identification. However, Paul Lapp's subsequent excavations there (1964) raised questions about identifying Gibeah with Tell el-Ful. J. M. Miller's literary analysis (1975) appears to confirm Robinson's earlier suggestion that Gibeah was located at Jaba (Arnold 1997, Gibeah, CD-ROM). Gibeah was later Saul's military fortress, if not also his home (1 Sam 10:26). Judges 19—21 indicates that Gibeah was a sizable town prior to Saul's reign. However, the excavations by both Lapp and Albright indicate that Tell el-Ful was not a major city in the twelfth to eleventh centuries. This has led some scholars to suggest that when the story of the Levite and his concubine was written down its location was given as Gibeah to discredit Saul and his family. Thus the story became part of the Saul/David polemic (McMurry 2007, 565-66).

At the beginning of v 30, the LXX inserts the following: ***And he commanded the men whom he sent saying, Thus you shall say to all the men of Israel, "Has there been such a thing as this from the days the Israelites went up from the land of Egypt unto this day?"*** The implication is that the Levite wanted the messengers to inflame the passions of the people with their question. The MT has rather the recipients of the dismembered parts of the woman speaking in exclamation about what has happened. The end of the verse in the MT is rather difficult, but the sense is clear. Both Boling (1975, 277) and Soggin (1981, 289) follow the LXX reading. Niditch (2008, 189) accepts the MT. The meaning of the verse is not materially changed whichever reading is accepted. The commentary below will follow the MT.

IN THE TEXT

■ **1-10** The story begins (v 1*a*) and ends (21:25*a*) with the declaration that ***in those days there was no king in Israel.*** Everything that happens in the account is under the condemnation that stable government was lacking and that the society was slipping into anarchy where ***each man did what was right in his own eyes*** (21:25*b*). Israel's pursuit of other gods had left them morally adrift. The worship of one God leads to the establishment of a single moral code that is derived from the character of God. As God is just, so his people must be just. The Ten Commandments require that God's people observe a high moral standard; not lying, stealing, committing adultery or murder. Polytheism has many gods with multiple reference points for determining moral behavior. The worship of Baal Peor included sexual immorality (Num 25:1-8). The Babylonian sun god Shamash, like the Sumerian Utu, was the guardian of justice. Babylonian fertility goddess Ishtar was less than moral. As the Israelites served the Canaanite gods, they became like the gods they worshipped.

The Levite (v 1b) **settled** (*gûr*, to sojourn, not an original or permanent resident; the same term used to describe the old man, v 16) in a remote part of the hill country of Ephraim, part of the central mountain region north of Jerusalem. His residence was in a remote part of the area and thus separate from that of Micah (17:1). He had taken a woman from Bethlehem of Judea as a concubine (*pîlegeš*, not a *zŏnă* [a whore or prostitute], such as Jephthah's mother, 11:1).

Who Was a Concubine?

The exact social position of a concubine is not known. It may have varied according to different cultures and different time periods. Evidently her position was somewhat lower than that of a wife. However, the relationship was recognized in society as a legal one. The mother of Abimelech, Gideon's son, was a *pîlegeš* (8:31). Abraham made a distinction between his son Isaac to whom he gave an inheritance and the sons of his concubines, probably Hagar and his third wife, Keturah, to whom he gave gifts (Gen 25:1-6). Bilhah, the handmaiden of Rachel, who was given to Jacob by Rachel, was a concubine (Gen 35:22). Her sons Dan and Naphtali, however, had equal status as the other sons of Jacob.

The young woman, possibly in her middle teens as she is later called a *na'ărâ* (vv 3, 4, 8), either had an affair with another man (v 2), or simply left her husband (see discussion above), and went to her father's house in Bethlehem. The Levite waited four months to go after her, allowing sufficient time to determine if she was pregnant (Schneider 2000, 253).

The Levite (v 3) decided to go after his wife and **to speak to her heart**; that is, to try and persuade her to return with him. The word "heart" in the Bible rarely refers to the emotions. The heart was viewed as the center of the person where the intellect and will combined to make decisions. He took with him a young fellow (*na'ar*) as his servant and two donkeys, one for himself and the other to carry provisions, and possibly for the woman to ride when they returned. The MT reads, **and she brought him to the house of her father** (LXX reads **and he came to the house of her fa-**

ther, which would be the expected reading). However, the MT reading indicates that the woman took the lead in presenting him to her father, possibly indicating her willingness to be reconciled to her husband. The father also probably hoped for reconciliation as he rejoiced to see him.

The following verses (vv 4-10) give an account of lavish hospitality. The passage functions as a contrast with the breach of hospitality that would occur at Gibeah (vv 22-26). For three days the father of the young girl and the husband ate and drank together. On the fourth day (v 5) the husband prepared to leave but the father persuaded him to eat before he left. The phrase is literally **sustain your heart with bread,** an idiom meaning that the person should take some food to sustain himself. Abraham made the same request to his three visitors (Gen 18:5; see also the same phrase in Ps 104:15). Generally only two meals were served each day, one in the morning and another in the late afternoon. The request of the father meant that the husband should stay until the afternoon meal. On the fifth day (v 8) the husband arose early and again the father persuaded him to stay until they ate. However, this time the Levite was determined to leave (vv 9-11). His father-in-law suggested that he stay the night and then rise early the next day and go not to his house but to his **tent.** The odd reference to his tent may have been a derogatory remark by the father-in-law indicating that it was time for the Levite to go. He could not ask him directly to leave as that would be a breach of hospitality. The Levite took the hint. His servant, his concubine, and his donkeys were prepared to leave. And so they left. Toward evening they came to Jerusalem, here called Jebus (Josh 18:28 and 1 Chr 11:4-5), after the Jebusites whom the Benjamites were unable to drive out (1:21). Jerusalem is about 5 miles (8 km) from Bethlehem, about an hour and a half walk. Verse 10 notes that the Levite had the two donkeys and his concubine with him. Placing this information at the end of the sentence gives it emphasis. He had what belonged to him, not just the donkeys but also the woman.

■ **11-21** The silence of the servant is broken only once (v 11), when he suggested to his master that they lodge in Jerusalem for the night. The master's response is ironic. He did not want to stay in a city of foreigners who were not of the house of Israel (v 12). So they pressed on to **Gibeah** where they hoped for safety, but would meet terror. Gibeah (see discussion above) has been identified with either Tell el-Ful, located 3 miles (5 km) north of Jerusalem on the road that ran to Ramah, or at modern Jaba, 5 miles (9 km) northeast of Jerusalem. **Ramah** (v 13) was located about 5 miles (7 km) north of Jerusalem, 2 km beyond Tell el-Ful on the same road from Jerusalem (Arnold 1997, Ramah, CD-ROM).

As the sun was setting (v 14) they entered Gibeah. The text emphasizes that the town was **Gibeah of Benjamin,** an Israelite town. Just inside the main gate of the town was an open area or square where business and court cases were often conducted (Ruth 4:1-12). Strangers could go to the square and wait to be invited into the home of a resident (Gen 19:1-3). Being generous and extending hospitality to strangers and sojourners was a duty of the Israelites. The law (Exod 22:21; 23:9; Lev 19:33-34; Deut 16:14; 26:12) required them to take care of those who were in need, especially the Levite who was not given an allotment as an inheritance (Olson 1998, 876). Yet *no man took them into his house to lodge,* a serious breach of hospitality.

An old man (no name ever given) entered the town after working in the fields (v 16). The text identifies him as old, as from the hill country of Ephraim, as a sojourner in Gibeah. The verse ends by noting that the people of the town were Benjamites. This tribal identification is important in the story. The Benjamites were not behaving in the way Israelites were required by the Law of the covenant with God. When the old man saw the Levite (v 17) he asked, *Where are you going and where do you come from?* The Levite responded (v 18) that his home was in the far region of the hill country of Ephraim and that he was traveling from Bethlehem of Judah to his home. Then he acknowledged his problem; no one had shown him hospitality by inviting him into his home. The Levite continued (v 19) by noting that he had fodder for the donkeys and enough food and wine for the three of them. Thus they would not be a burden on a host. The old man responded by offering hospitality to them. First, he pronounced a blessing, *Peace be unto you* (v 20). Then he assured them that he would care for their needs and finally urged them not to spend the night in the square. He was a gracious host (v 21), taking them into his house and feeding the donkeys. Traveling with sandals for shoes, or even barefooted, meant that the feet were dirty and needed to be washed. Washing the feet both refreshed and relaxed them. Then they ate and drank together. The hospitality given by the old man was complete.

■ **22-26** While they were enjoying themselves, literally *while they were doing their hearts good* (v 22), their meal was interrupted. The house was surrounded by men who then pounded on the door. The men are given a double identification, *men of the city* and *men who were sons of Belial* (v 22). The term "Belial" (*bĕlīyaʿal*) means "worthless" or "wicked." In the OT it describes evil, idolatrous, or immoral persons who opposed God and violated the covenant. The term later became a synonym for Satan, such as in 2 Cor 6:15, its only occurrence in the NT (Koester 2006, 421). They demanded that ***the man, the master of the house, the old one*** deliver the Levite to them that they might ***know him;*** that is, homosexually assault him (v 22). ***The man, master of the house went out*** to them (v 23) to plead that they not commit this evil (*raʿaʿ*). He addressed them as ***my brothers,*** emphasizing their relationship. To allow them to violate the Levite would be to breach his duties as host. He had extended hospitality and thus must protect his guest. The offense then would be against both the old man who would fail in his duty as host and the Levite who would be violated. He called their proposed action both evil and disgraceful (*nĕbālâ*).

In order to protect the Levite (v 24) the old man offered to the men the concubine of the Levite and his unmarried daughter (*bĕtûlâ*, a young woman, possibly married, but not in this case as she was still living in her father's house. The woman who was a virgin would be designated as one who had never known a man. See Gen 19:8 where Lot so described his daughters [private communication from Charles Isbell]). He offered to let the men humble (*ʿānâ*, "to humble or afflict," BDB, 776) them; that is, to rape them. They could do what was ***good in their eyes*** (v 24). To do what was right or good in one's own eyes was to act out of self-centered motives, unconcerned with what God required (14:3; 17:6; 21:25). The men would not listen to the old man (v 25), but wanted the Levite. The next phrase is ambiguous. ***The man seized his concubine and brought her outside to them*** (v 25). Was the man the Levite or the old man? Interpreters have differed. However, since the host is always identified by a double title, ***the man*** was probably the Levite who cast out his own concubine. One can only imagine the terror the young woman must have experienced. Her father is referred to as the father of the young woman (*naʿărâ* in v 4). She was probably no more than in her middle teens. The men not only raped her but also abused her all that night until the sun was about to come up the next morning. She made her way back to the house of the old man (v 26) where her master/lord (*ʾādôn*), a power term, not the standard "her husband," stayed safely until light, and collapsed on the threshold of the door.

The narrative here is similar to the account of Lot at Sodom (Gen 19:1-11). Lot, not a permanent resident of Sodom but a sojourner (*gûr*), offered hospitality to the two angels. They entered his house and ate. Men, in this case all the men of the city, came to the door of Lot's house demanding that Lot let them have the men/angels that they might know them; that is, homosexually assault them. Lot offered instead his two virgin daughters, but the men rejected the offer and nearly broke down his door in the attempt to get to the visitors. In this incident the angels protected the daughters, but the concubine had no heavenly protectors. The parallels are numerous as the original audience would have recognized. What had nearly happened to Lot and his guests had taken place in Israel itself.

■ **27-30** The next morning (v 27) the concubine's master opened the door to go on his way, only to find the woman there at the entrance with her hand on the threshold. There is no indication in the story that the Levite was concerned about the fate of the woman. Perhaps he had given her up as dead with nothing he could do to help her. Upon finding her at the entrance (v 28), he issued the commands, **Get up and let us go**. The LXX at this point in the text supplies, **And she did not answer him, but was dead.** Schneider correctly notes that "this is another case where the LXX may be correcting a passage that was too difficult for its readers to bear" (2000, 264). There is no indication that he felt any compassion for her. When she did not get up, he placed her on a donkey and went to his place, or home. The story is ambiguous again. Was she dead or only passed out? The next verse (v 29) describes how **he went into his house, took a knife, seized his concubine, and dismembered** (*nātaḥ*, a term used for dismembering sacrificial animals, Lev 8:20) **her at the joints of the bones.** Was she dead when the Levite found her in the morning? Did she die on the journey home? Did the Levite kill her when he dismembered her body? The ambiguity of the story leaves the reader to wonder about the motives of the Levite. Why did he go after the concubine after she had left him? Was it because his pride was offended, or did he have a real love for her? He certainly cast her out to the mob quickly enough to save himself. Afterward, he failed to display any concern for her safety or well-being. Did he see a kind of perverse retribution in what happened to her? She had committed fornication in seeking a sexual liaison outside of their relationship. Did he think it fitting retribution that she should be sexually exploited and abused? In every aspect of the story, the woman was reduced to a piece of property without her own dignity or value. Finally, her twelve body parts were then sent throughout the territory of Israel. Saul later acted in a similar manner as the Levite. Only he sent the dismembered parts of his oxen to the territory of Israel. His purpose was to rally the troops from the tribes to lift the siege of Jabesh-gilead (1 Sam 11:1-8). The Levite's purpose was to rally Israel to avenge his honor.

When all saw the body parts (v 30) they reacted in amazement. Rhetorically they asked if anything like this had been seen in Israel since the days when they left Egypt. What was it they were amazed at; the dismembered body or the action of the men of Gibeah? Again the story omits the details and encourages the reader to think about what happened. The Israelites were to consider it, to take counsel as to what they should do, and to declare their decision.

FROM THE TEXT

1. The woman forms a central focus for the story. She committed fornication, left her husband, and returned to her father's house. The Levite followed her seeking reconciliation. It was she who was given to the men. It was her body that was sent to the tribes. Never is she named. She like all the other characters in the drama remains anonymous. There is no indication that she had a part in the decisions concerning returning with the Levite or where to spend the night. She did have the ability to act on her own by returning to her father's house. The way women were treated forms one barometer of the spiritual health of Israel. At the end of the book Israelite society was deteriorating with everyone doing what he or she thought was right (21:25). The horrors inflicted upon the woman were indications of societal decay. This was not God's intention for humanity. Genesis 1:27 declares that both men and women were created in the image of God. While sin disrupts God's original intention for the relationship between men and women (Gen 3:16), that image of God was never lost. Redemption in Christ Jesus has provided restoration and reconciliation for all, both men and women (John 1:12; Gal 3:28). There are physical and functional differences between men and women that a society should take into account. However, societies that build structures that inhibit its citizens, male or female, from reaching their full God-given potential are to that extent unjust. The church in particular should provide support through its educational and institutional structures to enable men and women to respond fully to the calling of God on their lives. Societies do differ, and how the church works within them to preach the gospel has to be tailored to each individually. There is no master plan how every society should be structured. Healthy societies, however, will incorporate the principles of justice (for God is just), fairness (for God gives mercy to all), and equality of opportunity (for God calls each of us to be his children) for all their citizens.

2. Hospitality played a significant role in biblical cultures, not only in the OT, but also in the NT (Heb 13:2; 1 Pet 4:9). Travel was dangerous, and public places for rest were few at best. When traveling in the ANE a person or small group camping in the open were potential targets of thieves. People planned to stay with relatives or friends when possible. Travelers often had to depend upon the hospitality of strangers to travel safely. The Levite counted on the hospitality of the Benjamites in the town of Gibeah.

Modern travel is much different from ancient times. In developed countries travel is safe, and there are hotels in abundance. We do not feel the need to impose ourselves on others. In undeveloped countries, hospitality is still a feature of the societies. Travelers must rely on the generosity of strangers to provide for them safe accommodations.

Paul encouraged Christians to practice hospitality (Rom 12:13) and listed it as a trait of leaders in the church (1 Tim 3:2; Titus 1:8). While the same need for hospitality may not exist today as it did in biblical times, there are still opportunities for Christians to demonstrate it. Some families open their homes to foster children in order to provide a safe and loving environment for those who lack parents or who have for some reason been separated from them. Others entertain strangers who have special needs. One home provided shelter to a couple who were visiting a relative who was in prison. Giving shelter to those in need fulfills the teachings of Jesus, to love one another and to treat others as we would want others to treat us.

3. How corrupt can humanity become? The text gives a multifaceted portrayal of how sin corrupts what God has created. The woman was unfaithful to her husband. The Levite lacked courage and compassion. He sacrificed the woman to protect himself. He stayed in the house, safe from harm, but did nothing to aid the woman. The next day he showed no compassion, but upon finding her at the door, ordered her to get up and continue the journey. The town bullies perverted normal sexuality by wanting first to homosexually assault the Levite and then by raping and sexually abusing the woman. When people reject the laws of God in order to indulge their own desires, they become the slaves of sin (Rom 6:15-16). We do not know where sin will finally lead us, to what level of degradation we will fall. The Bible does not color over the hideousness of sin and the depths of depravity individuals and societies can plunge to. It offers an alternative path that includes repentance, forgiveness, and reconciliation with God and one another. By means of the sacrifice of Christ Jesus, we have access to a new lifestyle, living in conformity to the commands of God and the teachings of Jesus; a lifestyle empowered by the Spirit.

2. War Between the Tribes (20:1-48)

BEHIND THE TEXT

The chapter begins with all the tribes of Israel, with the exception of Benjamin, gathered at Mizpah. There the Levite gave his account of what happened at Gibeah. With the conclusion of his speech, he drops out of the narrative. The actors become the tribes themselves. The antagonists were Israel and Benjamin. Judah was chosen by God to take the lead in the battle. This forms a frame for the entire book, for in 1:2 Judah was chosen to take the lead in the conquest. The action moves from the convocation at Mizpah to the shrine at Bethel; back and forth between Bethel and Gibeah where the battles were fought; to the rock of Rimmon; and finally to the cities of Benjamin. The Israelite strategy for the first two battles was to confront Benjamin in a frontal assault. The last battle resembled Joshua's attack on Ai (Josh 8:3-23) with the use of troops waiting in ambush until the battle had drawn the defenders away from the city. At the end of the battle the scene shifts to the rock of Rimmon where six hundred of the Benjamites had taken refuge. All of the action took place in the territory of the tribe of Benjamin located in the central hill country just north of Jerusalem. The actors were the corporate tribes. Other than the Levite and Phinehas the priest, no other individual is mentioned. The chapter closes with the ominous note that after the battle, the Israelites carried out the ban of holy war in that they destroyed all the people and animals of the cities. The war of conquest had been applied to a tribe of Israel.

One of the continuing themes of the book is the search for leadership. When a crisis arose, a leader was called by God to rally the tribes and bring deliverance. In this narrative there is no leader. The tribes acted independently. They inquired of God as to which tribe should lead in the war against Benjamin but did not inquire if they should go to war. They assumed the rightness of their cause and applied God's holy war against Benjamin, to destroy the entire tribe, without divine authorization. Although the Israelites saw their cause as just, they acted independently of God. Only after two defeats did they inquire whether or not they should continue the war or declare peace. Within the context of the entire book, the intertribal war that nearly destroys an entire tribe was the result of the continuing spiritual decay of the nation. They were not faithful to worship Yahweh alone, but worshiped the gods of the other nations. They did not follow the guidance established in the law of the covenant, but pursued their own desires, doing what was right in their own eyes. At the end they turn against one of their own tribes and nearly eliminate it.

The numbers given for the combatants and those slain present a problem from a historical perspective. For the time period, they seem to be greatly inflated. The numbers are more in line with the number of troops mustered for battle during the seventh century when the Assyrian empire was ruling the ANE (see the discussion on numbers in the Introduction). Western culture since the Enlightenment (eighteenth century) has read numbers from a scientific and mathematical perspective. A number represents an actual counting. While the ANE could also use numbers in that way, particularly in business, numbers were also used to signify other concepts. In this passage the numbers have a theological function. The Israelites mustered four hundred thousand and the Benjamites twenty-six thousand, plus those from Gibeah (20:15-17). The odds were greatly in favor of the Israelites who should have overwhelmed Benjamin. The Israelites assumed that their cause was just and did not inquire of God whether or not they should go to war. Their initial strategy was to mount a frontal assault against the Benjamites. It was a disaster. In the first battle the Israelites lost twenty-two thousand and in the second eighteen thousand, however no losses for Benjamin were recorded; a total of forty thousand, ten percent of Israel's troops, to Benjamin's zero. Only during the third battle did Benjamin suffer losses, all but six hundred. In contrast to the high numbers given for the muster of troops and the losses, in the third battle the number of Israelites killed in the early part of the conflict were only thirty (20:31, 39), hardly a significant number of casualties when the previous numbers were in the tens of thousands. This lower number of casualties indicates that the numbers of troops historically engaged in the conflict were much lower. The oral stories passed down to the editors who were compiling the book in the late seventh century probably did not include the actual numbers of combatants, with the exception of the thirty lost in the final battle. The editors used the numbers theologically to state that superiority in numbers was not what mattered, but the will of God. Only after the Israelites approached God asking whether or not the war should continue did he give them victory.

Both Soggin and Matthews (2004, 192) reverse the order of vv 22 and 23. Soggin simply notes, "The commentaries are agreed in inverting the order of the two verses" (1981, 293). The order in the MT is odd. After the defeat of the Israelite forces of the first day, v 22 states that they went to battle again the second day. Verse 23 then describes how the defeated army of Israel wept before Yahweh the evening of the first day. Although not necessary, reversing the order makes sense. The NRSV also reverses the order, but the NIV does not.

Why did the Benjamites protect the guilty men of Gibeah? Why did they not surrender them for judgment? Few commentaries take into consideration the concept of tribal solidarity. In a tribal society, members protect each other. To attack one member of a tribe is to risk retaliation from any member of the tribe. Blood feuds between tribes have resulted in numerous deaths. Benjamin protected its own people even though they were guilty of a heinous crime. The other tribes' reaction illustrated the concept of corporate personality. Families, clans, or tribes were not thought of as groups of individuals, but as a single identity. The individual reflected the characteristics of the group. A child born into an Amorite family carried "Amoriteness" from birth. Thus a war to exterminate the Amorites would have been carried out on all, even the newborn. When Benjamin protected the guilty, it demonstrated that the whole tribe was marked by the characteristics of the few. And so judgment passed to the whole tribe, not just the few (Robinson 1935). Even today these types of reactions, both community solidarity and corporate personality, can be found in tribal communities. If a member of a family transgresses social norms, the family is often reluctant to give the member up to "outsiders" for punishment. If it does not itself punish the person, the entire family may not only be shunned socially but also be economically isolated so that no one will do business with them. Such social considerations do not justify the actions of the men of Gibeah, nor the refusal of the Benjamites to bring them to justice, nor the determination of the Israelites to go to war against them. They do, however, help explain why the tribes acted as they did.

IN THE TEXT

■ **1-11** Two qualities are stressed in v 1, unity and completeness. All Israel, *from Dan to Beersheba,* the traditional boundaries of Israel, plus those tribes from the Transjordan region of **Gilead** came together at **Mizpah** in Benjamin. The tribes in Gilead included Reuben and Gad (Josh 13:15-28). Half of the tribe of Manasseh was located in Bashan, north of Gilead (Josh 13:29-31). The term "Gilead" may stand for the whole area and all the tribes, the part signifying the whole. Mizpah possessed an ancient shrine dedicated to Yahweh. Samuel held a convocation there to choose a king for Israel (1 Sam 10:17). Little is mentioned of it during the period of the monarchy, but it was still regarded as a holy place after the destruction of Jerusalem in 586 B.C. (Jer 41:5) (Arnold 1997, Mizpah, CD-ROM). The tribes assembled together as a congregation unified in purpose, literally, *as one man* (v 1). **The chiefs** (*pinnâ*, means "corner" or "support"; it occurs with the meaning of "a leader" only here, 1 Sam 14:42, Isa 19:13, and Zech 10:14 [BDB, 819]) *of all the people of all the tribes took leadership in the assembly of the people of God* (v 2). They viewed themselves as a worshipping community assembled before God at the shrine at Mizpah. The congregation itself consisted of four hundred thousand foot soldiers who used the sword, or infantry. There was no chariot force or archers. The large number represents an overwhelming force. The text notes (v 3) parenthetically that Benjamin was aware of the convocation at

Mizpah but had no representatives there. The people then asked for an explanation of how ***this evil*** happened, but it is not clear whether they meant the rape and death or the dismemberment of the woman.

The Levite responded (v 4) to their question. Like Deborah (4:4), his identification is specific, listing his tribe and relationship: ***the man, the Levite, the husband of the woman who was murdered.*** The answer is brief and covers most of the details, but there are several changes compared to what the reader already knows. He identified Gibeah of Benjamin as the place where he and his concubine went to lodge. He then stated (v 5) that it was the ***rulers*** (*baʿălê*) ***of Gibeah,*** not the "sons of Belial" (19:22) or worthless men who surrounded the house. By accusing the leaders of the town, he made all of Gibeah responsible for the evil, not just a few lawless men. This became important later in the story when Israel demanded that the men responsible for the outrage be held accountable. The Benjamites, however, acting in tribal solidarity with the people of Gibeah, refused. Next he charged that the leaders intended to kill him, not homosexually rape him. In his indictment that they raped and killed his concubine, he omitted the fact that he was the one who threw her out to them. His cowardly act was omitted. It was only after the woman was dead, according to the Levite's story (v 6), that he dismembered her and sent her body parts to ***all the territory of the inheritance of Israel.*** By referring to ***the inheritance of Israel*** the Levite was invoking the ancient traditions of Israel. The land was given to them by God. ***The wicked and disgraceful*** (*nĕbālâ*, same term as in 19:23 and 20:10) ***act they committed in Israel*** was a violation of God's law (v 6). It was the responsibility of Israel to make an inquiry and to punish those guilty of breaking the covenant (Deut 13:12-18) (Niditch 2008, 202). If they did not act, then God could hold them responsible as well as Benjamin. He ended his speech (v 7) by calling on them to make a decision about what to do.

The immediate response (v 8) was a vow by all that they would not return home until the matter was dealt with. The text stresses the unity of the decision; ***all the people as one man rose up and said.*** They determined to hold Gibeah responsible. Two actions were decided upon. First (v 9), they would determine by lot who would lead in war against Gibeah. Second (v 10), they would apportion one in ten to supply food for the troops. The tribes were preparing to punish the inhabitants of Gibeah for their ***disgraceful action*** (*nĕbālâ*, 19:23 and 20:6). The section ends (v 11) with the statement that the men gathered against Gibeah, ***united as one man.*** The function of the sentence is to again emphasize the unity of Israel. Before the troops moved to Gibeah, they decided first to demand that Benjamin give up those responsible for judgment, and then to go up to Bethel to inquire of God.

■ **12-18** Although Deut 13:12-18 deals specifically with a case of idolatry, the actions taken by the Israelites were consistent with its requirements. First (v 12), they sent men to the tribe of Benjamin to inquire about what had actually happened. Second (v 13), they requested that the men responsible be handed over for punishment, in this case death. Refusal meant that all would be placed under the ban of condemnation and be totally destroyed. The Israelites requested that **the men, the sons of Belial** (*bĕlîyaʿal*, 19:22), not the rulers (*baʿălê*, v 5) of Gibeah, be surrendered. The writer has the Israelites requiring the persons actually responsible for the evil actions, not those whom the Levite blamed. By executing the men they would **purge** (*bāʿar*, burn out, consume; see Deut 13:5 [Heb, v 6]) **the evil from Israel.** The Benjamites, however, **refused to listen to the voice of their brothers, the Israelites** (v 13). In v 28 the Israelites will again refer to the Benjamites as "our bothers." Benjamin was committed to tribal solidarity, defending their own against outside aggressors. By handing over those responsible, or punishing the men themselves, they would have on the one hand betrayed their own kinsmen, but on the other hand remained faithful to the covenant with God. This was a test of their loyalty. To whom did their primary loyalty belong, the family or God? The history of Israel as traced in the book of Judges demonstrates that loyalty to God as evidenced in keeping the covenant, especially the command to worship Yahweh only, was not Israel's primary value.

The Benjamites then (v 14) gathered their warriors from their cities, mustering (v 15) twenty-six thousand foot soldiers (**men who draw the sword**), plus seven hundred choice young men (*bāḥûr*) from Gibeah. Ironically the worthless men, the sons of Belial of Gibeah, committed the crime, but the best of the city were called upon to defend them. Out of the total number of warriors (v 16) there were seven hundred choice young men **who were restricted in their right hand** (see the discussion on Ehud, 3:15, where the same phrase occurs). The phrase indicates either that they were left-handed or more probably ambidextrous. They were not regular foot soldiers, ones who drew the sword, but soldiers who used the sling with great accuracy. They did not **miss** (*ḥāṭāʾ*, the word often translates as "to sin," but used here in its original meaning of "to miss"). David used the sling to kill Goliath (1 Sam 17:48-49). The Assyrians had units composed of those who used a sling. It was a deadly weapon that could reach out a distance to kill an opponent. Israel mustered (v 17) four hundred thousand battle hardened men, an overwhelming force. The battle would not be won by the size of the army, however, but by the will of God. The Israelites first went to the shrine at Bethel, about 3 miles (5 km) northeast, to inquire of God which tribe should lead in battle. Bethel was an ancient holy site associated with both Abraham (Gen 12:8) and Jacob (Gen 28:10-22). Yahweh chose Judah to lead the battle. This forms a frame for the book as a whole. The book begins with Judah taking the lead in the conquest (1:1-2) and at the end of the book in the war against Benjamin.

■ **19-28** The first two battles were disasters for Israel. The Israelites arrayed themselves in a battle line before Gibeah (v 20), evidently trusting in their superior numbers for victory. Benjamin, however, struck down (v 21) twenty-two thousand of them. That evening (v 23, see discussion above about the order of vv 22-23) they lamented before Yahweh and inquired if they should go to battle again with Benjamin, their brother. Yahweh gave them permission but did not promise victory. For a second day (vv 22, 24) the Israelites attempted a frontal assault and were defeated, losing eighteen thousand this time (v 25). In the two battles, Israel lost ten percent of its force while Benjamin did not sustain any losses.

After the second defeat, all the Israelite troops and all the people (v 26), including probably those family members who had accompanied the soldiers, returned to Bethel. The rest of the day was spent in lamenting and fasting before the sanctuary of Yahweh. Evidently the battles began early in the morning and the adversaries broke off the conflict by afternoon, if not before. In the evening they offered up whole burnt or holocaust offerings in which the entire animal was consumed and peace offerings in which part of the animal was consumed and then the rest eaten by the worshippers. All of this took place at or in front of the sanctuary at Bethel. The writer emphasized the sanctity of Bethel by noting that at this time the ark of the covenant was there (vv 27-28) and the high priest Phinehas was serving before it.

The Ark of the Covenant

The ark symbolized the presence of Yahweh during the time of Israel's sojourn in the wilderness. It was Israel's most holy ritual object, later to be brought to Jerusalem by David and placed in the temple built there by Solomon. What happened to it later is unknown. Three suggestions carry the most weight. All relate to the conquest of the city and its subsequent burning by Nebuchadnezzar in 586 B.C. (1) The ark was buried by the priests under the temple mount to protect it. (2) Because the ark was covered in gold, the soldiers looted it and thus destroyed it. (3) It was taken as a prize of war to Babylon and never returned.

Phinehas was a contemporary of Joshua (Exod 6:25; Num 25:7). This indicates that the war with Benjamin took place earlier during the time of the judges and that the account is not in a strict historical sequence. The narrative's function is to illustrate the spiritual and social disintegration Israel experienced due to their refusal to obey God.

After offering the sacrifices, the Israelites again inquired of Yahweh if they should go out to battle Benjamin their brother or end the war. They were soundly defeated twice and realized that if Yahweh did not give them the victory, then their efforts, regardless of their overwhelming numerical superiority, were fruitless. How Yahweh was expected to communicate to them is unknown to us, possibly by means of a prophet or a priest. The answer they received was the command to go up against Benjamin again, coupled with the promise that he would give them into their hand.

■ **29-36a** This is the first of two accounts of the final battle. Soggin suggests that the second account, vv 36b-45, is from another source that supplements the first (1981, 293-94). Matthews correctly notes that "the editor is in fact employing a literary technique known as resumptive repetition to explain the apparent duplications of phrases." The narrative incorporates the two perspectives to give a complete view of the events. In the process the scene shifts from one perspective to the next necessitating some "duplication of phrases" so that the reader is able to follow the action (2004, 197).

The description of the battle begins with an editorial note (v 29) that the Israelites set some of the soldiers in an ambush around Gibeah. This duplicates Joshua's tactics at the second battle of Ai (Josh 8:2-8). The troops of Israel (v 30) took the field again as they had the two previous days.

Now begins the most detailed account of any battle recorded in the book. The Benjamites came out of the city of Gibeah (v 31) and engaged the Israelites in the fields along the roads that led to Bethel and Gibeah. Thirty of the Israelites were killed. The Benjamites assumed (v 32) when the Israelites withdrew that they were about to achieve another victory. However, their withdrawal was a tactical move to draw the Benjamites away from the city. The loss of only thirty soldiers reflects a more accurate accounting of casualties than the higher numbers given for the losses of the first two days (see the discussion above). The Israelites withdrew (v 33) to a site called **Baal-tamar** (location unknown, but obviously close to Gibeah) and reformed their lines. As the Benjamites pursued them, the city of Gibeah was left with only a token force to defend it. At this point those who were deployed in the ambush broke forth from their hiding place in **Maareh-geba**. The term may be a place name, the location of which is unknown. It has also been translated as **west of Gibeah,** a "place west of Geba" (Boling 1975, 282), "in the plain of Geba" (alternate translation, NSRV), "in the vicinity of Geba" (Soggin 1981, 296). Geba was located a short distance north of Gibeah. The Israelite force (v 34) engaged in a fierce fight with the remaining defenders. The main body of the Benjamite troops, however, were drawn away and were unaware that disaster was about to befall them.

The tide of battle turned (v 35) when **Yahweh struck down the Benjaminites in the presence of the Israelites.** The instrument of battle was the army of Israel, but the writer notes theologically that the Divine Warrior actually achieved the victory. Twenty-five thousand, one hundred Benjamites were slain. This account ends (v 36a) with the sad note that the Benjamites realized that this time they were defeated.

■ **36b-48** The second account of the battle gives more details about the ambush and the taking of the city of Gibeah. The Israelites withdrew from the city (v 36b) to draw off its defenders. The text (v 37) conveys a sense of urgency. ***The men who laid in ambush hurried and rushed at the city.*** Once they deployed inside it, they slaughtered the residents inside, literally, ***smote the entire city with the edge of the sword.*** The agreed on signal between the main battle units and those who had lain in ambush (v 38) was that when they were successful in taking the city, they would set fire to it. The column of smoke from the fire would be seen from a distance. Meanwhile, while the Israelites were retreating, the Benjamites killed thirty of them (v 39). The initial reaction of the Benjamites was that once again they were going to be victorious. This verse repeats much of vv 31-32.

The Benjamite troops also saw the column of smoke rising from the city (v 40). Mounce notes, "In ancient times the smoke of a burning city signaled its collapse." Once the flames began racing through the city, nothing would stop them until the city lay in smoldering ruins (1997, 329). When the Israelite (v 41) troops saw the smoke, they turned and held their ground. The Benjamites were terrified, for they knew they were facing defeat and utter destruction. The Benjamites then fled (v 42) on the road to the wilderness, which would be to the east toward the Jordan River valley. However, they could not escape the battle as the Israelites pursued them. It is not certain who also joined the pursuit, those in Gibeah to the west or possibly the reserve units that waited in a nearby town. They plunged into the midst of the fleeing soldiers, slaughtering them.

The battle is described in broad terms, not with precise details. Verse 43 begins by stating that ***the Benjaminites were encircled,*** and then notes that ***they were pursued from Nohah*** (an unknown location close to Gibeah); ***they were trodden down until to the east*** (literally, "from the rising of the sun") *of Gibeah.* Evidently at first they were surrounded and although they were able to break through the lines they could not disengage from the fighting. The losses (v 44) were extreme: **eighteen thousand, all these were valiant men.** Some (v 45) were able to break out and flee to the rock at Rimmon, but on the way another five thousand **were struck down** (*ʿālal*, "to deal with something a second time," "to deal harshly" [KBL 1985, 708]; another form of the word is used to describe how the men mistreated the Levite's concubine). They were pursued to **Gidom** (location unknown) where another two thousand were killed. A total (v 46) of those killed is given again (see v 35), twenty-five thousand. An epitaph of sorrow and honor describes the fallen, **all these were valiant men.** A remnant of six hundred (v 47) Benjamites took refuge at Rimmon for four months. The area east of Gibeah, which descends sharply to the Jordan River valley, has a number of rocky outcroppings and caves to which refugees might flee. The Israelites halted their pursuit of the refugees (v 48) and returned to the city; that is, Gibeah. All the remaining inhabitants plus its livestock were slaughtered. The people and cattle of the other cities of Benjamin were also killed and the cities burned. The war of destruction meant for the inhabitants of the land (Deut 7:1-2) was inflicted on Benjamin.

FROM THE TEXT

1. Throughout the book of Judges the tribes have had to fight for their existence. It seems that the Israelites were continually at war with the indigenous peoples or those who invaded their land. The ethical and moral questions that war presents to a Christian are some of the most difficult to sort through. What compounds the problem from a biblical perspective is that the conquest of the land by means of exterminating the indigenous people was ordered by God. The starting point of discussion concerning these issues must be the realization that there are no "good" wars. All wars are evil. The destruction of lives and property is inherently evil. The broader question arises, are there worse evils than war itself? Some Christians give a negative answer and take the position that a Christian should never be involved, directly or indirectly, in the killing of others. Other Christians recognize that there are evils more terrible than war itself, such as the systematic extermination of a people as happened in the last century, or the enslavement of a people that has been the history of humanity for thousands of years.

This passage was used by Joseph Fletcher, a close colleague of John Wesley, to denounce the American Revolution. He depicted those who participated in dumping the tea into Boston's harbor as "the sons of Belial." Those who rallied to their defense instead of giving the men over to authorities for justice were acting like the Benjamites. He approved of the royal proclamation calling for a fast, beseeching God to deliver the loyal citizens of the colonies, many who "have been deceived by the plausible and lying speeches of some of their leaders" or seized by "the epidemical fever of wild patriotism." Fletcher hoped that the colonists would repent of the war and cease the conflict, which he considered high treason. Evidently, he considered England's actions justified. (Quotations and materials taken from Gunn 2005, 263-64.)

In the OT the people of God were identified with a specific political entity, Israel. Its leadership was charged by God not only with religious duties but with maintaining civil and criminal justice as well as the protection of the people as a whole. War was often forced upon the state when others invaded the land. With the coming of the day of Pentecost (Acts 2) the church was no longer made up of an exclusive ethnic group, but included people from around the world; peoples from different ethnic groups and different political states. Ideally the church transcends national boundaries and should not be too closely identified with a specific government. Pragmatically, the church functions within specific political and cultural contexts. The members have loyalties to both God and their nation. It is easy for idealists to proclaim an absolute standard of no violence. It must also be acknowledged that unfortunately some who advocate pacifism have unjustly suffered personal hardships and social discrimination for their beliefs. However, it is more difficult to face the pragmatic questions that arise due to human avarice, greed, and lust for power. Communities maintain police forces to prevent crime. They are called upon to use violence when necessary to protect others. Armies are an extension of the police powers of a state. They protect the citizens from external threats of violence. What should be the Christian response when evil is perpetrated by nations? What should we do when our own nation is attacked? Are we our brother's keeper in a larger sense when we see other peoples being enslaved or exterminated? If we give up the use of violence, how can we then protect the oppressed?

2. Christians rejoice in the fact that God has brought redemption to us through the sacrifice of Christ. We have grown accustomed to thinking of God working in the areas of the spiritual and the individual. We become uncomfortable with the thought that he might be involved in the messy issues of political existence. Is God sovereign over all of humanity? Is he involved in the wars, famines, plagues, and natural disasters that make

up so much of human existence? Victory was given to the Israelites by God only after they dared to engage the question of whether or not they should be fighting their kinsmen. The battle was won only when God himself fought against Benjamin (v 35).

Is God involved in our battles today? In December 1944, during the Battle of the Bulge, the chaplain of Third Army was briefing the commander, General G. S. Patton Jr., on the spiritual status of the troops when Patton asked him if the soldiers were praying. The chaplain responded that they prayed in services. Patton repeated that he wanted to know if they were praying. He continued by saying that in a war there is the preparation for battle that included training and planning. But when the battle began, there was always an intangible that cannot be calculated. "Some call it luck," he said, "I call it God." The chaplain returned to his quarters and wrote out his famous "weather prayer." It was printed on one side of a 3 x 5 card, with the other side containing Patton's Christmas greetings to his troops. With Patton's permission, copies of the card were distributed to all the troops in Third Army. A couple of days later the weather moderated, aircraft were able to resupply the troops, and the siege of Bastogne was lifted.

Responses to our prayers are not always that quick in coming. Germany suffered twelve years under the rule of Hitler. Other dictators such as Stalin, Mao, and Saddam Hussein continued in power for many years, inflicting unspeakable cruelty on their own people. The Christian believes that the universe is not just a vast, cold, and empty existence. Beyond all the creation is a Creator who brings all peoples into judgment; there is a moral fabric to the universe and ultimately good will be victorious over evil. That victory, however, is often gained by God using the military forces of nations.

3. Wives for the Men of Benjamin (21:1-25)

BEHIND THE TEXT

This section is framed by the statements that there was no king in Israel at this time (19:1 and 21:25). The problem of leadership has been a continuing theme in the book. Waiting upon a charismatic leader to come forth to lead the tribes had proven to be an inadequate instrument to complete the conquest of the land and to maintain the covenant commitments to God. In this last chapter the congregation as a whole, led by the elders (v 16), takes action. No one individual speaks or acts. No savior/judge is raised up by God. The elders do not inquire of God what they should do. Plans are devised and carried out independently of God.

The problem faced belatedly by the congregation was the threatened extermination of the tribe of Benjamin. Their hasty action of going to war eliminated all but six hundred men. In their indignation over the death of the concubine and Benjamin's refusal to hand over the guilty, the congregation as a whole took two oaths; one that any who did not join in the battle should be put to death, and the other that none of the men would give their daughters to the men of Benjamin as wives. The problem of taking rash and foolish vows recalls the foolish vow of Jephthah (11:29-40). They thought that God demanded strict obedience, regardless of the situation. While the people wept before God over the situation, there was no consideration that they could repent of the vows and that God would graciously release them. Their poorly informed concept of God precluded seeking his forgiveness as a means of rectifying the situation. Instead they sought other ways of providing Benjamin with wives. First, they went to war again and destroyed an Israelite town, preserving only four hundred young women who were given to the surviving Benjamite warriors. The Levite had given his concubine to the worthless men of Gibeah to save himself. Here all Israel decided to forcibly take young women to give them to the Benjamites. The four hundred young women being inadequate for all the survivors, the elders had to devise a scheme to circumvent their oath. Two hundred of the Benjamites were advised to carry off the young women who were celebrating a festival at Shiloh. The chapter should be read with a sense of irony. There is no statement that the actions of the congregation were condoned or ordered by God. These are not examples of how to act in obedience to the will of God, but of what level of social anarchy the community had succumbed to.

IN THE TEXT

■ **1-7** This first section of the chapter sets up the dilemma that Israel faced; how could they insure that the tribe of Benjamin would continue? The seven verses form a chiasmic structure:

    V 1. The oath against giving a daughter to Benjamin is stated.
        V 2. The people weep sorrowfully over Benjamin.
            V 3. The people ask God how this could happen.
                V 4. The people offer sacrifices.
            V 5. The people ask who did not come to the assembly.
            The second oath is described.
        V 6. The people have compassion for Benjamin.
    V 7. The oath against giving a daughter to Benjamin is restated.
While at Mizpah (v 1) they had taken an oath not to give their daughters

to the men of Benjamin. It is possible that the oath had also included not taking any of the daughters of the Benjamites as wives for their sons, but with all the women slaughtered, that made the issue irrelevant. After the fighting was ended (v 2), the people gathered at Bethel and **lifted their voices and wept bitterly** before God concerning what had happened. At Bochim (2:1-5) the people had also lifted up their voices and wept before God. They were disheartened because the angel/messenger of Yahweh had told them that God would no longer drive out the inhabitants of the land, that the conquest was at an end. These two incidents of weeping provide another frame or inclusio for the book. The people rhetorically asked of God (v 3) why these events had taken place so that one tribe would be missing of Israel. There is no acknowledgment that they had acted hastily and without the authorization of God. They refused to own their part in the tragedy, seeking rather to cast the blame back onto God (v 15). On the next day (v 4) they arose early to build an altar and offer whole burnt and peace or well-being offerings. These are the same sacrifices that they made after their second defeat (20:26). In v 5 the reader is told about the second oath. The Levite had sent the dismembered parts of his concubine to the tribes, and they had responded by assembling before God at Mizpah. All the tribes, except Benjamin, were expected to send their warriors. The Israelites had taken a solemn oath that those who did not attend the assembly were to be put to death. The writer notes (v 6) that the Israelites repented of the slaughter of their kinsmen Benjamin. However, they were about to compound their guilt by slaughtering another Israelite town. Their dilemma is restated in v 7. They had sworn the oath not to give their daughters in marriage to the survivors, but they needed some way to provide wives for them. The stating of the oath in both vv 1 and 7 form a frame for this section. The problem facing the victors is set forth. The rest of the chapter describes their solution.

■ **8-14** Verse 8a restates the question of v 5, who did not come to the convocation at Mizpah? The answer (vv 8b-9) was that no one from Jabesh-gilead had come. Jabesh-gilead was located east of the Jordan River somewhere in the wadi el-Yabis, which flows into the Jordan about 20 miles (32 km) south of the Sea of Galilee (Edelman 1997, CD-ROM). The congregation as a whole (v 10) selected twelve thousand valiant warriors and ordered them to kill all the inhabitants of the town, including the women and children. The command is repeated in v 11; the town was placed under the ban (ḥerem, "devoted totally to destruction"). Every male and **every woman who had known, that is, slept with a man** was to be killed. The soldiers carried out the command. They also captured **four** *hundred young girls* (naʿărâ), *of marriageable age* (bĕtûlâ), *who had not known a male to sleep with a male* (v 12). They brought the women to Shiloh, not Mizpah. Shiloh was located in the central hill country on the road from Bethel to Shechem, about midway between the two towns. There Joshua convened the tribes to parcel out the land. There, too, was the tabernacle with the ark of the covenant set up (Josh 18:1-10) (Halpern 1997, CD-ROM). The mention of Shiloh sets up a connection with the next account, the capture of the young women of Shiloh. It also forms a bridge to the opening stories of 1 Sam 1—4, which are set at Shiloh. The note that Shiloh was located in the land of Canaan ties the account back to the opening chapters of the book. Boling notes that Canaan is mentioned seventeen times in 1:1—3:6. "Elsewhere in the book Canaan is mentioned only in the Deborah-Baraq material, where the opposition is specifically 'kings of Canaan' (5:19)" (1975, 292). The congregation then sent a message of peace (v 13) to the Benjamite warriors who were at the Rock of Rimmon and who accepted the women (v 14) as their brides. However, there were still two hundred men without wives.

Later the town of Jabesh-gilead would be rebuilt. In times of war residents of a town often fled to the many caves in the surrounding hills. Perhaps some of the survivors were among those who rebuilt the town. During the days of Samuel the town was attacked by the Ammonites (1 Sam 11:1-11). The newly elected King Saul responded quickly to relieve the siege of the town. After the battle with the Philistines at Mount Gilboa in which the Israelites were defeated, the men of Jabesh-gilead made a daring raid to reclaim the bodies of Saul and Jonathan from the walls of Beth-shean (1 Sam 31:11-13). It is possible that Saul acted so quickly and decisively because he was a descendant of one of the women from Jabesh-gilead and felt a kinship with the later inhabitants (Matthews 2004, 199). The people of Jabesh-gilead felt a deep loyalty to Saul, possibly not only because he saved them from the Ammonites but due to being blood-kin.

■ **15-25** The people were belatedly sorrowful about the war (v 15). In their sorrow, however, they shifted the blame on God for what had happened. In the ANE God, or the gods, were the primary causes of events. The sun came up each day because Yahweh (Israel) or Shamash (Mesopotamia) or Ra (Egypt) told it to rise up. If disastrous events such as plagues or droughts came upon them, the people would seek to find out which god was causing them so that they might in some way appease his or her anger. Yet people were able to act on their own, apart from the gods. It seems contradictory to the Western mind that the gods/God determined all things, yet humans had free will. Yet this was a common way of thinking about the world in the ANE. Therefore, the elders of the people (v 16) considered what they might do to supply the rest of the Benjamites with wives. They were facing a dilemma. They needed wives for the survivors lest a tribe (v 17) be wiped out from the people of Israel. Yet they could not give any of their daughters (v 18) to them because they had cursed any man who would give his daughter in marriage to the Benjamites.

The elders came up with a plan to get around their oaths. They were evidently meeting privately and not in full session with the people. Taking counsel at Shiloh (vv 12, 24), if their plans were public, the people of Shiloh would have been aware of them. The yearly festival dedicated to Yahweh (v 19) to celebrate the grape harvest, probably Succoth or Feast of Tabernacles, was about to be held at Shiloh. It was to this festival that Elkanah brought his family, including Hannah, each year to sacrifice to Yahweh (1 Sam 1:1-3). The exact location where the young women would be dancing is given in some detail: in the vineyards **north of Bethel, to the east of the road that ran from Bethel to Shechem, but south of Lebonah** (the only reference in the OT to this town, which must have been only a short distance north of Shiloh). The elders commanded (v 20) the Benjamites to lie in ambush (*'ārab*, same word used in 20:20 when the men laid in ambush around Gibeah) in the vineyards. When **the daughters of Shiloh** came out to dance in the vineyards (v 21) each man was to seize (*ḥāṭap*, occurs only here and Ps 10:9 where oppressors seize the helpless [BDB, 310]) **his wife from the daughters of Shiloh** and go (flee?) to the land of Benjamin. The elders assured the Benjamites (v 22) that if the fathers or brothers made a complaint to them, they would convince them to give up the women voluntarily and not go to war. They would point out that the women were not taken in battle as prizes in war to be rescued or ransomed, nor were they given voluntarily. Thus the men would not be guilty of breaking their oath.

There is no record that in the deliberations anyone spoke up on behalf of the women. Even the protests from their fathers or brothers were not to be recognized. They were victims as was the Levite's concubine. They were taken by force and made to submit to marriages. In the normal course of their lives, the women would have had little to say about who would be their husbands. The families arranged the marriages. Yet they were denied what little dignity and honor they would have been accorded through the negotiations prior to the marriage and the festivals that would have marked their entry into their husbands' homes.

The Benjamites obeyed the commands of the elders (v 23). When the women came out to dance, each seized (*gāzal*, "to seize violently," "tear away," "rob" [BDB, 159]) one of them. The men with the women returned to their ancestral lands, *their inheritance,* and rebuilt the towns that had been destroyed in the war. Then all the Israelites departed from Shiloh (v 24). Each returned to his tribe and family, to his ancestral lands, *his inheritance.*

The stories should be read ironically. The Israelites were in a dilemma of their own making, although they shifted the blame onto God (vv 3, 15). Like Jephthah, the Israelites had hastily taken foolish vows. Unlike Jephthah, they tried to find loopholes by which they could circumvent the vows. The results were horrendous. The first result of their scheming was the annihilation of another Israelite town. Except for four hundred women who were to be given to the Benjamites as wives, all the inhabitants of Jabesh-gilead were killed. When the supply of women from Jabesh-gilead was not enough, another scheme was devised by the elders. The violent words used to describe the actions have shock value. The remaining Benjamites were commanded to lay in ambush (*'ārab*) and each seize a woman like an oppressor seizing the helpless (*ḥātap*). The Benjamites obeyed and each violently tore a woman away (*gāzal*) from the group and then fled home before the father or brother could react. While the Israelites turned to God in sorrow, weeping, and offering sacrifices, there was no inquiry made to God about the situation. God was not an actor in the drama. The people made their own decisions. Thus the story and the book end with the telling statement (v 25): *In those days there was no king in Israel and each man did what was right in his own eyes.* Social and spiritual anarchy was the final result of Israel's experiment with self-rule. There is also irony in this final verse as it speaks on two levels. Was there no king in Israel? Certainly there was no human who ruled over them. That institution was established later when the elders later went to Samuel to ask for a king. God spoke to Samuel, saying, **Listen to the voice of the people in all that they say to you. For they have not rejected you, but me they have rejected from being king over them** (1 Sam 8:7). Certainly they had a king, the God of Israel. Yet they had no king, for they did what was right in their own eyes; not what he commanded.

FROM THE TEXT

1. The book of Judges is to be read as part of a larger work that includes the books of Joshua, Samuel, and Kings. The compilers and editors (Dtr) wrote the books to account for the fall of Jerusalem (586 B.C.) when the temple was burned and survivors were carried off to Babylon. With the loss of the land, the temple, and kingship, those carried into exile were de-

moralized. They questioned why God permitted this great tragedy to befall them. The Dtr intended to demonstrate from the history of Israel that the people continued to break the covenant established between God and Israel at Mount Sinai. Because Israel did not follow the covenant by directing their worship exclusively to Yahweh, the curses of the covenant came upon them. As a final act of punishment designed to call the people to repentance, the nation was carried into exile. While the people had to go through the horrifying experience, there was hope that if they called upon God in true repentance, he would restore them (Deut 30:15; 1 Kgs 8:46-51).

Judges traces the continuing spiritual and social decline of Israel from the time of the deaths of Joshua and the elders of the generation that began the conquest of the land (2:6-10) to that of the rise of the monarchy in the days of Samuel. When the people worshipped other gods, God brought the curses of the covenant upon them in the form of oppression from other peoples. When the people cried out to God, he then graciously sent a judge to save them. The cycle repeated itself and the people drifted slowly into spiritual and social decay. The last stories of the book should be read as a portrayal of the end results of their sin. There are no heroes. No saving judges dedicated to the will of God. In most of the scenes God is absent. The people often acted without regard to the will of God. As a result of their sin, Israel turned against itself, almost annihilating the tribe of Benjamin and destroying the Israelite city of Jabesh-gilead.

The book presents in graphic detail the results of sin as a warning to its readers. God calls for the exclusive loyalty of his people. The worship of other gods leads to spiritual death and social chaos. The reader is called upon to reflect not only on the history of Israel but also on his or her personal life. The gods that seduced Israel were visually portrayed in wood, stone, or metal. The modern gods of power, greed, sexuality, spiritual apathy, self-indulgence, and a host of others speak to our inner thoughts. They sing an alluring song that appeals to our self-centered nature, but their promises are false. Their end is not freedom and life, but slavery and destruction.

2. In the last chapters women are depicted as commodities to be seized for the benefit of men. In Israel as in all of the ANE, women were second-class persons at best. In these accounts they were treated only as sexual objects subjected to the demands of men for the purpose of providing for the survival of their inheritance. It is inappropriate to look back at history and pass judgment on others by standards of a different era. However, even by their own legal and theological standards, the women were badly treated. Israel believed that both the male and the female were created in the image of God (Gen 1:27). In these accounts it is clear that Is-

rael fell far short of treating women as persons who bore God's image. The spiritual health of a society can be measured in some part by how it treats the vulnerable segments of the society (Exod 22:21-27; Deut 24:17; 27:19). The seizing of women and forcing them into marriages debased them; it turned them into commodities, not persons. A society that seeks to promote justice will protect the vulnerable and create opportunities for all its citizens to develop their God-given abilities and talents.

www.ingramcontent.com/pod-product-compliance
Lightning Source LLC
Chambersburg PA
CBHW070806230426
43665CB00017B/2513